LORDS OF THE RINK

Ian Young & Terry Walker

LORDS OF THE RINK

IAN YOUNG & TERRY WALKER

POLESTAR
BOOK PUBLISHERS

Published by Polestar Press Ltd.
1011 Commercial Drive, Second Floor
Vancouver, BC
Canada   V5L 3X1

The publisher would like to thank the Canada Council, the British
Columbia Ministry of Small Business, Tourism and Culture, and
the Department of Canadian Heritage for their ongoing financial
assistance.

Cover design by Jim Brennan
Cover photograph by Chris Relke
Editing and Production by Michelle Benjamin and Julian Ross
Printed in Canada by Best Book Manufacturers

Canadian Cataloguing in Publication Data

Young, Ian, 1946-
　　Lords of the rink

ISBN 0-919591-73-6
　　1. Hockey—Goalkeeping. 2. Hockey—Goalkeepers. I.
Walker, Terry, 1949- II. Title.
GV848.76.Y68 1994   796.962'27 C94-910608-9

LORDS OF THE RINK

Foreword *by Ian Young* 9

The Making of a Goaltending Guru *by Terry Walker* 14

The Roots of Nobility 21

Goaltending: The Psychological Game 25

Discussion With The Pros 43

A Closer Look At Goaltenders 63

      Tom Barrasso 65

      Ed Belfour 66

      Sean Burke 66

      Mike Fountain 66

      Grant Fuhr 66

      Jeff Hackett 67

      Dominik Hasek 68

      Kelly Hrudey 68

      Curtis Joseph 68

      Kirk McLean 69

      Felix Potvin 69

      Bill Ranford 70

      Damian Rhodes 71

      Mike Richter 71

      Patrick Roy 71

Peter Sidorkiewicz...72

Mike Vernon 72

Kay Whitmore 72

Royalty From Earlier Eras

Johnny Bower...73

Gary Cheevers 74

Roger Crozier 74

Ken Dryden 75

Tony Esposito..75

Glenn Hall 76

Bernie Parent 77

Jacques Plante 78

Terry Sawchuk 78

Gump Worsley 79

Random Thoughts From The Crease 81

A Comprehensive Review of Goaltending Fundamentals 85

Stance 86

Angles...96

Skating & Motion 103

Ice Shots 111

Rebounds 117

Deflections 121

Screen Shots 126

Breakaways 131

Two-on-ones...142

Two-on-nones...145

Award-Winning Goalies

Hart Memorial Trophy 148

Calder Memorial Trophy 148

Vezina Trophy 149

Conn Smythe Trophy 150

William M. Jennings Trophy 151

Hockey Hall of Fame 151

All-Star Goaltenders 152

Milestones in Goaltending History 154

About The Authors 180

A book of this nature cannot be written without family support. I am deeply indebted to my wife, Donna, who showed compassion and encouragement during my time commitments to this project; and to my daughters Lindsay (5) and Jennifer (3), who proofread the material. I love them all dearly.

— Ian Young

For the patience and understanding of my wife Mary Jane, and our children Kimberly, Ryan and Allison. Never has a former goalie been happier to face a four-on-one.

— Terry Walker

Kirk McLean, Lord of the Rink (Relke).

FOREWORD
by Ian Young

Those of us with a maple leaf tattooed on our hearts will never forget it.

Hamilton, Ontario. September 15, 1987. Wayne Gretzky drops a perfect pass to Mario Lemieux in the deep slot. The Magnificent One coasts closer to the crease before wristing a shot high into a corner of the net. Seventeen thousand and thirty-six fans almost blow the roof off Vic Copps Coliseum while the voices of millions more, coast to coast, erupt in patriotic rapture.

Moments later, it's final. Canada 6, Soviet Union 5. Our third Canada Cup win in four tries, and the maple leaf is where it belongs—flying high in triumph over the entire hockey world.

The celebration was underway.

Some of my more intense friends claim it took them days to come down from the adrenalin "high". For Canadians, hockey is that important.

And that's what's so ironic. We have a sport that inspires intense nationalist pride, one that's so important to the collective psyche that it partially defines our national character. Tales of shinny feats from the stars of earlier eras serve as a cultural thread that binds our past to the latter-day successes of Gretzky, Coffey, Lemieux and company. The proof is in the hundreds of thousands of youngsters, parents and coaches who make up that substantial subculture known as minor hockey. For those people, hockey gives purpose to the relentlessly frigid nature of Canadian winters. And yet, sadly, for as long as little Johnny and Jacques have been stickhandling their way across frozen Canadian ponds, the poor goaltender has been largely ignored.

Ask a goalie how he got his start in the crease and he'll probably tell you that he was the worst skater in the neighbourhood. If not, it was a peculiar quirk of fate that landed him between the pipes. Either way, it's a non-developmental system that relies on luck.

In my own situation, it was the quirk of fate scenario. When I was a young lad, the goalie on our team decided to play forward.

I was the only one who volunteered to replace him, and went from being the worst scorer on the team to the best goalie.

I find it interesting that Canadians aren't the only ones who find their way to the crease in a roundabout way. Vladislav Tretiak, the great Soviet goalie of the 1970s and early '80s, says that he was attracted to hockey as a ten-year-old because of the uniforms. In his case, it wasn't a Maple Leaf or Canadiens sweater, but that of the Soviet Central Army sports club. Unfortunately, his offensive skills weren't good enough to land a position on the first team and the uniform was still out of reach. But at the time, the team had no goaltender. Tretiak volunteered for the position, and the rest is hockey history. Even in a hockey program that prides itself on rational thought and a scientific approach to the game, the birth of its greatest goaltender had everything to do with a young boy's aesthetic appreciation of hockey apparel.

Then, once young goalies are entrenched in the position, they're on their own. When a young player puts on the pads, so begins a career as a practice "target". Even in hockey schools, you'll find the goalie standing by the boards, waiting to go into the net and take a turn facing shot after shot from forwards with only one thing in mind—the goalie's embarrassment. The emphasis is clearly on offensive hockey, on scoring.

Unfortunately, it's a bias that pervades the entire hockey world. Ask people to name their favourite player. Almost without exception, they'll name Gretzky or Lemieux or Yzerman or Hull or some other goal-scoring whizbanger. Will they ever name a goalie? Or a defenceman, for that matter? Forget it. They'll always go for the glamour guy.

I say it's time to change that and shift attention to the most important person on the ice—the noble goaltender.

When I was ready to embark on my junior hockey career in the summer of 1963, all six NHL clubs showed a lot of interest. I signed with the Boston Bruins organization because they promised me off-season help in the form of on-ice sessions with former Canadiens great Bill Durnan and ex-Bruin goalie Long John Henderson. Just one thing went wrong: I never saw them. In fact, in my four years of junior action I got practically no help whatsoever. Is it any wonder that recruiting a good goalie is mostly a matter of luck? Even a player who shows all the promise in the world at one level of play might have technical flaws that become all too apparent when the competition is stronger and quicker.

Still, I was determined to become the best goalie I could be. At one point, I arranged for a week of facing shots from American Hockey League scoring ace Dick Gamble. But it wasn't easy. By 9:30 a.m. I was on a Scarborough bus to Oshawa before transferring to a second bus that took me into Bowmanville. I'd spend seventy-five min-

utes facing shots and then head home, often not arriving until 5:30 p.m. or later. My team's contribution? Well, they paid for the bus fare and the ice time. *But there was no one there from my team to watch me!*

My junior career had its good and bad sides. I had the opportunity to play at Oshawa with the likes of Bobby Orr and Wayne Cashman. A Memorial Cup berth and a pair of first team all-star selections promised to carry me to the realization of a lifetime dream: a career in the NHL

As I was on the verge of signing with the Boston Bruins, the dream was shattered. A Mickey Redmond slapshot hit me in the face (those, of course, were the days before most goalies wore masks). The bones above and below my left eye were shattered and I was left with 4% peripheral vision.

With the exception of a one-season fling in university hockey as a one-eyed goalie, my playing days were over. But by 1983 I was back in the game, coaching goalies for my old junior club, the Oshawa Generals. Since then, I've played a role in the development of goalies who went on to NHL careers—Peter Sidorkiewicz, Kirk McLean and Jeff Hackett. A fourth goalie of mine—Mike Fountain—was drafted by Vancouver in the summer of 1992 and has been involved with Canada's national team program. He and Fred Brathwaite, a fifth graduate of our Oshawa program, are moving into the world of NHL hockey.

It's that kind of success at the junior level

that led to offers from NHL clubs. I'd al-ready done some work with Kelly Hrudey while he was with the Islanders when the Toronto Maple Leafs took me on as Goalie Consultant part way through the 1990-91 season. Shortly after that, the Vancouver Canucks contacted me to do the same for them. Slowly, hockey organizations are beginning to recognize the need to pay more attention to goaltenders. But in all too many cases, the help that's offered is still inadequate, or inconsistent at best, and some-times even counterproductive.

Look at it this way. Everyone assumes that NHL goalies are masters of their trade, but even though they may have better-than-average experience, co-ordination and ath-letic skills, that doesn't mean their tech-nique is as sound as it could be. For exam-ple, Greg Millen is a good goalie who's spent well over a decade playing in the world's most prestigious league. As such, he should be lauded for his accomplish-ments. But for a large part of his career, Millen had a habit of confronting players coming down the wing by skating right at them. He'd still be moving out when the shot was taken. Now, let's recall a similar goaltending tactic that played a key role in Darryl Sittler's cup-winning overtime goal at the first Canada Cup tournament in 1976. As Sittler broke in off the wing, Czechoslo-vakian goalie Vladimir Dzurilla came out, came out, and came out some more. So high was Dzurilla that had Sittler shot, he prob-ably couldn't have hit the end boards, let alone the net. So Sittler simply took a cou-ple of extra strides, outflanked the charging European goalie, hit the wide open net, and ignited another of those Canadian nation-wide parties.

What Millen and Dzurilla both had in common was a move that effectively put all their eggs in one aggressive basket. But a really good forward, like Darryl Sittler, will steal that basket and crack the eggs on your ego. Now, if either Millen or Dzurilla go out and teach young goalies a move like that, is this a good thing? Or will improper goaltending tactics be passed on to the next generation of puck-stoppers?

For the sake of future expressions of nationalist pride, I hope we can avoid such a scenario. Instead, our task as educators of tomorrow's goaltending greats is to de-velop a legion of confident, knowledgeable disk deflectors, tough enough to stand tall, come up with the big save, keep their teams in the close games, and inspire confidence in their teammates. They must become, in truth, Lords of the Rink.

But before they're ready to mount the Throne of Goaltending Awareness, they must be willing to work. If improvement is foremost in their minds, the goalie coach's responsibilities are greatly simplified, re-duced to four simple requirements:

1) the ability to impart sound technical knowledge;

2) experience at a sufficiently high level

of competition, in order both to understand and to lend credibility to the lessons;

3) through explanation and trial-and-error, the ability to convince the young goalie that something useful and benefical is being taught; and

4) the trust and friendship of the players; they won't play—and certainly won't improve—for someone they distrust.

If you can successfully clear these hurdles, you've entered the golden realm of goaltending influence. Now you're ready to direct the development of tomorrow's goaltending stars.

That's what I've been attempting to do for the past several years. However, the job has just begun. My intention over the next several years, through my work with young goalies and written works like this book, is to improve the understanding of goaltending for all hockey people, to de-mystify the position and drag it—kicking, if need be— out of the dark ages and into the era of modern hockey. To make a contribution— humble though it may be—to the future of the sport I love.

—Ian Young, 1994

Ian Young in nets as Oshawa challenges the Toronto Marlboros, 1966 (Ian Young collection).

THE MAKING OF A GOALTENDING GURU

by Terry Walker

Growing up in the Toronto suburb of Willowdale, I shared a common dream with tens of thousands of Canada's hockey-mad youngsters. Someday, I felt, I'd sign a pro contract and get the chance to emulate the on-ice feats of my hero Johnny Bower, one of the greatest stand-up goalies to ever slap on a pair of pads. Realistically, my playing days never held the promise of a career in the NHL, but I was competent enough to land a league MVP award at the midget level (that old wood-and-tin trophy still enjoys a place of honour in my living room), and eventually earned a hockey scholarship at a small American college before enjoying a one-year playing stint in Europe. Several years later, my dreams giving way to an encroaching middle-age paunch, I devoted five seasons to coaching young goaltenders at the minor hockey level. If truth be known, I fancied myself a bit of an expert on the position.

And then I met Ian Young.

I was playing old-timers hockey at the time, determined to continue this goal-tending thing until I got it right. Never one to give up too easily in the dream department, I still clutched at emotional straws, hoping against all odds that somehow, somewhere, a pro scout would catch my act and conclude, "Gee, just what we're looking for. A balding, diminutive, overweight, near-sighted and over-the-hill goalie with two bad knees."

Ian was staying in shape working out as a forward with a group of old-timers, his puck-stopping days deep in the past. I vaguely recalled his earlier playing days and the promise of goaltending greatness that accompanied his exploits with the junior Oshawa Generals. He was a two-time all-star in the Ontario Hockey Association (now the Ontario Hockey League) while starring with an Oshawa team that boasted the likes of Bobby Orr, Wayne Cashman and Danny O'Shea and that went to the 1966 Memorial Cup finals. But before you could say, "Sign on the dotted line, kid," a Mickey Redmond slapshot shattered Ian's hockey future while providing the best possible argument for goaltenders to wear face masks. It happened on January 21, 1967. Young's left eye was permanently dam-

aged by the puck, leaving in ruins the hockey future of the big kid with the quick reflexes and the "can't miss" tag.

Just how good was Ian Young? Check out the headlines:

"Ian Young Tremendous in Goal"
"Can Ian's Heroics Continue?"
"Goalkeeper Plays So Capably, Injured Orr Hardly Missed"

The 1966 run to the Memorial Cup finals included playoff wins over the St. Catharines Black Hawks, Montreal Junior Canadiens (with coach Scotty Bowman) and the Kitchener Rangers of the Ontario Hockey Association; North Bay of the Northern Ontario Hockey Association; and the Shawinigan Bruins of the Quebec Junior "A" Hockey League. There was one amusing note to the final game of the St. Catharines series. When a fight broke out late in the game, Ian and Black Hawks' goalie Larry Holmes, both seemingly bored by the fisticuffs, confirmed the camaraderie that exists within the goaltending brotherhood by passing the puck back and forth the length of the ice. Working on their clearing-the-puck skills, no doubt.

But Ian Young's playing days included much more than occasional displays of nonchalance. After Oshawa knocked off the Montreal Junior Canadiens, general manager Wren Blair (later the General Manager of the Minnesota North Stars) said, "Ian Young was brilliant beyond description." And coach Bep Guidolin, after another typical Young performance in the Shawinigan series, said, "When we needed him, he was there. He saved us tonight, and in our OHA playoffs he beat the Montreal Junior Canadiens almost single handedly."

Wren Blair was prompted to make a more general evaluation of his guy between the pipes: "You always need strong goaltending to win in the playoffs…and Ian has been fantastic…He looks every bit as good as Bernie Parent did for Niagara Falls last year, when they won the Memorial Cup. There is absolutely no question in my mind that Ian will be in the National Hockey League before long, particulary with expansion coming."

Toronto *Globe and Mail* writer Rex McLeod called Ian "…the most accomplished goaler to come out of the Junior "A" series in several seasons," and during the Memorial Cup finals against Edmonton, McLeod made the observation that, "Bobby Orr is acknowledged as Oshawa Generals' most valuable player, but there are several members of the Edmonton Oil Kings who will cast a vote for Ian Young. [Young] has played so capably in the last two games of the Canadian junior hockey final that the injured Orr has hardly been missed."

You could never really say that an absent Bobby Orr would "hardly be missed," and at the end of that season Orr was front and centre to accept the Auto Workers Credit Union Trophy as the most valuable Oshawa General. Ian had to settle for a miniature

trophy for finishing second in the voting.

The following season, Orr and Cashman and others had gone on to bigger and better things, leaving Ian behind to tend goal for a barely mediocre Oshawa club that wallowed near the bottom of the league at the halfway mark in spite of his allowing the second-lowest goals-against total. And the printed accolades continued.

"…*Young, all-star goalie for two years running, was brilliant.*"

"*Oshawa goalie Ian Young kept the Generals in the game…*"

"*The Oshawa goalie has been like Atlas, carrying the team on his back…*"

Constantly under siege but never willing to raise the white flag of surrender, Ian had opposition players scratching their heads…literally. An article in the *Oshawa Times* included the following: "Ask London Nationals who Ian Young is and they will tell you "Houdini". Young repeatedly stopped prospective London scorers as he led Oshawa Generals in their 2-2 tie with London…London captain Walt McKechnie illustrated the feelings of this team when he stood on the blueline and scratched his head after the Oshawa goaltender had made another difficult save."

Long-time Bruins' general manager Harry Sinden gave his opinion of the future-that-never-was when he said of Ian, "He was definitely in our plans as the next Bruins' goalie. He was outstanding."

But then came Mickey Redmond's

slapshot, and Ian had to accept the fact that his dream of a big league goaltending career would go unfulfilled. And that's tragic, really. For most of us, the shattered dream is due to insufficient talent. For a few, it's because of a waning interest in the sport. But to lose it due to injury, in a sport where injuries usually mean a temporary absence from the game, would be almost too much for most athletes to handle. Fortunately for Ian, he had other qualities that made him unique, and years later he was able to use those qualities to re-enter the game in a different capacity. On January 14, 1967—exactly one week before Ian's accident—an article appeared in the Toronto Maple Leaf game program under the title "Ian Young, Top Junior Goalie". It was written by Toronto sportswriter Frank Orr. "Young," wrote Orr, "shares a boat with many goalies. Hockey's reluctance to provide specialized coaching plus the fact few ex-goalies become coaches means the young goalie is on his own. Although a coach who was a forward or defenseman during his playing days can offer some tips, there are few who can teach the fine points of guarding the net."

Such insight was rare in those days, and Ian backed up the author's point while offering an early indication of his future hockey involvement. He told Orr, "Of course, my coaches have been some help, but much of what I've learned has been through trial and error. I've tried to study Johnny Bower and Glenn Hall, the way they play the net and things like that. For instance, I try to be a stand-up goalie, but there are times when a goalie must drop to his knees…The best place to learn is in practice. If a player scores on me in a workout, I ask him why he was able to score. I want to know if I'm giving him too much net to shoot at."

Here was the curious, analytical mind of a hockey coach-in-the-making, a young man with the willingness to learn and improve his understanding of the position. If that meant consulting with the "enemy"—forwards—then so be it. Today, after more than a decade as goalie coach with the Generals and several stints as a goaltending consultant with NHL clubs, Ian recalls, "I used to do that a lot, asking my teammates in practice how they were able to score on me. And I was reminded of it when Eric Lindros was in Oshawa and he used to come out to my special workout sessions with our goalies. He was always the first one to volunteer to take shots, and told me he got a lot of out it. By listening to me talk to our goalies, he was learning what we were thinking and figuring out ways to beat us!"

We know that Eric Lindros' attention to detail is paying off. And Ian's coaching sessions with his goaltenders have had the desired effect as well. In his first decade working with Oshawa puck-stoppers, he not only helped win a Memorial Cup in three championship appearances, but also sent Peter Sidorkiewicz, Kirk McLean, Jeff Hackett, Mike Fountain and Fred Brathwaite to professional careers. We can only guess at what the next decade will produce.

Young has had a couple of appearances on Don Cherry's "Grapevine" television show, and it's obvious that Grapes is a fan. Cherry says, "Coaches don't know how to train goalies. Practices are set up for forwards and defencemen because most coaches were forwards or defencemen when they played, and how can they tell goalies what to do? They'll just throw the puck out there and have guys hammer it at the goalie. Ian was one of the first [to work with goalies], and maybe the best. It's probably not nice to say, but maybe his injury was a blessing in disguise. All of a sudden, Ian was forced to look at goaltending from the outside and learn to think about it. If you think of it, all of the great coaches in hockey like Pat Quinn, Pat Burns—and me, of course—we were never star players. But guys who had to sit on the bench a lot watched the game and figured it out. Ian's the same thing. Because of his injury, he got a chance to do that."

If you truly love the game, the itch to play is a tough one to scratch. A few years after his injury, Young embarked on the comeback trail as a one-eyed goalie. He was in his final year of finance at Waterloo University when the school's hockey team talked him into enlisting. As it turned out, he must have done something right out

there. He made the League all-star team. But more importantly, he was forced to further develop his understanding of the position. "I had a blind spot that made it hard to pick up the puck as it approached the net. I'd see the puck, lose it, then have to pick it up again. So I concentrated on positioning and angles," he says. "I learned to compensate. For instance, I learned that if a guy comes in on the wing and winds up for the big shot, generally speaking he'll go to the far side. So I trained myself to be almost ready to move before the shot was made. And if a guy tried a wrist shot, I learned to watch his lower hand. The lower it slid down the stick, the higher the shot would go. If that lower hand stayed high, chances are it would be a low shot. And on breakaways, if the forward started to straddle the puck as he approached me, I knew he was going to try a deke. In possible deflection situations, I learned to move to the point of deflection. And on screen shots, I had to know what was going on around me. Where were their guys, where were our guys. That kind of thing."

Shortly after that, during a trip to Boston to visit his old buddy Bobby Orr, the two of them got together with Phil Esposito and Gilles Gilbert for an all-night session of revelry and hockey talk. Near the end of the evening, after Young told the NHLers of his Waterloo experience, they suggested he come to the Bruins' camp next fall. With that as his incentive, Young worked out in

Orillia all summer with a group of pros including the likes of Orr, Mike Walton, Vaclav Nedomansky, Phil Russell, Bill Barber and Billy Harris. "Things didn't start out very well," he remembers. "Right off the bat, Nedomansky took a shot that I didn't see until it came flying back out of the net. And Harris buried a slapshot from an incredibly sharp angle. I knew right then that I was going to have to work even harder on figuring out angles. Things slowly got better and later in the summer, Phil Russell asked me to stay out an extra few minutes so he could work on breakaways. I stopped him eight or nine times in a row, and that was the first indication that things were starting to come together."

At the end of the summer, Ian was one of eleven goaltenders at Boston's training camp. He saw five of them cut before he was offered a minor league contract with Binghamton of the American Hockey League. Here, at last, was vindication. He had proven his ability to play at the professional level.

But there was still the reality of the eye injury, and no guarantee that others wouldn't make decisions on his hockey future based on his damaged eyesight. And so, armed with a degree from the University of Waterloo, the one-eyed goalie with the advanced understanding of goaltending technique gave up his playing days for good and embarked on a career in finance.

In the early 1980s, Ian was approached by Oshawa general manager Sherry Bassin (who eventually became the General Manager of the Quebec Nordiques). It seems the Generals' number one goalie was having problems, and Bassin asked Young for a helping hand. And so, without the young goaltender's knowledge, Ian watched a few games, took a pile of notes and then went to work on Peter Sidorkiewicz. Thus began an Oshawa coaching connection that's continued to this day.

One athlete who gives a lot of credit to Ian Young's coaching techniques is Damian Rhodes of the Toronto Maple Leafs. They worked together when Young tutored goalies in the Leaf organization during the 1991-92 season. "It was a very vital period in my career," says Rhodes. "If Ian wasn't there, I wouldn't be where I am today. I was fighting the puck and playing with no confidence at the time. But he made me do drills that had me moving more, moving out on the play, and he introduced the half-butterfly move for low shots. So he altered my style a bit, although he told me he didn't want to change my style. He wanted me to do what was natural for me. He made sure I knew that I was still very much in control of my own game. A lot of this game is mental, and Ian thrives on helping guys keep a healthy, positive outlook."

Ian Young's involvement with the game doesn't end with his Oshawa coaching or a few goaltending consultant jobs at the NHL level. He's evaluated goalies for Canada's national junior team program, and he runs a goaltending school in Whitby, Ontario that attracts students of the position from across North America, purposely restricting enrollment to ensure a low student-to-instructor ratio. He's also developed and marketed several practice devices to help goaltenders develop their play. Ian's "screen shot apparatus", in particular, has given hockey's coaching fraternity a safe but effective means of combating their goalie's feelings of hopelessness while facing the dreaded screen shot. With all of his contributions, it's no wonder that the Hockey Hall of Fame in Toronto has acquired one of Ian's Oshawa sweaters for display.

During the process of completing this book, Ian and I spent considerable time in enthusiastic discussion and debate of the subject that's close to the heart for both of us. While he never claimed that his way of playing the position was the only way, he always impressed me with his ability to not only evaluate a goaltender's overall game,

but to break it down into its component parts through precise attention to detail. Whether it's a discussion on positioning and motion under a certain set of circumstances, or listing several reasons for holding the stick or trapper in a certain position, his arguments are always consistent and well-considered. When you add that to a love of the subject matter and the ability to communicate with young athletes, you've got a recipe for success. And when it comes down to it, isn't that what you're looking for in an educator?

There's no doubt that the premature end to his playing career lingers as a deep disappointment. As he says, "It still gets me in the stomach that I never got a chance to play." Understandably, his metamorphosis from player to coach must have been an emotionally painful process. But when all is said and done, who can deny that Ian Young has successfully made the transition from pro goalie could-have-been, to goaltending guru?

Bill Ranford—Lord of the Rink (Relke).

THE
ROOTS
OF NOBILITY

Hockey fans sitting in the stands have the same impression, more or less, of the two puck-stoppers opposing each other during a game. Both goalies have helmets, pants, sweaters, blockers, trappers and leg pads that may differ in colour, but are, generally speaking, of similar size and shape. It would be easy for these fans—especially the younger ones—to think that goalkeepers had always assumed this general appearance. But as Charles L. Coleman documented in his scholarly three volume work, *The Trail of the Stanley Cup*, nothing could be further from the truth.

When the earliest published rules of organized hockey were printed in 1899, the regulations as they applied to goaltending and goalie equipment were so different that it's safe to say that only the size of the goal itself—6 feet wide by 4 feet high—has remained unaltered.

In just about every other way, the position was different in hockey's early days.

At one time, only goalies in Ontario were permitted to stop the puck with their hands, although that may not have been the smartest thing to do, since the earliest puck-stoppers wore ordinary leather gloves.

They used a stick that was no different than those used by the defencemen of the day, and as late as 1913, it was decreed that a goalie stick couldn't be wider than three-and-a-half inches at any point.

The earliest leg protection consisted of ordinary shin pads, although in 1896 a Winnipeg goalie named G.H. Merritt started a revolution in goaltending gear by wearing cricket pads on his legs in a Stanley Cup series in Montreal.

And of course, there were no face masks.

During the 1931-32 season, the NHL opted to use the Ross puck. The manufacturers claimed it didn't roll. But George Hainsworth and some of the other goalies in the league objected to the puck, saying it rolled as much as the old Spalding puck. Also, Hainsworth was convinced that the Ross puck—which had a bevelled edge—curved like a baseball when it was shot. The

league finally reverted to the old puck.

The six-by-four foot goal dimensions may have survived to the present, but today's hockey fans would find it difficult to recognize any other features of the earliest "net". To begin with, there was no netting. The goals consisted of two poles with flags on top of each one. Until 1900 there was no crossbar, and goal judges used nothing more than their own judgment in determining whether or not shots were too high.

Even the goal line painted on the ice didn't make an appearance until 1903, and wasn't enshrined in the official rules of a league until another ten years had passed.

But the rule which most clearly separates the early days from contemporary goaltending is the one that stated: "The goalkeeper must not during play, lie, kneel or sit upon the ice, but must maintain a standing position." By 1913, a goalie leaving his feet faced a $2 fine for the first offence, and a $3 fine and a five-minute penalty for a second infraction. Another offence cost $5 and ten minutes in the box, while infraction number four called for a costly $10 and a match penalty. The rules were modified shortly after that for a playoff series between the champions of the National Hockey Association and the Pacific Coast Hockey Association. For a first offence, a goalie leaving his feet was given a warning. A second offence called for a two-minute penalty, with no substitution in goal permitted.

Think about it! No butterfly, no stacked pads, no desperation lunges across the crease. I guess you could call it the era of the true standup goaltender!

Then, during the National Hockey League's first season of 1917-18, a most revolutionary rule was evoked. It seems that Ottawa goalie Clint Benedict brought to the game a flopper's style, and because they feared he would make a mockery of the game by drawing penalty after penalty, league officials decided to permit goalies to leave their feet.

From that moment on, there were almost as many goaltending styles as there were goal-tenders...everything from the traditional standup play of Canadiens' Georges Vezina, to the flopping Clint Benedict, and the roving Hugh Lehman, who often thrilled the fans by skating far out of his net to clear loose pucks.

When you combine their skills, improved equipment and the right to leave their feet to the 1921 rule that gave goalies the right to pass the puck as far as their own blueline, and then add the fact that there was no such thing as an icing call (giving defenders under pressure the right to clear the puck down the ice time after time), what you have is a Golden Era of Goaltending...a time when shutouts flourished and goals-against averages fell through the ice.

But it didn't happen right away.

In the 1920-21 season, Clint Benedict's five shutouts was a regular season record.

But five years later, Ottawa's Alex Connell had 15 in 36 games. And the following season (1926-27), the 220-game schedule yielded 84 shutouts.

One year later, Canadiens' George Hainsworth had 13 shutouts in 44 games and an almost unbelievable 1.09 goals against average. But the goaltending story of the year was the six consecutive shutouts recorded by Alex Connell. Since three of them were scoreless ties—and tied games went to 10-minute overtime sessions—Connell's scoreless streak ran to a remarkable 460 minutes, 49 seconds. That amounts to more than 7 games and 2 periods of straight time.

Hainsworth really put it all together the following year. In 44 games, he posted 22 shutouts and a 0.98 goals-against average. But it was Roy Worters of the New York Americans who won the Hart Trophy as the League's most valuable player. In fact, it was a glorious season for *all* big league goalies. Each full-timer had a GAA under 2.00, with the league average sitting at 1.46.

But perhaps the most impressive statistic of all is that in 220 regular season games, there were 120 shutouts. Fifteen games ended in scoreless ties. As much as this might please those of us in the goaltending fraternity, such a paucity of goal scoring was too much for the paying public, and NHL officials set out to reverse the game's defensive trend before the 1929-30 season. And so, whereas hockey up to this point had been primarily a stickhandling game with no forward passing, new rules were introduced to allow forward passes within any of the three zones—offensive, defensive and neutral.

The result was immediate and dramatic. By season's end, the average goals against average was 2.96—more than double that of the previous year. And instead of 120 shutouts, there were just 26. A balance between offence and defence had been achieved, more or less. Certainly, there were still periodic rule changes that seem a little bizarre by today's standards—for instance, automatic goals awarded when a defending player threw his stick in the defensive zone, or limiting the number of defensive players allowed in the defensive zone before the puck was carried into it—but for the most part, the sport was now free to develop into the great game we have today. And the goaltender was ready to take his rightful place as hockey's magnificent Lord of the Rinks.

Curtis Joseph (Relke).

GOALTENDING: THE PSYCHOLOGICAL GAME

You, the Noble Goaltender, take your rightful and honourable place between the pipes. Before long, your six-by-four foot fortress is besieged by enemy warriors, pounded by galvanized rubber disks catapulted at speeds approaching 100 miles per hour. Quickly, a pair of well-directed missiles find the mark. They may have been "good" goals—no fault of yours—but coach Mike Mean'un, who has a reputation for doling out swift and decisive punishment for lapses in performance, pulls you from the game. Humiliated, you find yourself replaced by a back-up nobleman of lesser rank…

There's a scramble in front of the net, but you've located the puck and used your superior training to place yourself correctly. Just then, a most nefarious opposition forward skates past and uses his stick to take your feet out from under you. Somebody puts the puck in the vacated net, prompting one of your own defence to skate over and say, "Come on, you've *got* to have those…"

The onrushing forward cradles the puck with the blade of his stick. Before he even takes a shot, you go down. But the puck hits the open trapper. You throw your hand into the air, and everyone in the rink thinks it's a spectacular splits save. The applause is deafening, but you know that plain luck has masked the classic mistake of going down too soon…

A shooter at the point winds up for the shot. You come out ten feet, and the puck hits your pads. The TV commentator says, "That's the way to play it; challenge the shooter and take away the angle." Meanwhile, there are enemy players at both sides of the net. If the puck was passed to either one of them, you'd be a Royal Kingfish out of water and the puck would be in the net. And yet, the comment that went coast to coast and found the ears of hundreds of thousands of people—including a truck-load of young goalies—is that this is the way to play it…

Four separate scenarios; four incorrect ways of interpreting goaltending situations.

And that's why the starting point for a discussion of goaltending psychology is this: When confronted with critical analysis of goaltending, *always consider the source..*

Is it coming from a coach who spent his playing days as a forward or defenceman, and doesn't have the time or inclination to properly assess the position because he has 18 or 20 other players to worry about during games and practices?

Consider the source.

Is it coming from parents and fans who may or may not have played the game, but even if they did, never saw the need or had the knowledge to properly understand the position and what it involves?

Consider the source.

Or is it coming from television and radio broadcasters—even those at the NHL level—who can often be counted on to blame goalies for "bad" goals when, in fact, the guy with the pads wasn't to blame? For that matter, many of these "experts" are sometimes incapable of pin-pointing the reasons for a goal even when the guy between the pipes is at fault.

Consider the source.

As for criticism from teammates—well, that's a little tougher to take. After all, the Lord of the Rink deserves and expects the support of his teammates. But even if it does happen, what makes *them* such experts on goaltending?

So, as I say, consider the source.

WHO SAYS *THEY* KNOW?

You've heard it all before: "That shot hit the five hole; it's a bad goal." Or, "He moved too early for that shot and couldn't react to the deflection." But when these comments are thrown in your direction, just remember: They're not facing those shots, *you* are...and you're all alone out there.

Oh sure, it's a team game. Forwards are expected to backcheck and have—or should have—defensive responsibilities. And the defence, by definition, defend. Their job is to protect the goal and the goalie. But when that puck finds a small opening in the 24 square feet you must protect, others will often find a way to deflect the blame in your direction.

After all, stopping the puck is *your* job.

If it goes in, *you're* the sieve...the "target" that disappeared at an inappropriate time.

And as the humorists in the crowd will never tire of reminding you, *you're* the one who has a "sunburn on the back of your neck" because the goal light went on.

Sportswriters will go to great lengths to find a scapegoat for a loss, and more often than not, that scapegoat turns out to be the poor goaltender. But in a large number of such cases the writers' ignorance of the position robs them of credibility. Take the case of the hockey scribe who described a 20-foot slapshot that caught the short side of the net. "The save should have been made," he claimed, because the goalie, "...had a clear view of the puck."

Well, I'd like to ask that writer a question: If a puck travels about a third of the distance that separates a baseball pitcher's mound from home plate, and hits an uncovered part of the net while moving about as fast as a Nolan Ryan fastball, does he think he could stop it?

Maybe. But first, let's see if he can catch a bullet between his teeth!

Let's face it. You're playing a position that by its very nature will attract a lot of double-guessing by teammates, coaches, fans and media members. I don't expect you to like it, but you may as well get used to it.

But as I say...consider the source! Goaltending is *not* their area of expertise.

But *it is mine.* So believe me when I say that I've always felt that the psychology of goaltending is as important as any other aspect of the position because your mental approach has a direct impact on your performance, and therefore on your career. And since you have to be your own boss during games—you're alone in that crease, my friend—you have to rely on yourself to develop and maintain a positive outlook.

Just as a negative outlook will produce negative consequences for your play, a positive outlook increases your chances for positive performances, and a prolonged career.

So how do you create that positive mental

outlook? Simply speaking, from taking negative experiences and dealing with them in a positive way. It's easy to criticize a goaltender, and very easy for that goalie to get down on himself as a result. But it won't help anyone—except the opposition—if you get down on yourself and allow that criticism to remain a negative. Step number one—and I'll say it as often as I have to—is to consider the source. If people are yelling at you because of a five-hole goal, or say you're going down too much, or complain that you're coming out too far—or not far enough, for that matter—the first thing you've got to ask yourself is this: *What makes these people such experts*?

Forget them. If you're faced with a problem in your play, it's up to *you* to turn that negative into a positive. I'll get into that in more detail later, but before I do I think it's important to point out that even at the highest levels of the game, people constantly mishandle their goaltenders and create the basis for possible negative results.

Example: Look at Mike Keenan and his handling of Chicago goalie Ed Belfour. It's common knowledge that Belfour was being pulled far too often. What's the philosophy behind that? Does anyone really think that a goaltender can maintain a consistently positive mental approach to the game if he's being pulled every time a coach thinks he's made a mistake?

The fact that Belfour continued to play so well was a tribute to his mental toughness under trying circumstances. He was an all-star and Vezina Trophy winner *in spite* of Mike Keenan's yanking tactics, not *because* of them.

When Keenan took over as head coach of the New York Rangers, he was still up to his old tricks. After goalie Mike Richter helped the Rangers rack up a ten-game unbeaten streak, he stopped the first seventeen shots he faced in a game against the Florida Panthers. Halfway through the second period Florida scored and Keenan pulled Richter from the game. Judging from Richter's comments after the game, the decision did not sit well with him.

There's no reason a coach has to do that, just as there's no reason a coach has to yell and scream at the guy with the oversized pads. Goalies have far too much pride in their game for anyone to consider any of these "techniques" a productive way of handling problems. You can't pull a player every other game and still expect him to maintain a maximum positive attitude. Over time, our confused monarch is going to start looking over his shoulder, thinking, "Oh oh, here it comes." If one shot gets by him, he won't be the same for the rest of the game because he'll be worrying about being yanked. Goalies can do without that kind of unnecessary pressure.

Sure, sometimes you've got to give a guy a little jolt to get him going. But a coach has to know the individual and recognize the contribution he's made to the team.

> *"A goalkeeper should never be reproached for his mistakes during the game. On the contrary, he should be constantly encouraged."*
> —*Vladislav Tretiak*

It would be like Vancouver's Kirk McLean going in there, game in and game out, nursing a 2.50 goals against average, winning all sorts of games, and then having a terrible outing. Do you get down on him? Of course not. He's put you in the playoffs, in contention. Everybody's entitled to a bad game once in awhile, so give him that right. In fact, any screaming that's done in this situation should be directed at the rest of the players to pull up their socks and support the guy who's won those games for you all year long. If a goalie goes out there and gives you solid performances while winning game after game, and then suddenly has a stinker, the troops have to rally around him. They have to say, "Hey, this guy's off tonight. We've got to backcheck a little harder and win it for him. We've got to show him we appreciate his efforts."

But too often, the psychological well-being of our blue-blooded puck-stopper is totally ignored.

Here's an example—speaking of Kirk— of how a goalie at the highest level of the game can be denied the mental preparation time he needs leading up to a game. As every goalie knows, getting psyched before a game—thinking about their big shooters, evaluating their offensive tendencies—is as much a part of playing as facing enemy shots. But during one game-day morning skate at Maple Leaf Gardens, neither Kirk nor teammate goalie Troy Gamble knew who was going to start that night. Just before game time, Gamble was called aside by coach Bob McCammon and told, "Troy, you're playing." So when he resumed his warmup laps around the rink, Troy turned to McLean and said, "Kirk, I'm playing tonight." Believe it or not, that's how guys are told sometimes, even at that level! True, the appropriate time to relay that information to your goalies depends on the individual. But I certainly don't think you should show up at the rink for your morning skate and find out only then whether or not you're playing.

Ideally, a goaltender should know days in advance whether or not he's expected to play in a particular game. That way, he can focus his workouts and mental preparations towards that game. The coach should be talking to the goalies—by the way, a lot of them don't—and say, with all the respect and reverence owing to the position, "My Lord, you're playing Saturday night in Toronto." That way, when you practice on

Wednesday or Thursday, you'll already know that your number's been called. And believe me, that removes a lot of unnecessary pressure. Instead of operating in an emotional vacuum, guessing whether or not you're going out there, you can prepare with confidence and direction, secure in the knowledge that it won't be a last minute, spur-of-the-moment coaching hunch that's throwing you in the nets. Besides, this approach has the added advantage of creating improved communications between coach and goaltender...and I'm all for that!

Here's another example:

When Peter Sidorkiewicz left Oshawa, he was an aggressive, play-the-angles goaltender who used the butterfly to his advantage. (That, as you'll see later in the book, is what I try to teach.) He was drafted by Washington, traded to Hartford, and when he became the Whalers' number one goalie, they told him they wanted him to stay in his net, stand up, and let the defence do the work clearing the rebounds. In my opinion, Peter's game changed at that point; he wasn't the same type of goaltender he was when he left junior hockey and as far as I was concerned, he wasn't as effective. But that's what they told him to do. However, being a technically sound goalie, he continued to play at the National League level.

You've got to consider the source. Is there any hockey coach who knows better than Peter the style of play that best suits him? I think not!

When I played, I certainly wasn't immune to unproductive treatment at the hands of hockey's powers-that-be. When the Boston Bruins signed me at the age of 15 to play for the Oshawa Generals (those were the days when NHL clubs ran farm systems that included junior clubs), the Oshawa newspaper ran a picture of another goalie who was coming to camp. Since he had two years of junior experience in Thunder Bay, the article concluded that he would be the number one goaltender.

Well, that burned me up.

All modesty aside, I'd been an all-star every year I played and won several championships. But now I was being told—by the press, at that—that I wasn't going to make the club. Well, a couple of things happened. One, I got angry. Two, I went out and had a tremendous camp, beat out the other guy, and earned the right to start the season against the Montreal Junior Canadiens.

You'll hear more about that game as this book unfolds, but for now I'll do a quick summation: they had a star-studded lineup and although they beat us 6-4 (the last goal an open-netter), I was chosen third star of the game.

So imagine my surprise when I got to the dressing room and ran into my extremely irate general manager who yelled and screamed at me for letting in the fifth goal—a deflection that went in one side of the net while I was moving to the other. He told me it cost us the game, and fined me ten dollars…a significant sum, since I was being paid twenty a week.

How do you think I felt? I was chosen third star and blamed for the loss. That's a good way to confuse a 15-year-old!

Later—much later—that general manager apologized to my parents for that incident. It turned out he was on his way to the dressing room with the score tied and, hearing the roar of the crowd, turned to a fan and asked what happened. The answer he got was, "Young blew one from the blueline." The deflection wasn't even mentioned.

I knew his criticism was unjustified, that the goal was the result of a wicked deflection. But for me, the damage was done. I became a Lord in Exile, sent down to the Junior "B" Whitby Dunlops.

Although I still practiced with the Generals, my confidence wasn't what it should have been and I spent two years playing with the Dunlops. Unfortunately, no one was there to urge me to turn that negative into a positive.

Still, without even feeling particularly good about my game, I must have been doing something right. Both years I managed to make the Junior "B" all-star team, beating out a pretty good kid who was roaming the crease for the Etobicoke Indians at the time. Our games against them were great battles, your classic 2-1, 3-2 games, 45 shots each. And when all-star voting time rolled around it was me—not Ken Dryden—who got the nod.

Following my second year with Whitby, I rejoined the Generals, became a first team all-star, and was on my way to the Memorial Cup. But I still blame that one incident when I was 15—and my inability to handle it properly—for retarding my development. Now I realize that I was too sensitive to criticism and let it play on my mind, rather than deal with it in a productive manner. In short, I let it affect my performance. *When it's unjustified criticism, you're better off not thinking about it too much.*

How should you deal with negative reactions from others? Well, first of all, *consider the source*. But if there's some justification for the criticism, you have to make a very honest assessment of your ability, and what you did wrong. If, for instance, you've been pulled from a game after giving up a goal, then analyze the situation. Only you know if it was a bad goal, and whether or not you could have done something else to prevent it.

If it *was* your fault, then your response has to be, "Well, it's going to happen from time to time; that's a bad one out of my system. It's in the past and I'm not going to let it bother me forever. Now it's time for me to correct the fault." Then, your next time out, you've got to stuff it up your coach's shirt. *Show* the guy what you're all about by playing the best game of your life. But remember…you're on your own to do that.

SUCH A LONELY GUY. . .

When I talk about goaltending responsibilities with the guys I coach, I break it down this way: You've gone through a year or two working with me, either on my team or at my goalie school. But the moment you skate onto the ice for a game, Ian Young's not working with you any more. When that guy shoots from the wing and picks the short side, you have to be the one to understand that you were too deep in the net, or too far from the short side post. If you've been trained well enough to understand that, the next time a similar situation occurs you should be mentally prepared to correct the mistake and position yourself where you want to be. In short, *become your own goalie coach.*

The very nature of the position reveals that you have to find a way to analyze and correct your own mistakes. We know that the defence can't go out there and be scored on. We know a forward can't go out there and be scored on. Together, they can make ten times the number of mistakes made by a goaltender, but they'll never be scored on. *You're* the only one with the nobility of spirit necessary to accept the honour of that awesome responsibility. So if you're going to play this game, don't go out there worrying about bad things that might happen; hold your head high, and make adjustments to your game when necessary.

Heading into every game, your attitude has to be, "I'm going to show everybody in the rink how good I am. I'm going to show them I know how to play this game, and I'm going to gain the respect of everyone." You can't afford to go out there hoping nothing bad happens to you. If you hit a stretch where things just don't seem to be going well, remember that it's highly unlikely that anyone you deal with knows more about goaltending than you do. Sure, a lot of players will offer opinions, insisting that,

Late in the '91-92 season, when he was with Toronto, Grant Fuhr gave up five goals in a tie at home with New Jersey. He didn't look particularly good on any of them, and the catcalls rained down in punishment. Not only did he have to re-focus his attention after every soft goal, but he had to block out the taunts that followed, and the sarcastic cheers each time he made a routine stop. Afterwards, he shrugged off the boos, saying, "It's part of the game, there's nothing you can do about it. It was probably one of the worst games I've had. I don't need anyone else's help realizing I had a bad game. I know it."

"This guy's a good goalie," or "That guy's a bad goalie." But that's from *their* perspective; it has nothing to do with a *technically knowledgeable* perspective. So let's be honest: *You're* the one who knows best, and nobody knows more about your game than you. So you've got to become your own coach from shot to shot, from game to game, and find a way to turn potential losses into wins.

NEVER A DOUBT. . .

Every goaltender goes through periods when nothing seems to be working. After two or three bad games in a row, you might even start talking to yourself. But remember: *never doubt yourself.* You've got to play this game with confidence, so take a look at your track record. If you can look back and know that you've played well in the past, and *know* that you have a high level of ability, and *know* you've cracked the roster of team after team all the way up, then why would you doubt yourself all of a sudden? You have to keep working hard. It always turns around.

The mental toughness to get through those bad periods has to come from within. Every time you hit the ice, you've got to nurture a positive attitude. So if the whole world is yelling at you for letting in a bad goal, the only person who can turn it around is *you.* As I said earlier, negatives get turned into

positives by an honest appraisal of your abilities and game performances. By doing that, you'll know if the criticism was incorrect; or if it was justified, in which case you're going to use that knowledge constructively to improve your play and avoid similar mistakes in the future. Either way, the appraisal—and the correction, if necessary—has to come from you.

Understand that there may be times when the turnaround takes a little longer than you'd like. A bad game, one more, then another, and you start to get over-anxious and lose confidence. You're convinced that your feet are encased in cement. But it's a matter of accepting that there are peaks and valleys in this game. Let's face it, if you played to your fullest potential every time out, you'd have shutout after shutout. We know that's unrealistic; things are going to go against you in this game. Instead of thinking you've lost it—even if you've had three or four rough starts in a row—you've got to rise above it and address the problem areas.

It happens to the best of them. I remember getting a mid-season phone call from Kirk McLean. He said, "I'm just not moving well. I can't get into it...I'm just not moving any more." Did that mean he'd put on a hundred pounds? No. Did it mean his skate blades were no good all of a sudden? No. He was the same weight, and his blades were fine. Simply put, he was going through an awkward period during which he felt physically uncomfortable. It's going to happen occasionally to every goaltender, but it always turns around...as it did for Kirk.

Whatever you do, don't go out at times like that and make a major overhaul to your style. That could *really* mess up your game. However, it might be necessary to address some smaller issues.

For example, when I worked with Jeff Reese he was going through a rough period. He was getting caught by short-side shots high to the trapper side. His glove was resting on his pad too much instead of being out and open, facing the puck. He needed a minor technical adjustment, a little work at practice, and the problem disappeared. Often, it's that simple.

So don't forget what got you there in the first place!

WHEN GOALS COME EARLY. . .

One of the best goalies I ever played against—and one I admired greatly—was Bernie Parent. He was a tremendous angles goaltender who left very little net showing when he left the crease. He possessed great reflexes and anticipation. Bernie was a brilliant goaltender, a natural. He and Doug Favell were the backbone of a great Niagara Falls junior team. Bernie won a Memorial Cup with them one year, and when I started out in junior hockey, he was my hero. One day at the Niagara Falls arena, I was stand-

ing there minding my own business and Bernie walked up and said, "How are you, Ian?" I couldn't believe it...he was actually talking to me! I was never one to pass up an opportunity to improve my knowledge of the game, so I said, "Bernie, I played years of minor hockey and got used to lots of shutouts and one-goal, maybe two-goal games. Now all of a sudden, I'm playing junior, and sometimes I'm giving up 5 or 6 goals a game. But the worst feeling is three minutes into a game when I've already let in a couple. Fifty-seven minutes to play, and it's already 2-0! How do you handle those situations."

Bernie said, "You know what? Those two goals? You can't get them back. Are you going to spend time worrying about it? Are you going to lose your focus because you're worrying about what happened in the past? *You've got to look at the next shot as if it was the first shot of the game.*"

That was great advice, but today, as a coach, I'll take it one step further: Regardless of what happens—it could be 5-0 after five minutes—play it tough. That next shot could be your career!

Get them out of your system.

Hand-in-hand with that is the need for an immense amount of pride in your game, because if you allow yourself to play at less than 100% efficiency, the only ones who will suffer are you and your teammates. *Don't let them—or yourself—down.* Forget the past; look to the future.

THE BUTTERFLIES. . .

When it comes to frayed, pre-game nerves—the butterflies that go along with pre-game preparations—there's no greater example than that of Hall of Famer Glenn Hall. Legend has it that Hall got so nervous that he threw up before every game.

But Hall was a great goalie who never fell prey to that occasional goaltending psychological pitfall known as "seizing up". Those who do get hit by this particular affliction lose the aggressiveness that makes them innovative in their game. Fluidity disappears, they stop flowing with the play, and their moves become mechanical.

In Hall's case, severe though it was, the butterflies disappeared once the game began. That was because of his style. He played high, challenging the shooter and pulling back with the play. That movement allowed him to get into the game and stay loose. Rather than stand and let them come to him, he went after them. Aggressiveness was probably his abdominal salvation.

Anyone who has ever lived with a goaltender knows that they can be a very different person on game day. Some get very quiet, even sleepy. Others are short-tempered. If you happen to share living space with one from the latter category, it's best to stay clear. But don't worry...it's really nothing more than the reality of awesome responsibility intruding on the tranquillity of others.

Several years ago, I read a hockey study that compared degrees of nervousness before games. The study set out to determine

Here's how Jeff Hackett looks at the psychology of goaltending: "Most hockey coaches don't think goaltending is very complicated. They think all you have to do is react to the situation, use your reflexes, and make the save. But it's a lot more complicated than that. The mental part of the position is the most difficult. There will always be your 'down' times. But you can't cave in. You've got to shake off the bad goals and the bad games. People don't know how hard that is, adjusting yourself mentally for the next shot. It sounds easy, but sometimes it's pretty hard. The really great goalies do it easily. They have a way of focussing on the next play. In Oshawa, even if I let in some bad goals, I knew I'd be playing the next night anyway. That gives you confidence, and you can get prepared for the game. But in the NHL, that doesn't happen. You can end up sitting out the next two weeks. That's tough on you."

which players—or more accurately, which positions—were most affected. It concluded that wingers, probably preoccupied with evaluating their latest haircuts, were the least affected. That is, on average, they spent little time in nervous anticipation of the coming battle. Defencemen were a little higher on the pre-game agitation scale, which befits their role as protectors of hockey's lords of the frozen realm. (It's interesting to note that defencemen on weaker teams had longer periods of pre-game anxiety than those on good clubs.) And centres, accepting the responsibility of offensive creativity, spent even more time than defencemen preparing themselves mentally for the approaching confrontation. But of course, the keepers of the crease were by far the most responsible. According to the study, the butterflies convened much earlier; in some cases, pre-game jitters set in as early as 10 hours before game time. And unlike defencemen, the duration of pre-game nerv-

ousness increased for goalies who played on better teams. This makes sense. After all, responsibility for a loss by a strong team that usually dominates its opposition is more likely to be laid at the feet of that team's goalie. On the other hand, a goalie whose team is routinely outshot by a wide margin doesn't experience the same type of psychological pressure, since he isn't likely to be blamed very often for losses.

But either way, goalies on any kind of team will suffer a more acute form of pre-game jitters than their teammates. So if goal is your position of preference, learn to live with the butterflies. They go with the territory.

For some of us, handling pre-game pressure is a simple matter of routine. But that can become a problem in itself, occasionally requiring intervention from a competent goalie coach. When Peter Sidorkiewicz first played at Oshawa, he did everything the same way on every game day. He'd get

In his book The Game, *Ken Dryden wrote about a feeling that occasionally hit him on the day of a game. "Slowly in my stomach and legs," he wrote, "I get a feeling, a gnawing uneasiness, then in my chest and throat a fear.* I don't want to play tonight. *I don't want the hours of anxious waiting that must come first...I don't want the two and a half hours that will come at the end, hours I can't control, that will make me work and sweat, that might embarrass me, that will give me a mood to carry around until the next game. I don't want it, any of it." It seems even Hall of Fame goalies can experience severe cases of pre-game butterflies.*

up at the same time and go to the rink at the same time. He'd hit a ball against a wall—supposedly for his reflexes—and he'd go through his stretching exercises and pre-game warmups the same way. I respected his self-discipline but to me, it was a mechanical approach that was restricting his development.

At that time, Peter's game lacked smoothness and was taking on a predictable and staccato-like appearance. He always played certain situations the same way. One day I said, "Go out and have a good time the night before a game. Stay up late and play the game a little tired if you have to, but get out of your regular pattern. And when the game starts, use *all* your tools. Instead of always using the skate on a low shot, try the butterfly. Try different things and develop your game. Instead of always standing three feet outside the crease with your glove on your pad when the puck is dropped, stand up straight in your crease. Try something different, and see what happens."

In other words, change your pattern, your mental approach to the game. Go out there and enjoy it!

So one day, Peter went out and washed his car, something that wasn't part of his normal game-day pattern. Now, it wasn't much, but it *was* a change. Not long after that, Peter made a great trapper save in a playoff game when he challenged a shooter by coming way out of his net. I'm convinced that by making a break with his usual pre-game routine, Peter had also made an adjustment to his game. He had given himself the behavioural flexibility to alter a goaltending approach that, until then, had become too static and predictable. Chalk one up for psychological flexibility.

LOOK OUT FOR NUMBER ONE

When I was playing goal, the crease belonged to me. It was what gave me the room to execute the moves I needed to make in order to stop the puck. Penalties—or a defenceman's fists—confronted any opponent who dared trespass in the area. I played secure in the knowledge that the crease belongs to one guy…the goaltender.

But not today. The game has changed.

Today, players will do anything they have to do in order to disrupt a goaltender's game. As a result, the goalie is forced to endure unprovoked attacks of all kinds. Sticks shoved in your rib cage or jabbed at your skates or poked at your mask are as infuriating as sticks that are used to lift your lumber off the ice while a shot is on its way to the net. And yet, these are some of the milder forms of the psychological and physical intimidation that are practiced by so many forwards these days. How about the players who yank your feet out from under you, or better yet, the ones who skate right over you, or purposely fall on you, claiming they were forced into you by a defenceman?

These are nothing more than blatant attempts to determine the outcome of a game by injuring the goaltender.

As long ago as the 1926-27 season, the NHL felt a need to protect its goalies. A major penalty was assessed for "cross checking, bodying or charging the goalkeeper." One can only hope that hockey's will to protect the guy in the crease will once again grow that strong.

One year, in the OHL finals against Sault Ste. Marie, the play was in Oshawa's end of the ice and then headed back up ice. When the puck was well outside our blueline, Tony Iob, who had been checked in the corner by one of our defencemen, skated over to Mike Fountain, our goalie, and slashed him behind the knees. Mike crashed to the ice in pain. Not only did the referee miss this, but far more importantly, it could have resulted in serious injury. Fred Brathwaite was our backup goalie, but he was already out with an injury. Luckily, Mike was okay and continued to play, but Iob's stupid slash could have left us without competent, junior-level goaltending in a championship series.

That strikes me as a pretty easy route to victory. And unfortunately, it's a too-common tactic used by hockey teams at all levels.

The following year, we had a pretty passive defensive corps. They weren't very good at clearing the front of the net. So Fountain spent most of the season not only getting attacked physically from all sides, but also facing a ton of screen shots through opposition bodies that weren't being cleared from in front of the net.

Well, the screen shots were one thing. But the physical abuse he had to endure was an altogether different matter. And since I subscribe to the theory that at some point you've got to be prepared to stand up and be counted, I went to Mike with a suggestion. "That crease is your territory," I told him, "and *nobody* has the right to hit you in there. So if anybody so much as skates through your crease, he's fair game. Slash his ankles, hit him in the ribs, knock him over with your blocker…do anything you have to do to keep him out of your crease!"

Two changes resulted from this admittedly direct approach. After Mike nailed a few guys, they weren't quite so eager to encroach on his area; and it forced our defencemen to come to his defence. So even if a goalie picks up a penalty for removing an opponent's ankles with surgical precision, at least his defence will get into the game and come to his aid. And let's face it…that's what you wanted in the first place.

Remember, nobody in this game seems to care any more about the health of the goaltender. Certainly, we know the opposition has never bothered to send a get well card. They're far too obsessed with scoring, beating you, and increasing goaltenders' insurance health costs. However, their irresponsible actions—even if they say they just want to throw you off your game psychologically—can damage or end a career. So I say this: If hockey's powers-that-be allow that kind of behaviour to continue, you have to stand up for yourself.

Once again, we see that what's needed is mental toughness—in this case, the determination to combat all physical attempts to throw you off your game...or knock you out of it.

FEAR OF FAILURE

We know that goaltenders are a spectacular species. Overlooked in victory, they're often handed ultimate responsibility for a team's failure. Being alone in a front-and-centre specialized position, a goalie has to accept an existence that includes a career-long affliction known as "fear of failure".

No other members of a team can feel the same way because, unlike the Lord of the Rink, they're not the last line of defence. Mistakes can be theirs without ultimate cost. So the possibility of fear of failure, and the embarrassment factor that goes along with it, is borne largely by the lonely goaltender. But goalies who let this non-productive attitude take control are forgetting what the game is all about!

During my minor hockey days in the Toronto area, I was fortunate to play with winning teams comprised of fabulous people. I couldn't wait to get home from school so I could go out and play hockey; I couldn't wait to get out on that rink and catch that puck in warmup; I couldn't wait for that tough situation in the game so I could come up with the big stop; I couldn't wait for that buzzer to sound so we could celebrate another win; I couldn't wait to get back to that dressing room and hear the jokes and happy

In The Game, *Ken Dryden describes the psychological aspects of goaltending this way: "Because the demands on a goalie are mostly mental, it means that for a goalie the biggest enemy is himself. Not a puck, not an opponent, not a quirk of size or style. Him. The stress and anxiety he feels when he plays, the fear of failing, the fear of being embarrassed, the fear of being physically hurt, all are symptoms of his position, in constant ebb and flow, but never disappearing. The successful goalie understands these neuroses, accepts them, and puts them under control. The unsuccessful goalie is distracted by them, his mind in knots, his body quickly following."*

comments. In short, I couldn't wait to experience every aspect of the game. Today, *I won't allow my goaltenders, at the junior or pro level, to feel any other way.* You've got to treat the game as if it's still minor hockey. There's no big difference, really. If you've reached a level of competence at one level of hockey by being that way, why would things change at any other level? But for some reason, goalies put unnecessary pressure on themselves, and that pressure tends to make them mentally soft or technically staccato-like in their motion. So if you enjoyed the game as a peewee, even when that puck beat you low to the stick side, why wouldn't you still be having a ball when that shot beat you in a game against the Kamloops Blazers, or the University of Alberta Golden Bears, or even the Montreal Canadiens? Put it in perspective! The dimensions of the net haven't changed, and the size of the playing surface hasn't changed. So why wouldn't you look forward to coming to the rink and facing that next shot? Believe me, it all goes back to those minor hockey days in freezing arenas, when you had to have your trapper warmed up before games and the only sounds were the vocal urgings of a handful of enthusiastic parents and the slapping of sticks against pucks and pucks against boards.

Let's look at it: You've had great games; you've won awards; you've won championships—or at least came close—and you've played 40 or 50 games a season and

experienced playoff hockey. Does fear of failure make any sense at all?

In the days of minor hockey, you went to school, studied, went home for dinner, then went out and played a game. There were no complications; it was *fun*. Why should that change just because you're getting older?

Remember your past glories; remember the three shutouts in a month; remember the big, last-minute save in that 4-3 win. They're much more meaningful than the occasional soft goals and losses. Remember: Your bad moments were always the exception, not the rule. *Feel good about yourself!*

I can't think of too many great goaltenders who played a bad game when the chips were down. Why? It's *because they find a way to turn a negative into a positive by turning fear into an asset.* When they hit the ice, they're mentally prepared *not* to fail. I'm a big believer in that…if you won't fail, you *won't fail*.

I should point out that the mature goaltender is the one who has the courage to accept responsibility for goals against. And for him, that responsibility is more than a state of mind—it's a code of honour that governs those behind the mask. Unfortunately, the noble intentions inherent in such a notion are often absent in the psychological makeup of those I consider to be mere pretenders to the goaltending throne.

And when that necessary mental outlook is absent, it can have a devastating impact on team play.

> *"Many times, I was certain I would fail. Many times, I did not want to play, afraid of being humiliated if I did. But I always managed to cope, and found a way."* —Ken Dryden

TEAM PLAY, GOALIE STYLE

More often than I like to admit, I've seen goalies who refuse to look into a mirror and accept responsibility for goals against. Instead, they're quick to point out the mistakes of others. But the bottom line is this: In spite of who's to blame, you won't get much sympathy from anyone if pucks enter your net with great regularity, and you start blaming others. Deflecting blame is another way of letting negatives affect your game by not addressing your own responsibilities.

Instead, look at it this way: Here's an opportunity to turn a negative into a positive...and a chance to prove yourself.

A negative can be a giveaway in your end of the ice; a negative can be an uncovered forward in front of your net; a negative can be a defenceman allowing an opponent to go around him. But in each case, if you make the save and cover up for the mistake, the team will benefit.

If they score, they score. But look at it as a challenge. Make the save, and you'll gain the respect of your coach, general manager, teammates and fans.

Grant Fuhr has made a career on his reputation as a goalie who makes the Big Save. He's highly regarded for doing that regardless of giveaways in his own end. So don't get negative and place the blame elsewhere; look at the mistakes of others as opportunities to shine.

If a teammate gives away the puck with a bad pass up the middle, don't sit back and say, "Well, if I don't make this save it's okay, because it isn't my fault." *Go after it!* Get aggressive and make the save. If you do, your teammates' reaction will be, "Way to go. Great stop!" And as anyone who knows hockey will tell you, a big save can inspire a team's bench. It means that much!

So don't let negatives stay negatives. Find a way to turn them into positives.

I'll take it one step further. I'm a big proponent of team play and I like guys going to bat for each other out there. But since the noble goalie is a lonely monarch at the best of times, you've got to settle in and play your own game. *If you play well, team success falls into place.* And as an important part of that success, *you've fulfilled your role as a team player.* The monarch who acts wisely oversees a prosperous and contented realm.

Never underestimate the effect a goalie's

performance can have on others. Players get an emotional lift when their guy between the pipes comes up with a big stop. On the other hand, a team's mental outlook can also crash to the ice if you're playing poorly or don't appear to be putting in the effort. And how about the opposition? Their spirits can just as easily soar or sag, depending on your ability to come through in key situations. Clearly, *your* positive mental outlook—and the big plays that flow from that—are necessary for the healthy psychological perspective of the team as a whole.

That's how important you are to the team concept.

Communication with defencemen can help; being an understanding off-ice buddy to your teammates can help. But it's only when you can go out aggressively game in and game out, and make the big save week after week, that you can become highly regarded. Only in that way can you earn your spurs as a great goaltender. And when that happens, your team is going to win games. To me, *that's team play from a goaltending perspective.*

Kirk McLean consults with Kay Whitmore (Relke).

DISCUSSION WITH THE PROS

I've always felt proud that three of my junior proteges have achieved their dream of making it to the top of their profession. Having my own dreams shattered before making it to the NHL is a disappointment that will stay with me as long as I live. But like the parent who realizes hopes and aspirations through the accomplishments of his or her children, I find my chest swelling with pride whenever Peter Sidorkiewicz, Kirk McLean or Jeff Hackett pull rabbits from hats and mystify the world's best players.

Take that, evil shooters!

I began coaching with Oshawa in 1983. The team was concerned with Sidorkiewicz's play and asked me to work with him. That first year, we changed a lot of things in his game, not least of which was a tendency to be too intense and take the game too seriously. Unnecessary worrying can have you mentally fatigued before the game even begins. Over time, Peter learned that the only time you *have* to get serious is when the puck is dropped, and not necessarily the morning of the game. He ended up winning an OHL title and went to the Memorial Cup, where he was the top goalie and won most valuable player honours.

After Peter, Kirk McLean entered the picture in Oshawa. Kirk was a highly-touted goalie who came out of the Don Mills Flyers organization of the Metropolitan Toronto Hockey League. At first he didn't think he needed any help, but when things didn't go so well, the shock turned him around.

At first, he wasn't as aggressive as he should have been. Instead, he stayed deep in his net, depending far too much on reflexes. But Kirk is probably the best athlete of the three, and was always good on his feet. As a result, once he learned his angles, he could stay with the puck in most situations.

By the time Kirk McLean left Oshawa, he was a quality goaltender. I knew he was one of those guys destined for great things.

Then, it was Jeff Hackett's turn with the Generals.

When Jeff first came to camp, I didn't know anything about him. One day, I was sitting in the stands watching an intrasquad game when Jeff's side fell behind 5-0 after one period. Despite the goals against, I turned to Sherry Bassin, our general manager, and said, "This kid's a good goaltender. I like him."

When I came back the next day for a second look, Jeff wasn't there. It turned out he'd gone home to London, Ontario, apparently convinced he couldn't play Junior hockey. I was upset because I was sure we'd lost a good one. He came back for another shot the next year, and the rest is history. He beat out our number one goalie in his rookie year and played the championship game in the Memorial Cup. Next year, he was the OHL's all-star goalie and played behind Jimmy Waite on Canada's gold-medal winning team at the world junior championships in Moscow. Then he was drafted by the Islanders in the second round. All in the space of two years.

Not bad for a kid who went home to play Junior "B" because he didn't think he was good enough to play in the OHL.

Peter, Kirk and Jeff have worked for years as instructors at my summer goalie school. Whenever we'd get together for a few laughs after work, more often than not the conversation would come back to the subject we hold most dear to our hearts. I'd like to invite you to one such discussion. Unfortunately, Hackett couldn't make it on this particular occasion, but Sidorkiewicz, McLean and I rambled on about our experiences in the game, talking about everything from our goaltending theories to our pet peeves and some truly ridiculous moments.

Enjoy it.

MEMORABLE MOMENTS

Peter: At the world championships in Stockholm in the late '80s, I was the third Canadian goalie there. Grant Fuhr hadn't shown up yet, so I was the backup for Sean Burke. We were beating Poland 9-0 with five or six minutes left in the second period. So Dave King walks down the bench and says, "Peter, why don't you go in for awhile?" I mean, we're up 9-0! So my attitude is kind of like, "Gee, thanks Dave." He throws me in there, and we're shorthanded at the time. Right away, they come down on me on a 2-on-1. The first guy drops it, and the second guy steps into it as hard as he can. I'm a little nervous because I just got in the game, so I went down a little early, and the puck hits me right square in the head! It shakes me up a bit; I'm kind of wobbly. So the puck goes back to the point, there's another shot, and I finally freeze it. Well, the guys are laughing so hard...they think it's funny! Dave Babych was *killing* himself laughing. Here I am, in the game for just a few seconds, and I'm almost dead!

Kirk: If we're talking about embarrassing moments...We were playing Montreal and in the first 5 minutes, we're losing 5-0. I'm thinking, "Take me out, take me out." It was 7-0 after the first period. A nightmare! Another time in Long Island—this one made TV bloopers, by the way—Mikko Makela came in on a breakaway. He made a deke, left the puck—I think he did it on purpose—I went with him and the puck went straight in the net. He gave it the old "stick-around-the-puck" thing, it went in, and I'm flopping all over the place. And in Toronto one night—I always play lousy in Toronto, *always*—Dan Daoust's coming down the wing. It was a good game, about 3-3 going into the third period. We went up 5-3 and lost 7-5, somehow. But anyway, Daoust comes down the wing and he's cutting towards the net. I thought he was going to pass it across. So I anticipated the pass, went across, but he lost the puck and it went straight in the net. I felt like an idiot.

Peter: We were playing Chicago one game—it's 1-0 for us late in the second period. Steve Thomas dumps it in, a little looper, and I end up fielding it like an infielder in baseball. I catch it and all of a sudden Randy Ladouceur, my defenceman, is skating to me, saying, "Here! Here! Here!" I was going to freeze it, but all of a sudden he's yelling for it. I put it out to the side for him, and he panics! At the last second it hits his skate and goes in. The fans are booing me like crazy, they're just going nuts! What a stupid goal. I gave up two goals to Chicago in two games that year, and both goals were stupid like that. The second goal, Chicago was in town, and we're winning 3-0 halfway through the third period. I went out to field the puck with Jeremy Roenick coming down one way and Sylvain Cote, my defenceman, coming down the other way. So I shoot it and all of a sudden my defenceman peels off, it hits his skate, goes right to Roenick, and he's got an empty net. Dumb.

Ian, you said something once about a game you saw years ago, and somebody came in on Gary Smith?

Ian: Yeah. Doug Jarrett was playing with the St. Catharines Blackhawks and he took the puck in from the left wing, in across the front of the net, and Gary Smith—"Suitcase" Smith—was playing nets for the Toronto Marlies. And I *know* that Jarrett didn't mean to do it. But Jarrett cut in front of the net, Suitcase went across with him, Jarrett lost the puck and it kept going right in the net, tantalizingly slow.

Kirk: And after it goes in, you feel about one inch tall. But what can you do?

Peter: Your teammates more or less joke about it because they make some pretty stupid mistakes too and we bail them out a lot. When something stupid like that happens, they joke about it more than get mad about it.

Kirk: They can make mistakes and the team can get away with it. But we're the last line of defence and that's what shows up. Everybody gets ticked off at the moment, but afterwards they forget it.

Ian: In the pro game, it's understood. You don't go out of your way to embarrass someone. You're not going to let in a goal like that on purpose. The defenceman's not going to let a guy go around him and drive in on purpose. Wayne Gretzky isn't going to have a breakaway and go in on net and shoot wide on purpose. It's human nature. As pros, they know that.

Peter: You mention Gretzky. I stopped him on a breakaway once. I've had pretty good success against him.

Kirk: So have I, but he's something else to watch.

Peter: Lemieux's scary—some of the things he does.

Kirk: They're two totally different hockey players.

Peter: Gretzky makes the whole team go. Lemieux's great, but I'll take Gretzky any day.

Kirk: He throws passes and you don't know how they got there.

Peter: Gretzky sees the ice. All the good players see the ice. Gretzky makes plays and passes that you wouldn't even think of making. He throws the puck out and all of a sudden someone is there.

Kirk: He's got his play made before he gets there. I've watched him closely when we play them. When he's on the bench and there's a dispute or something and everybody's talking to the ref, he'll come right off the bench and get right over there. Around the league, other captains and assistant captains, they don't do that. They sit on the bench and wait for the coach to tell them to go out there.

Peter: He has a lot of influence and he knows that. And he uses it to his advantage. He'll bitch and complain when things aren't going well for his team until he starts getting some calls his way…

THEIR START IN HOCKEY. . .

Kirk: I grew up in Toronto and played for Don Mills Flyers. I had a goalie coach there, Dean Dorsey, who was a kicker for the Toronto Argonauts and Ottawa Rough Riders. At the time, he'd just finished playing goal for Sault Ste. Marie Greyhounds. As a coach, I guess he was pretty good. At that time, when you're a kid, you're playing on natural talent. You just stop the puck any way you can. But he taught me a few things. Years before that I went to the Scarborough Lions Hockey School and afterwards, there was a goalie school and my dad and I would

sit there and watch them. I remember there was this instructor who was like a drill sergeant. But I liked the goalie masks. I played one year at left wing in the house league and halfway through the second year we needed a goalie. Two of us put up our hands. We split duties that season, then I became number one. I was a good skater because my dad always took me to the public rink and made me go in the corners and skate backwards, that sort of thing. I always enjoyed skating. I still like to go out skating.

Ian: Well, every goalie suddenly reaches the point where he's got to be honest about it. When you reached midget or junior, how did you feel on your feet? Did you feel pretty good out there? If you did, then you can generally take it that you were a pretty good skater.

Peter: I think I've always been a pretty decent skater. I was strong on my feet—not necessarily the quickest, but you don't have to be the quickest. You have to be agile and have good balance. You get guys running into you but I don't find myself being bowled over. Guys will run into me pretty good, but I always think that I hold my own and I think I have pretty decent balance. I'm strong on my skates.

Ian: There are so many things happening at the pro level that you've got to react and make your move quickly. You know whether or not your feet are letting you down. But there's also the psychological part of the game.

Peter: The psychological part is at least 90% of the game, if not more. It's unbelievable—when you get to the pro level, it's all mental.

Kirk: You've got everything to deal with. You've got the fans, the media, and you've got the number of games you play.

Peter: Night in, night out, you've got to go out there. One night you can go out and get shelled 8-2, and you've got to go back out there the next night and somehow stop the puck. That's where your mind comes into play. You look at guys who play for any length of time, they've got to be mentally strong. It's a real psychological game.

Kirk: You're in the limelight…

Peter: The pressure is on us. You know, I sit there and I look at other guys—forwards and defence—and they're joking around before the game. But I haven't seen a whole lot of goalies joking around before a game.

Kirk: Only if they're not playing.

Peter: Right. When you're playing, you've got to be focussed because when the game's on the line, you could dictate the outcome. If you're playing well, you can win the game; if you're playing awful, obviously you're going to lose it for the team. The way

you play has a big effect on the team.

Kirk: It's often up to you to get the team started. If the players aren't doing well, you know you've got to be on to keep them in there. You want to be a leader.

Peter: You've got to love this game. Remember that time in Sault Ste. Marie when we were working at Paul Theriault's hockey school? John McLean [New Jersey Devils] and Joe Cirella [Florida Panthers] were with us and we'd come home at night and we'd start talking hockey; it's three o'clock in the morning and all of a sudden we started talking about 2-on-1's. Before you know it, we're all up on our feet and playing a 2-on-1, talking about how we should do this and do that, how the role of the goalie is this, and the defence's responsibility is this. Here we are in the middle of the night, and we can't think of anything better to do than talk about 2-on-1's.

We played in Belleville and they have an Olympic-sized rink. The majority of our games are in regular size rinks—you know, 200-by-85 feet—and all of a sudden you go into Belleville. It's a lot wider and you get lost out there as a goalie…especially the way *we* play. Ian has us out of the net often with a lot of motion. I remember being out there and a guy's coming down the wing. I think I've got him and all of a sudden the guy shoots and I swear it's going six feet wide. But when I looked around, the thing's in the middle of the net. I'm thinking, "How did that happen." But you can lose your net totally. You really have to stress angles and know where the net is at all times.

Kirk: On that rink in international hockey, you've got to play a totally different game. You've got to stay in your net and let things come to you a little more. It's lateral movement and reflexes. If you don't stay close to home, they'll have a whole open net...and they'll *still* throw it back to another guy.

Peter: You *can't* let guys get behind you.

Kirk: I always thought it was exciting playing against the Soviets. I played them to a 1-1 tie with first place on the line at the world championships. It was quite an experience. Those guys can move the puck around quickly, especially on their own ice surface. They just fly! You need a lot of strength on your feet.

Peter: You have to be *aware*.

Kirk: I've found that most guys in the NHL like to go upstairs with their shots.

Ian: Well, it's because the butterfly is much more a part of the game than it used to be.

EQUIPMENT

Peter: Right. And nowadays, a lot of goalies are a pretty good size. When they go down they cover the bottom part of the net really well. Look at guys like Mike Liut and Sean Burke—if you shoot low, you won't have as much luck as you would if you went upstairs.

Kirk: So many goalies now are six feet tall or better. I think I'm small — I'm 6'1/2". There aren't too many Mike Palmateer types these days.

Peter: People see me off the ice and they can't believe how small I am. I'm 5'9". On the ice, I look so big.

Kirk: They're just looking at the padding.

Peter: I don't like to *feel* the puck.

Kirk: You want to stop it, but you don't want to feel it. I cut a lot of things out of my padding.

Peter: I do too. I cut a lot of padding out of my pants.

Kirk: Even my belly pad. And I've got a small helmet. And I think my glove is way too big. I like to have a small glove.

Peter: I haven't had a glove I've been comfortable with for about three years.

Ian: Nowadays, it's hard to imagine a goalie getting hurt with a shot. But in the old days, count the bruises! Under the knee, on the pads, on the arms or shoulders, on the rib cage—I mean, you hurt after *every game*. Today, the goalies are so well protected and the equipment is so much lighter…it's so much more practical. I think you had to be a better goalie back then because you didn't have the equipment.

Peter: My second year of junior, I got a one-piece pair of shoulder and chest pads and I couldn't believe the difference. I wasn't afraid of the puck any more. Before, you'd wear two pieces — the chest pad was one piece, the shoulder pads, another piece. Well, you'd bend over and the padding would buckle, and I used to come home with marks on my shoulder from the pucks. I had bruises on my shoulders all the time. I'd wonder why my shoulder would be hurting all the time. Well, it might be those few hundred shots I took!

Ian: What I don't understand is the *size* of the equipment. There are supposed to be limits, but look at the trapper for example. With the cheater on, that's like saying, "Here's a beachball for a hand." I know it's an add-on to cover more of the net, but I don't think it should be allowed. It's far too much. There's no control! You can't grab anything that hits the cheater, the puck just drops.

Peter: All this stuff is custom made, but everything is so big now. I don't like a big glove, either. Finding one that's comfortable is really tough. Maybe with the big trapper and the cheater, you can stop a few more pucks. But you can't *handle* the puck.

You can't *shoot* with it. You can't grip the stick any more. I can't, anyway.

Ian: Another place they've allowed cheaters to come into the game is at the base of the pads, right around the blades. They put little plastic pieces down there, stitched into the pads. It's possible on an ice shot, for example, that if you lift your stick off the ice the puck will go under your stick but hit the cheater and stop. I don't think they should be allowed—I think there should be a standard pad. If they want the pad to come right down to the ice level, then fine. But don't start adding on.

That's what they've done with the trapper. Why can't the trapper be made in one piece rather than having all these add-ons? Before you know it, they're going to stick pieces on the net! Why not put a cheater in the upper corner? In some of today's trappers, the pockets are immense! My concern is in the hand, the fingers. There's no control of the thumb and the finger area of these trappers. They close like two pieces of wood coming together, rather than clenching the puck. Those trappers are too concerned with protecting the hand, rather than practicality.

And sticks. The only people that curved blades benefit are the stick manufacturers. Can a goalie shoot the puck better with a curved blade? Maybe, but only because you don't have to work as much. And it can't be as comfortable on the backhand. And you know those sticks with the bent shaft so you can—supposedly—pick up your stick easier when you've dropped it? If I was playing the nets, it wouldn't kill me if I didn't have the bend in the shaft. I'd play the same game. And I don't ever recall having a problem picking up my stick.

But the worst thing is shots at the neck. I got hit in the throat many times, and coughed blood from it. Today, I can't believe that there are still guys who don't go for some kind of neck protector. But the biggest thing about equipment today is that they've made immense strides. It's almost impossible to hurt a goalie with shots now. The goalie's got more of a chance to get hurt going down in a scramble or when a guy drives to the net than he has from a puck. I'm not saying that improvements can't be made, but overall the equipment is exceptional now. In the old days, shots would bruise my hands. I never see goalies with really sore hands now—the protection is so good.

SHOTS ON GOAL. . .

Peter: Everybody says you've got to be crazy to be a goalie. But physically, the game's not that tough. It's *mentally* that the games are toughest. But in practice, it gets a little scary physically because you have all these guys coming down on you. The worst ones are the guys in slumps, because if you have a player who hasn't scored in 20

games, he'll be doing his damnest to score every time he comes down on you…just to build his confidence. So every time he comes down, he's hammering the puck every chance he gets. He doesn't care who's in there. He doesn't care if he kills you or 10 other guys. He just wants to score so that in the next game he's thinking, "Oh, gee, I scored 10 goals in practice yesterday. I'm really going to be hot tonight." I like the snipers—they come down and *loft it at you,* they *float* it at you. They don't care if they score in practice because they know they're going to go out there tomorrow night and score.

Kirk: Yeah. They're all Gretzky sometimes. When you're not playing well and you want to bear down and work hard, and guys start pulling the old "puck-between-the-legs" stuff with eight passes back and forth in front of the net, you just want to shoot right back at them. I've never shot at the head, but I've gotten fed up with guys screwing around so I just get the puck and fire it back at them.

Peter: Bobby Holik is the most dangerous man you want to meet on a rink. He comes down and shoots it as hard as he can, every single time. He just *pounds* it, and 6 out of 10 shots are shoulder height or higher. One day he came down on me in practice and hit me square on the forehead. Well, I just lost it, screaming and yelling, and (coach) Rick Ley was almost on the ice laughing so hard, because I went nuts. I'd never done that before in my life. But Bobby's always shooting upstairs. These guys—once in awhile, it gets away from them. But every day you've got things going up around your ears and finally I yelled, "Stupid jerk...what do you think you're doing?"

Ian: Glenn Hall says that Bobby Hull used to terrorize him in practices, that he would hammer the puck at him. Evidently, Hull loved to hit guys with the puck...and you know how hard he could shoot.

Kirk: When a guy does that to me in practice, I'll shoot it back at him. I'll just snap the puck into his ankles. They get pissed off at you for doing that, but they get the idea.

Peter: Part way through the season, maybe they're having a rough time and you're having a rough time so a lot of guys will come down in practice and do something dumb, and every once in awhile you hit them in the back or whatever and they get pissed off, just as you were pissed off at them. It happens. Tempers flare. You live with guys seven or eight months a year, you're with them all the time, and when things aren't going well, tempers are short.

Kirk: One year in junior, we were doing a drill and one guy was knocking my goalie stick. That drives goalies nuts! So finally I swing around and slashed him big time and we started fighting. The next year, the day before a playoff game, he comes down, rips one, hits me in the head, and cuts me

open...right through a wire mask!

Peter: I've got a wire mask story. I was with Binghamton in the American League and we were playing St. Catharines. One of our guys comes down in warmup and hits me right in the head, and I was digging the paint out of my forehead! That mask dented in at the nose and the forehead and the plastic coating around the wire was actually stuck right in my head! And it wasn't even a hard shot. If it was a hard shot I would have been history. It was an easy slapshot, but it was right at me. You know how those can freeze you? I missed the rest of the practice, but then I went out there and shut 'em out.

Ian: This guy I know who played goal in Europe tells the story of a teammate in practice who hammered him into the boards behind the net. This is in *practice*. My friend was so ticked off he heaved his stick at the other guy. He missed and it landed out at the blueline. Later, the jerk came down and said, "What are you so upset about? You'll have to put up with that in a game." Can you believe it?

Peter: Torrie Robertson! There's a guy who almost killed me every year in training camp. Hell, this guy had already made the team. But he's a tough guy, and felt his job was threatened every year. And why should he care about me—I was a rookie. So I cleared the puck, and all of a sudden he nailed me with an elbow, right in the head.

Almost knocks me out. It's a scrimmage in training camp and he's nailing me in the head! He hit me every year!

Kirk: How about all the times when a play comes down on you, and a defenceman backs up and runs right into you? You move over to make a save and the defenceman runs right into you. They do that a lot, especially in practice because they kind of ease up.

Ian: They never turn and say, "Are you okay?" They just break back with the play as if it was to be expected.

Peter: How about when you freeze the puck and get the big pileup, and you get pissed off at the guy on top of you? Meanwhile, it's your defenceman that shoved him into you.

Ian: You know, if we print all these stories, no one will want to be a goalie!

FITNESS & CONDITIONING

Ian: A few years ago I was down in New York having dinner with Kelly Hrudey and Terry Simpson. The Islanders had put Kelly on a program that said when he came back to training camp, he had to bench press X number of pounds and run a mile in a certain period of time. But I found it really hard to base a guy's ability to play goal on running a certain time or bench pressing a certain amount of weight. So I said to Terry Simpson, "Why is that a concern of yours for Kelly?" And he said, "Because in the National League, some of these forwards are pretty tough." And I said, "Well, what are you telling your defencemen to do?" It's that kind of thinking that tells me people in the league don't understand goaltending. To me, his argument should be with his defence.

Peter: I go to training camp every year and I'm supposed to bench press so much. Well, I'd get up there and almost kill myself. I'm not a weightlifter—I'm playing *hockey* in the National *Hockey* League. Why should I have to bench press that much?

Ian: I don't think you should. An hour session of what I do with you is more beneficial for a goaltender than the other stuff. They're not thinking of the goalie; they're thinking of the other players. You shouldn't have to do that kind of thing.

Peter: You should have good wind, good legs, and be strong enough upstairs because you have to carry all that equipment. You have to be in good all-round shape, but the important thing is your wind and legs.

Ian: On another level, it's a psychological game. The only person who can actually control the mental approach is the guy in the net. No coach can tell you how to do it Certain things happen to you over the course of time. You walk into a dressing room and don't like some of the guys...they're not your buddies any more, for whatever reason. All of a sudden, you've got to play with a bunch of strangers. Or you get out there and give up a bad goal, or let in 6 goals, and you've got to come back stronger for the next game even though no one's telling you how to react to it. But at least that's a human problem. Right now, it's so technical, so serious...lifting weights, running a four minute mile. A lot of the fun seems to have been taken out of it.

PRE-GAME PREPARATIONS

Peter: The game has gotten so technical, conditioning concerns and everything else. You've got to have fun. That's one of the biggest things Ian helped me with—to have fun with the game. You've got to have fun out there. When you get to the rink, you get ready to play hard. But you can't worry about it all day long, because by time you get to the game, you're worn out mentally. Some of these forwards never seem to worry about it. Some of them don't think about it until the game's over: "Oh, I scored two goals!" I don't really get into it now until I wake up from my pre-game nap in the afternoon. Then I slowly start to focus. I try to get rid of everything else and think about who I'm facing.

Kirk: I wake up late. We have a morning skate at say 10:30 in the morning, get home

by 11:30. Then I eat my pre-game meal at 12:30 or 1 o'clock. And I like to snooze so I'm in bed afterwards till about 4 or 4:30. Then I get up and start to think about it. Sometimes when you're lying in bed, you start visualizing things on the ice. And you fall asleep and when you wake up you're all excited about the game, go to the rink, and feel like you're at home again so you can relax a little, slow down a bit.

Peter: You build up to it gradually, and in the warmup you get it going a little more. And by the time the game starts, you're right into it. You're still relaxed, but you're focussed now. You're ready to go. There's such a fine line between relaxation and being too screwed up. You've got to be wired, but not too wired. You've got to be relaxed, but you can't be too relaxed.

Ian: When you played in Oshawa or in minor hockey, you didn't spend all day at school thinking about the game. But when the game started, you performed. Now you're more mature and a professional athlete, but that's no reason to change. When you decide to get focussed, you get focussed. But you've got to remember the days you spent out on the pond with the boys when you were 10 or 12, playing hockey. That's what the game's meant to be. If you keep the game fun even though you're playing pro, you've got half the battle won.

Kirk: As soon as you get into the money, it

changes a little bit. You get conditioned into a daily routine.

Peter: Your environment conditions you to get too serious sometimes. Everything is hockey, hockey, hockey and before you know it, you're walking around like some robot. You've become a product of your environment.

Kirk: It's the exact same thing every day. In minor hockey, you went to school and then maybe played a little road hockey, and you didn't care what you ate an hour or so before you went out on the ice. Now you've got to eat at 1 o'clock because the carbohydrates have to kick in. And some people say you shouldn't really have more than a two-hour nap because it might work against you and make you tired. And then you get into the psychological part — it gets too technical.

Peter: That's because the game has gone from recreational hockey to a business. But you attitude has to be even keel—that's an important directive for any goalie. You can't get too high or too low.

CELEBRITIES. . .

Peter: Ivan Lendl lives in Greenwich, Connecticut. He came out to practice one day to play goal. Mike Liut was with us and Mike went down to one end; I stayed at the other end, giving Ivan a few pointers. He's got all the equipment, and he loves it. He says his dream was to be a goalie. So we're having a great time—I'd go in goal for awhile, then he'd go in—and he wasn't bad, actually. Good reflexes, but not very good feet. But he loved every minute out there. He had some pictures taken during the course of the practice and one of them was him leaning on the net with LENDL on his back, and he had it doctored so there's this big flame around his head. We were in the playoffs against Boston one year and he sent me that picture. He wrote on it, "This is what you look like right now, Peter. Keep up the great work." I got it framed.

Kirk: You know what I like? Sitting on the bench in L.A. and John Candy and Andre Agassi would be sitting there. There's a little glass partition there, and you give a little glance and there they are!

Peter: It was weird in Hartford. Hartford's not the hockey capital of the world, but there we were with Gordie Howe walking through our dressing room regularly, and Ivan Lendl would come down to watch us and talk to us, and Bobby Orr is down there quite often. So there we were with two hockey Hall of Famers and one of the best tennis players ever. It's unbelievable. Gordie Howe came out to practice three or four times a year. You can see why he was great. The guy's what—65 or something? He comes down and switches hands on you! It's not hard to see how he played so long. He's a big man, he's taken care of himself, and he's got great hands.

Ian: He's also a terrific person, a classy guy.

Peter: When I was a minor league goalie trying to make the Whalers, we were going to Washington for an exhibition game. I was supposed to start. I got on the bus, really nervous about it, and who sits down beside me? Gerry Cheevers! He was doing the games on TV, so he sits down and starts cracking jokes…"Hey, you're not nervous, are you?" We were late for the game because the plane was late, so we raced straight to the rink and Cheevers says, "Hey, it's better this way, kid. You don't have to think about it as long. Just go out there and play."

SUPERSTITIONS

Peter: Every year, I become less superstitious. Usually, I tie my right skate up first and put my left pad on first. I think when you're younger, you're a little more superstitious and try to do everything the same way. But as you get a little older, you decide it doesn't much matter.

Kirk: I'm superstitious. Nothing major, but for instance, during a game, I never drink out of the water bottles on the net. Never. Stupid things like that.

Peter: I *hate* to look at the clock.

Ian: Yeah, I used to be like that too. It goes so slowly when you watch it.

Peter: The only time I'll watch the clock is in the final two minutes or so, in case I want to freeze the puck.

Kirk: Well, Ian used to break it down into segments, three segments per period. Ten minute and five minute segments. And I do it, too. But now it's every two whistles, every two stoppages I look up at the clock.

Ian: The game really does drag, though. It's a long game out there.

Kirk: And now more so, because of the commercials.

Peter: I try to keep track of things like how much time's left in a penalty.

Kirk: I'm the opposite. If there's not those two whistles, I'd rather not know.

Peter: I'd rather just sit there as the game goes along, and all of a sudden hear, "Last minute of play in the first period." That's the best feeling in the world. One minute. Okay, now I'll shut 'em out the rest of the period.

Kirk: I'm different in that if my two stoppages haven't come up and there's a penalty call or something, and it's only the first whistle, I try to ignore the guy announcing the time. I don't want to hear how much time's left.

Ian: I would never drink water. Back when

I played we had chocolate and orange slices between periods, and I'd never take water. I'd never have more than maybe one little piece of chocolate or one slice of orange because I thought it would make me too heavy.

Kirk: Me too. But at the end of the game, I'd be dehydrated. When it comes to superstition, my attitude is whatever's working, stick with it. As soon as it starts to fail, try something else.

Ian: When I was in the Memorial Cup, my aunt sent me some heather from Scotland. I put it between my knee and my pad, figuring this was a good luck charm. We lost in six. But you always try to get the advantage. When I put the heather in my pad, the first thing that came to my mind was, "Ah, it's not that heavy. It's not going to slow down my leg."

Kirk: I've got a real four-leaf clover in the back of my mask.

FEEDBACK

Kirk: Sometimes coaches will call you in before a game and tell you you've been playing lousy. But their perspective of a bad goal might not be the same as ours. You'll see something they don't see…like a deflection, for instance. And that happens all the time.

Peter: If you let in a goal through your five-hole, look out. It doesn't matter if it was shot from two feet away, or went 100 miles per hour. If it goes through your five-hole, it's automatically a bad goal. What are you supposed to do? Stand there with your pads together and let everything else in? Or are you going to give up that odd one through your legs? You look at all the good shooters and that's where they score, through your legs. Because most of the time, that's the only opening they have.

Ian: In the old days, the way to play goal was to keep the legs together and come out to the edge of the crease, and that was your angle. But in the old days, wingers stayed in their lanes and the play was more A to B. It was more direct to the net, which made it easier to play the angles. Nowadays, with the influence of the Europeans and the flowing motion, the cross-overs, the picks, it's more important than ever that a goalie has motion in his game and is aware of the situation as it develops. We know that half the coaches and announcers out there are critical of the five-hole goal. They don't understand that the guy over there was wide open for the pass. If I'm standing still, I can cover the five-hole. But I've got to open up to move for the pass. If I don't, my feet are dead and my options for the pass are gone. And how can I get over there if I'm standing still? Not only do I have to cover the four corners, but I have to be aware of that player at the side of the net. So I've got to open my legs slowly to keep movement as an option.

I'll tell you, there isn't a goalie in the National League or anywhere else who doesn't get his ire up when someone wants to talk about five-hole goals and how bad they are. A lot of coaches will complain about goals going between the legs, but I have two comments: One, why did they go in, and two, are they in fact "bad" goals?

Kirk: That's where the mental part comes in. Just forget it.

Peter: It has to go in one ear and out the other, and away you go to the next night.

Kirk: But if the coach figures it's a bad goal, sometimes you say to yourself, "Uh oh. Now I'm not going to play for the next eight games."

Ian: And then there's the media. They think they're experts, and you'll never win an argument against them.

Peter: I try not to read the paper. Sometimes reading the paper affects the way you think. If you play a real good game, they're writing about the great job you did. But you've got to keep it on that even keel, and one of the ways you do that is by not listening to all the media types or reading all the press clippings. And in the American markets, half the reporters don't know much about hockey.

Kirk: But the scary thing is that they write it down and the people read it, and that's what they believe.

Ian: A lot of players will read their own press, and if the press gets negative on them, *they* get negative. But you can't let that stuff affect you. If it does, don't read it. If a guy writes that you let in a bad goal and you don't agree, are you going to get upset, just because some reporter who's never skated is making a comment on your ability to play goal. You can't let it bother you. But that comes back to the individual. I can't emphasize enough how important a goalie's mental outlook is to his performance.

COACHING

Kirk: I guess it comes down to educating people. Most fans, coaches and reporters don't care how the goalie makes a save. They think if he stops it, he stops it, and if he doesn't, he doesn't. If a long shot goes in, they think it's a bad goal. We've got to educate people!

Peter: Name another sport that treats players the way goalies are treated. In baseball, every team has a pitching coach. In football, they have a quarterback coach, or some kind of offensive co-ordinator, and defensive coaches. So everyone has a coach. And as hockey goalies we can either win it or lose it in the majority of games. Goalie coaches? Everybody has a different philosophy, but if all teams had some kind of a goalie coach who could work with the goalies every day, it would help. And not just the physical stuff, but the *mental* part. If you get somebody in there who's played 10 or 15 years in the NHL and knows what young goalies are going through, he could coach them through tough situations. But that doesn't happen in the NHL. A few teams do have goalie coaches, but a lot of them are part-timers. Some might be scouts who come out once in awhile to help the goalies. Or some have one guy, but he's busy working with the minor league and junior goalies. Maybe if you had a goalie coach around all the time you'd rely on him too much, and you wouldn't try to work things out on your own. On the other hand, you do need someone around to coach you through the rough times, someone who's been through it and knows what you're thinking. Because of the nature of the position, we think differently than the average player. One thing I know for sure — when it comes to pressure, any player who's played this game for 10 or 15 years in the league, in that whole time they haven't gone through anything like what we go through *every night*. No one can argue with that statement. We have a different outlook; we're a different breed. And in most cases, there's nobody there to help us with those thoughts and pressures. If there was, we could rectify problems quickly rather than heading into a prolonged slump. And if you *do* have a long slump, they'll bring in someone else.

Ian: That doesn't make sense. If you're good enough to be there, they should spend time figuring out what's gone wrong, rather than bringing in some other guy. If you have a problem with your powerplay, you work on it. But the problem is, the people who are coaching understand powerplays, not goaltending. It's easier to work on the powerplay if that's what you know. The problem with a lot of goalie coaches goes right back to minor hockey. Very few people understand the position. That's where the void is. There's no proper, quality coaching unless you fluke into it. So you get to the junior or NHL level and you've never had quality instruction. You learn how to play angles based on the fact they beat you low to the stick side, or you learn about the proper way to butterfly because they went to the five-hole on the deke. You learn by experience. That's pretty sad! Even at the NHL level—and I've seen it—coaches make statements about goaltenders that are the farthest thing from the truth. You have an unqualified person telling you that you played a lousy game, or you shouldn't go down so much, or you left too many rebounds, or why didn't you have the five-hold covered on that goal. They're the ones that don't understand the game, yet they're also the ones who are harming this individual. A large part of coaching is psychological, and you have to keep your people positive. The guys I coach, if they let in a five-hole goal, I support them. Then at least they know the guy they're working with is supporting them. But how many goalies have that kind of support?

Kirk: When you get to the National League, they're not looking for what style you play. They just want you to stop the puck. They couldn't care less if you were the best technical goaltender in the world if you lose every game. They'd rather have someone who wins 10-9 every game than someone who loses 2-1 every game. You know, I could easily name half-a-dozen guys in the NHL with the worst styles you've ever seen, but they stop the puck. Ed Belfour is one.

Ian: And Grant Fuhr. He's a totally reflex goalie. But he's so *quick*.

Kirk: There are very few technically sound goalies in the NHL.

Ian: Just because you're in the National Hockey League, it doesn't mean you're really technically sound.

Kirk: I don't think there are two goalies in the league who play the same style. I think Mike Liut's pretty technically sound.

Ian: And Clint Malarchuk.

Kirk: I think so, too. And for a big guy, Darren Puppa's pretty good technically. I like Puppa as a goaltender.

Ian: Me, too. I'll give you an example of a guy who *doesn't* play a textbook game of goal, but he won a Molson Cup as a 21-year-old for the Maple Leafs. Peter Ing. You'd never say he was a technically sound goaltender, but he got the job done. And he was playing for one of the worst teams in the NHL at the time.

Peter: It makes a big difference who you're playing with. Sometimes a goalie is only as good as the team in front of him. A lot of goalies won't get recognition when they play for a bad team. They're out there making good saves, but eventually you'll give up one or two bad goals. And that's all anybody will look at. If you're playing behind a really good team, you're called on to make four or five big saves a game. If you make them, more often than not you're going to win. But if you play on a really bad team, you've got to make 15 or 20 real good saves. That makes a big difference.

WHAT IS TO BE DONE?

Ian: A young guy at our hockey school went back to his minor hockey team and a goalie coach there told him about a couple of things he should be doing. The young guy said to this goalie coach, "That's not what I was taught at the Ian Young Goaltending School." Now, who's right? At some point, somebody has to be right. You guys who coach at my school are going to be closer to right than some guy who never passed midget hockey as a player. And it's the technical level that's been reached by you three that has to be passed on to young goaltenders. When I put my name on the line, I know I can't go wrong having Peter Sidorkiewicz, Kirk McLean and Jeff Hackett on my side, because you guys know the game. But you'll even get differences in opinion among people at the highest level of the game. Of course, I always had the albatross that I never played in the NHL, so a lot of kids will say, "Who's Ian Young compared to someone like, say, John Vanbiesbrouck?" Let's face it…he's played all those years in the NHL, and I didn't. Well, Peter mentioned Paul Theriault's school up in the Soo. I was the guy in charge of the goaltending program up there, and John Vanbiesbrouck was one of the instructors. We broke off to the nets at one point and John was down at the other end of the ice teaching something altogether different than something we just talked about. The problem is this: I'm not saying he was right or wrong, but you have to go with a standard approach. You can't always have different opinion. For example, if I said to a young goaltender, "Come out to the edge of the crease and you've got your angle," and then Peter said to him, "Come out five feet,"— who's right? There's got to be solidarity in your approach. I think that's why, in our school, we don't step on each other's toes. And those young goalies leave our school with a sound and basic approach to the game. We never claim it's the only way, but we say, "Here are our reasons for believing in it." And it works.

Peter: Over the years you get a number of different people working with you, from minor hockey on up. Everyone has a different approach and nobody's totally right or wrong, but you've got to figure out what works for you and discard the things that don't. Somewhere along the way, try to establish a game that's consistent. You want to play consistently, and I think—the way Ian teaches the game—we try to go out and play the game the same way, night in, night out. One night we might give up eight goals, but the next night we're going to go out and play the same way. We're not going to change our whole game, and I think that's the biggest thing. Over the long haul, we're going to have success because of that.

Ian: I'm not saying that my theories and philosophy are the be-all and end-all of goaltending. It's like in my school: we never teach the poke-check, but we never discourage it because we know it's going to happen. What bothers me is the number of people who are given a high-profile forum to talk about goaltending, but are really missing the point — they think they're right, but they're not. And I think that's the cancer in goaltending circles. A lot of people who offer their services don't really understand the game. Although their heart's in the right place, their technical competence might not be what it should be. If you're going to provide a goaltending forum for minor hockey, you've got to have a standard approach to the game. That won't happen until we raise the level of coaching and overall knowledge of the game, until we create a level of goaltending coaching that will enable us to properly develop goaltending. That means the development of a nation-wide goaltending institute, something that could live on corporate sponsorship and address the problems of minor league coaches and goaltenders and give them the structure to nurture goaltending skills and understanding through minor hockey days right up to the professional level. It's a revolutionary concept. But because we've won four out of five Canada Cup tournaments, we're in a bit of a Catch-22. Since we win so often, everybody says we've got to be the best. And that includes goaltending. Theoretically, at least, that means we don't have to concentrate on developing better goaltenders, and in most cases all you hear from people after Stanley Cups or Canada Cups are obvious state-

ments like, "You need great goaltending to win." Okay, let's look at the goalies we're talking about. After the 1976 Canada Cup, was Rogie Vachon the best goalie in the world? In 1984, was Reggie Lemelin the best goalie in the world? And today, is Grant Fuhr the best goalie in the world? Is Bill Ranford the best goalie in the world? Is Jeff Hackett the best goalie in the world? I mean, how do you know what the "best" is, when in fact the only way most goalies develop is through their own natural ability — they learn by trial and error. We have no way of knowing what "best" really means. It's assumed that goaltenders who reach the NHL are the best in their trade. But if we agree that there's very little coaching right through to the NHL level, how can they be the best they can possibly be? We're sitting with a false standard for goalies. That standard could be a lot higher if teaching is standardized throughout the hockey world. My idea of a goaltending institute can combat the problem.

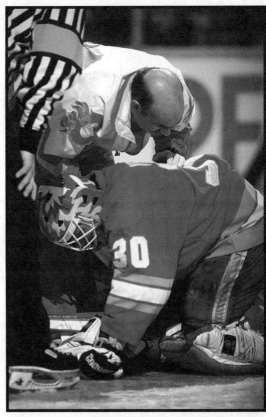

A Calgary trainer gives a shaken Mike Vernon a closer look (Relke).

A CLOSER LOOK AT GOALTENDERS

You'll never hear me claim that the goaltending style I teach is the only way to play the position. Students at my goalie school are offered a technically sound foundation and a lot of hard work, but I know they'll use that as the basis for the development of a style that most suits their individual skills.

I once saw a brochure advertising a "School of Standup Goaltending". How can that be? It's appropriate to stand up in certain situations, but you've got to go down in others. That's why the butterfly has become such a prevalent and effective addition to the goaltending arsenal. You can't just play the standup style of goaltending any more; you have to be able to do other things as well. This should be obvious to anyone who follows the game with more than passing interest, but even knowledgeable sports columnists can miss the point. For instance, I've read several articles that refer to Kirk McLean as a standup goaltender. That's absurd. Kirk may stand up a little more than some goalies, but that's not his predominant style. Kirk goes down with the best of them. What is a standup goalie? A standup goalie is Bernie Parent. But not Kirk McLean. As far as I'm concerned, that's a pretty good example of the difficulties encountered when evaluating goaltenders. If people see Kirk maintaining his feet in a few situations where some goalies might be flopping on the ice, then all of a sudden he's a "standup goaltender".

It's true that classifying goaltenders—and rating them, for that matter—can be a tricky proposition. I read a magazine article that claimed quite authoritatively that Vladislav Tretiak was the best goalie in hockey history. Now, it's true that Tretiak had several superb games against European, Canadian and NHL clubs. He was so exceptionally quick that he could get away with sticking well back in the net—a common trait of European goaltenders. But I can't help wondering how he would have handled an 80-game schedule with all that travel and constant intensity.

Tretiak first came to the attention of Canadian hockey fans during the historic 1972 Summit Series between Team Canada and the Soviet Union. He played all eight games in that series, finishing with a 3.88 goals against average. Most Canadians remember Ken Dryden at the other end of the ice in that series, because he played in both the shocking first-game loss at Montreal, and the dramatic, Canadian face-saving final game victory. But Dryden, who won six Stanley Cups and five Vezina Trophies during a splendid NHL career, has admitted having some less-than-brilliant outings against the Soviets. In that 1972 series, he played four games—winning two and losing two—and had an uncharacteristic 4.75 goals against average. What a lot of people seem to forget when they discuss the series is that Tony Esposito—who played the other four games, winning twice and tying once—had the best goals against average of the lot at 3.25.

My point is this: We all know that Tony Esposito was an excellent goaltender, but is it fair for us to assume that he was better than Tretiak or Dryden because of his accomplishments in that one series? And by the same token, is it fair for anyone to call Tretiak the greatest of all time when his exposure to us was, at most, a few games each season while he played behind Red Army and Soviet National teams that ranked amongst the strongest in the world? I think Tretiak was a great, great goaltender. But I'll say it again: It would have been interesting to see him over an 80-game season. Or several of them. With the Ottawa Senators.

There are a lot of good goaltenders in the National Hockey League today, and they're all a little different. Some are excellent angles goalies, some rely on reflexes more than positioning, and some go down earlier—and more often—than others. When I watch games, it's hard for me not to take mental notes and develop independent impressions of the goaltenders. With that in mind, I offer these thoughts on some of the game's premier puck-stoppers. Keep in mind that I'm more familiar with some goalies than I am with others, and in some cases, these observations are based on minimal exposure to the goalie in question.

Tom Barrasso makes the stop (Relke).

TOM BARRASSO

Playing for the talent-laden Pittsburgh team has got to be one of the toughest jobs in the world. But Barrasso—one of the big goaltenders—has made huge stops, game in, game out. He's played very consistent, and he's got solid strengths: an excellent trapper, and he's quick on his feet. I always thought he used his butterfly too much, but he could fall into that category of goalies that you don't want to tinker with too much because he's won Stanley Cups. He's played within his means, and he's done the job. I think his career was rejuvenated when he left Buffalo to join the Penguins, and at times he's played some outstanding hockey.

Barrasso is a great example of a pro you'd put on your team simply because he knows how to win.

ED BELFOUR

Ed Belfour is a great example of that new style of goaltending you also see in Curtis Joseph and Felix Potvin. He has that exaggerated opening in the five-hole, so a lot of people assume that all you have to do is shoot through it. But he's a perennial Vezina Trophy candidate, so it can't be that simple. Belfour is extremely quick with great desire. He's aggressive on the puck, not in the technical sense of coming out to challenge, but in the way that he reacts to the puck quickly and goes to it. He redefines his angles by moving to the puck. Belfour goes to the butterfly quicker than most because his knees are so close to the ice due to his exaggerated stance. And after he goes to the butterfly, he doesn't stay down unless the puck stays in close. If the puck goes out high, he's back up quickly.

SEAN BURKE

I like Sean Burke. He's a gifted goaltender with great ability to place himself wherever the puck is going. He's big and uses his size to his advantage, and he's quick with great reflexes. When he's playing with confidence, he's tough to beat. Sometimes he has the tendency to drop his trapper too much because he goes into a low crouch, but I understand he has an excellent attitude and is highly coachable. With a good team in front of him and proper coaching, Sean Burke could be one of the best in the league.

MIKE FOUNTAIN

I will be amazed if Mike Fountain does not become a star in the NHL. Not only does he have great desire to play, but he's unbelievably quick, especially with his legs. He can get up and down quickly, move laterally really well, has a terrific sense of the puck and understands how the game should be played. When Mike's deep, it means he's playing possibilities around the net. And he knows when to challenge so he doesn't get burned. He has an outstanding attitude, and works hard in drills. He's primarily a butterfly goalie. He was a 1992 second-round pick of the Vancouver Canucks.

GRANT FUHR

Grant Fuhr relies almost exclusively now on quickness. He plays deep in the net and loves doing the splits. Unfortunately, he gives up a lot of rebounds—he wears big pads and he'll make the save, but not concern himself with rebounds. He was always the guy who made the big save under high pressure situations. He'll never be remembered for low goals-against averages, but he was the perfect goalie for the high-flying Oilers teams of the 'eighties. Grant knew he could give up four or five goals and still win, and when those two or three key shots came his way, he usually found a way to make the impossible stop. When it was 4-4 or 5-5 and the opposition got a breakaway, he'd make the save. And that's where money goalies make money. My suggestion to Fuhr would be to not rely as much on quickness. Instead, he should combine his existing quickness with some technical adjustments, and he'll be back where he was.

JEFF HACKETT

Jeff Hackett is extremely quick. When he first came to Oshawa, he gave up five goals in the first period of an intra-squad game. He went home after that, but I was so impressed by his potential that I commented that Jeff Hackett would become a great goalkeeper. He came back the next year, and I would say that in his rookie year with the Generals, Jeff Hackett never played a bad game. He has tremendous quickness, and great leg speed in dropping to his butterfly. He worked hard at becoming sound laterally, and at cutting down his angles, and put together his goaltending package in his two years at Oshawa. I knew Jeff Hackett would become a force in the NHL.

Jeff Hackett displays perfect form (Relke).

DOMINIK HASEK

Hasek's a typical European goaltender in that he plays in the crease all the time. He depends a lot on reflexes and reading the play. Hasek's biggest asset is his puck sense. He's always right on the puck, or never far from it. He has an exciting quickness, reacting with great speed to situations. He doesn't have to be quite as strong on his feet as other goalies because he stays deep in his crease and he doesn't need nearly as much movement in his game. But again, his puck sense and concentration level are his biggest attributes. He doesn't play the highly technical game of North American goaltenders who often rely a little bit more on playing the angles. He's playing at the same level in the NHL as he did in Europe, which is an astounding accomplishment. If you look at other European goaltenders in the NHL, very few have had the same effect as they had back home.

KELLY HRUDEY

My impression of Hrudey is that he's more a natural ability goaltender than anybody else in the game. He's serious about his job, and he gets it done. He's got a solid attitude, and comes to play every night. He'll do anything to stop the puck: he'll dive, fall to his knees, stand up, he'll do a two-pad slide across the net...whatever it takes to get the job done. I don't think Hrudey's style is as technically competent as it could be, but he's got tremendous drive and desire to be good at what he does.

CURTIS JOSEPH

Late in the 1992-93 season and right on through the playoffs, Curtis Joseph went from relative mediocrity to superstar status. He has a unique style, but it's not one you would teach to a young goalie. Technically, it leaves a lot to be desired. On the other hand, if the style works for Joseph, if he's stopping 60 shots and winning games, why would you try to change the way he plays? Curtis Joseph goes down in the wierdest and most awkward way. This style does cut off the five-hole quickly—he bends his knee in a bit as he goes down, so the moment he turns in, he cuts off the five-hole. And when he lays the shaft of the stick flat on the ice, he takes away shots along the ice. But with this new style, used by people like Joseph and Potvin, goalies tend to give up a lot of bad rebounds because they're not under control. And when the rebounds bounce out front, the goalie is down. That's the problem with that style—you're down all the time. If you just drop to the butterfly and extend your pads, you've covered the entire lower net, too. And with the butterfly, you're more upright, and ready for shots. One thing to remember about Joseph is his combative spirit. Sometimes, technical play isn't as important as an attitude that says the puck won't beat me.

KIRK MCLEAN

Kirk plays some situations deep in the net because he depends so much on his puck sense and quickness. He's got tremendous speed, great foot strength, superb technical knowledge and a strong trapper. Because his reflexes and speed are so outstanding, he can play deeper in the net than most other goaltenders. He's great at anticipating the play. When a shot's about to hit him, he knows where it's going. And he's very strong at controlling rebounds. When you combine quickness, technical competence and the ability to read the puck well, you're going to stop a lot of pucks.

FELIX POTVIN

When I was with the Leafs, I asked Floyd Smith and Tom Watt why they were going for a big-name goaltender when they had Felix Potvin down the road in St. John's. They had Peter Ing, playing for the worst team in hockey at the time, in one of the toughest cities to play in, and he won the Molson Cup as the team's top player that year. They had Jeff Reese, who was getting better and better, and was playing pretty solid in goal for a team that didn't have much going for it. I told Smith and Watt to play these two young goaltenders and see what they can do, and bring in Potvin in

Kirk McLean—outstanding speed and reflexes (Relke).

January, and he'll take over. I regard Felix Potvin as a franchise hockey player. Some people criticize him in two areas. They claim he goes down too much, and that he stays too deep in his net. But in the 1993-94 season, he was voted to the all-star game. Sooner or later, goalies like Potvin have to be given credit for outstanding quickness and reflexes, as well as shot anticipation. What's more, Felix is unflappable in net, and that's a perfect psychological attribute for any goaltender. For years to come, he'll continue to be one of the elite goaltenders in the NHL. I couldn't wait to work with him, but unfortunately, I never got a chance to because Cliff Fletcher didn't retain my services after he took over the Leafs.

BILL RANFORD

Bill Ranford is a goalie with good size and good intensity. He plays a little higher in his net than a lot of others, and he is primarily a stand-up goalie who exhibits great reflexes. He has good feet and a quick trapper, and is usually on his feet and in position for the second shot. That's what I call strong on your feet, unlike goalies who constantly dive across the crease, effectively eliminating their options even if they stop the initial shot. Ranford has great mental toughness and a will to win, which he proved during Team Canada's victory in the 1991 Canada Cup, and again during Canada's world championship triumph in '94.

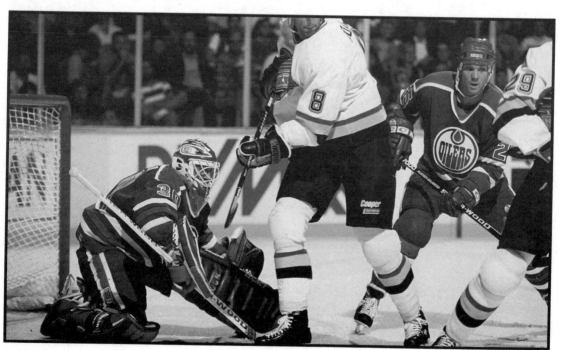

Bill Ranford—good feet and a quick trapper (Relke).

DAMIAN RHODES

I worked with Damian Rhodes when he was with Newmarket and I worked for the Leafs. I don't think Damian is quite the goalie that Potvin is, but he's come a long way and is capable of playing in the NHL. He's had to work on his butterfly because it wasn't a natural move for him. When I started working with him, he was far too erect—he wasn't fluid enough in his play. Now he opens his stance a bit, challenges more, and gets around his crease a lot better. Reflexes were never an issue with him. It was a case of building confidence and changing his style a bit—it was as if he was playing with clumps of cement in his skates.

MIKE RICHTER

For a while, the Rangers' combination of John Vanbiesbrouck and Mike Richter was one of the best—if not the best—one-two goaltending punch in the NHL. When Richter is on, his reflexes and movement are so quick it's almost impossible to beat him. He was outstanding for the American team at the 1991 Canada Cup tournament, and almost carried them past Team Canada in the finals. His game is a pretty nice combination of the standup and butterfly styles, although he leans more to the standup. He has a sound trapper, and reacts quickly to situations. A complete goaltender, when he's on top of his game.

PATRICK ROY

Roy is a reflex goaltender with a predominantly butterfly style. He's not that aggressive, in that he doesn't come out and challenge—he's always deep in his net. But nobody gets away with playing the butterfly style as deep in the net as he does without great puck sense. He's a natural athlete. He knows where to be, and he's got great reflexes. Of veteran goaltenders in the league, Roy is in the top three. During Montreal's Stanley Cup win in 1993, Roy got up in the dressing room between periods of a final series game in L.A. The game was tied, and he asked his teammates to score

Patrick Roy—a natural athlete (Relke).

one more goal. That's all they'd need, he said, because the Kings weren't going to get any more on him. They didn't. Montreal won the game in overtime. After, Canadiens' captain Guy Carbonneau said that after watching Roy for eight years, he was ready to believe his goalie when he said the opposition wouldn't score. That has to be the ultimate compliment for any goalkeeper.

PETER SIDORKIEWICZ

Peter is more of a standup goalie than the other goalies I coached at Oshawa. He has a great love of the game and has developed a high degree of technical competence and has managed to maximize his ability. He'd be the first to tell you that he's not the best goalie in the NHL, but he's also the kind of player everybody wants on their team, because of his effort and the way he plays. Without question, Peter has got to position himself well in the net to play the game, and that's where his strength lies. Peter's got a sound butterfly technique and a very quick trapper, but he also knows the game through strong positional play so he's able to make the tough saves. In Ottawa's first year, he literally held the franchise together. He made the all-star game and played well there, showing everybody that he was a capable goalkeeper. I don't think he really had an opportunity to show that until he got to Ottawa. Peter is not a spectacular goalkeeper but he gets the job done efficiently.

MIKE VERNON

Vernon is more of a standup goaltender. He relies a lot on his quickness, reflexes and experience. He's had a lot of outstanding years in Calgary, playing efficiently by playing his angles well. He has a fast trapper, and will long be remembered for a big glove save against Vancouver in overtime of game seven of a divisional semi-final in 1989. Calgary went on to win the Stanley Cup, and that makes him a winner.

KAY WHITMORE

I've always liked him. I was a consultant for the national junior team in 1987, and he was one of five goalies. After watching him for awhile, I told him, "I don't know how this is going to work out as far as selections are concerned, but I really believe you're the best goalie here." That national camp had Troy Gamble, Sean Burke and Kirk McLean. Kay has extremely good reflexes, is very quick with the pads, wastes no time getting back on his feet after going down, and brings a lot of energy to his game. He also has the ability to focus, an important attribute for a goalie in a back-up role. Kay has the knack for giving shooters what they don't expect to see. For instance, a forward comes down the wing and looks up, expecting to see the far side. Instead, Kay has given them the short side. Most forwards will get confused and blow the shot. In short, Kay likes to play with their minds.

ROYALTY FROM EARLIER ERAS

One of the biggest differences between today's goalies and the Bowers, Sawchuks and Worsleys is that the latter group placed tremendous stress on reflexes. Today, the big thing is quickness. That's part of the evolution of goaltending. Not that reflexes aren't important, but in the old days, youngsters were told that goalies should stand up, and they needed fast reflexes. Today, because of the butterfly, there isn't the same emphasis on standing up. In the old days, there was more predictability to the game. There was the drop pass and the shot; the pass to the wing and the shot; the pass to the slot and the shot. That's probably why goalies stayed deep in their net and relied on reflexes. Today's goalies have greater need for quickness, moving from post to post, moving out and coming back, and reacting to guys driving through and across the crease.

Bernie Parent and Glenn Hall are my picks as the all-time greatest goaltenders. (I have a leaning for Patrick Roy as well, but he's still playing so I won't include him here.) Parent was the standup goalie, Glenn Hall the butterfly man. My ideal goaltender would be someone with a combination of their two styles.

Johnny Bower—a heart-and-soul player (Imperial Oil-Turofsky/Hockey Hall of Fame).

JOHNNY BOWER

Johnny Bower was a classic standup goaltender. He would play the top of his crease with his feet together, and counted on taking away the net and blocking the shot. In the sixties, a friend went to a Maple Leafs practice and sat behind the net, watching Bower at work. To this day, he still marvels at Bower's ability to give the shooter a corner of the net, and then take it away. As the forward came in on goal, Bower would leave a few inches on the short or far side. As the shooter unleashed his shot, Bower would close the opening and make the stop. Bower also loved to do the splits. And he had a trapper that seemed to flap in the breeze when he snared a shot, but I think that had more to do with the type of trapper they used. Bower's greatest move was his poke-check. Guys would drive in on goal and even though they knew he was waiting to use the poke, he would still pull it off. I think the secret to Bower's poke-check was the quickness of the move. There's a good lesson for young kids—good shooters watch where the goaltender is going, good shooters see a goalie's hand moving up the stick shaft preparing for a poke-check, so they're mentally prepared, giving themselves a better opportunity to counter it. But Bower's move was so fast—as the shooter got to a certain point, driving to the net, Bower's stick was out there. You need tremendous eye-puck co-ordination to do that not only well, but consistently. Bower was a heart-and-soul guy, a high-character competitor who would throw his face in front of the puck if that would save the day. As a result, teammates loved to play for him. He'll always be remembered as an all-time goaltending great, and when I was growing up he was one of my heroes. He may not have the same amount of talent as a lot of others, but he had heart, and heart took Johnny Bower a long way: 15 NHL seasons yielded four Stanley Cups, four Vezina Trophies, and a first team all-star selection.

GERRY CHEEVERS

Cheevers' biggest attribute was his strength on his feet. He was a strong skater who could react quickly to play around his net. Cheevers was a great athlete and such a good skater that he even played forward in some junior games with St. Michael's. When I played junior, I worked hard on my skating partly because of what I knew about Gerry Cheevers. He was able to go down, get up, move laterally, come high, go low …whatever it took. He also improved with experience, a reflex goaltender with an above average trapper who stayed near the top of his crease in what was basically a standup style. He became a money player who came up with the big save at the right time, and the Bruins loved to play in front of him. His 13 years in the NHL yielded a pair of Stanley Cups with Boston in 1970 and 1972.

ROGER CROZIER

He was another Glenn Hall clone, like Tony Esposito, who would come far out of his net to challenge the shooter. He was the smallest of the three, and his physical stature probably helped with his quickness, which was considerable. Crozier had an exclusively butterfly style of play and a good trapper, but his size didn't prevent him from playing 14 NHL seasons that produced a Calder Trophy and a Conn Smythe Trophy to go along with a first team all-star selection in 1964-65.

KEN DRYDEN

As I mentioned earlier, Ken Dryden and I had some classic battles in our Junior "B" days. He played with the Etobicoke Indians and I was with the Whitby Bees, and it wasn't unusual for us to play 2-1 or 3-2 games with each of us facing over 40 shots. So not only did I get to follow his brilliant NHL career, but years earlier I watched him do his thing at the other end of the ice. He was so tall and lanky that sometimes he looked awkward, but he was a natural who used skills learned elsewhere to help his goaltending. For instance, he was a good baseball player, so few pucks got past his trapper. He had huge, size thirteen skates and used them to good advantage. To me, the classic Dryden move was to drop to one knee and kick out the puck. And he was smart. He read the play well and knew where he had to be, when he had to go down, when to stay on his feet; he put the whole package together. For a big man he was quite agile, although I've never thought of Ken Dryden as a goalie who moved forward and backward a lot. He moved side to side as the puck moved back and forth out front. He often had a problem against the Russians because of the fast-flowing European style of play. But when you look at some of the things he did at the NHL level—not only the championships but the high level of consistency while playing under the pressure that goes with being on a perennial contender like the Canadiens—you can't help but be impressed. Some people think that a great team can win championships with an average goalie, but that's not true. The goalie on a winning team still has to come up with big saves at key points. Dryden had greatness. When Montreal beat a formidable Bruins' team in the 1971 playoffs, the Canadiens' greatness didn't win that series—Ken Dryden won that series.

TONY ESPOSITO

Tony Esposito was a Glenn Hall clone. They both had the inverted "V" stance, both came out and skated back with the play, both went to the butterfly then got right back up, and both had post-to-post quickness. Neither would hesitate to come out 15 or 20 feet to take the angle and then back in with the shooter. But for both of them, the main claim to fame was their butterfly. Tony was a bigger goaltender who would drop to the butterfly from chances in close, keeping his body erect so guys couldn't get the puck past him, even if they shot high. He was tremendously quick. I look back to the 1972 Canada-Soviets series—Canada wouldn't have won that series without Tony Esposito. Although he never played with an outstanding team in Chicago, he was exciting to watch and racked up a pile of shutouts—76 in his career—to earn the nickname "Mr. Zero". He was a first team all-star three times, and a second team pick twice. Fittingly, both Tony Esposito and

Glenn Hall had their numbers retired by the Blackhawks at the same time. In a moving pre-game ceremony on November 20, 1988, Esposito's #35 and Hall's #1 were lifted to the rafters at Chicago Stadium.

GLENN HALL

I admired Glenn Hall immensely and he was instrumental in the development of my own goaltending style. Everything I teach today concerning motion and challenging the shooter came from Hall's example. He would overcompensate sometimes, but

Glenn Hall—a goaltending pioneer (Imperial Oil-Turofsky/Hockey Hall of Fame).

that's not such a bad thing. I tell my goalies that when they're moving out on a shooter, it doesn't matter how far out of the crease they come as long as they're on the centre line. Of course, you've got to be aware of your ability to come back or react laterally with the play. It was nothing to see Hall come 20 feet out of the net, then move back as the puck advanced on him. He introduced motion to the position. Hall was also the first goalie to use the quick butterfly move. He challenged aggressively and when he went into the butterfly, he was right back up. You never saw him flopping around in his crease. You had to see him do the down-and-up movement to appreciate how quick he was. Old-time players and fans know that one of hockey's oldest axioms is that players should shoot low to the stick side. Today that doesn't really apply because of the prevalence of the butterfly move, and since Hall was the man who introduced the butterfly, that makes him a goaltending pioneer. His motion, quickness, use of the butterfly and a very quick trapper add up to an 18-year NHL career highlighted by one Stanley Cup, 3 Vezina Trophies, and 7 first team all-star selections. Four times, he was named to the second team. Hall also holds the goaltending record for most consecutive complete games with an almost unbelievable total of 502. Without a doubt, the iron-man of goaltending—the man they called "Mr. Goalie"—knew something about playing the position.

BERNIE PARENT

Bernie Parent was the greatest standup goaltender of all time. He was quick with his feet, and his positioning was perfect. We talk about the telescoping theory of angles and how goalies strive to come out to the ideal spot on an angle. Parent never went beyond that point. He would never take an extra foot. He was always on that centre line, and knew exactly how far he had to come out to achieve the optimum angle. Not only were you looking at a competent and quick goaltender, you also had an athlete who knew angles and blocked off the net perfectly. In situations where the puck is passed from one side of the net to the other, most goalies will come across with the two-pad slide to try to block the shot. But Parent always moved across while staying on his feet. He didn't have a weakness. Even in goal-mouth scrambles, he was able to stay on his feet rather than flop around on the ice. There were always situations where he had to leave his feet, but when Bernie did so, he was always quick at getting up. He had great quickness, superb lateral motion, tremendous angles play and a maturity and mental toughness that was there even during his junior days. Professionally, Parent played 13 NHL seasons with Boston, Toronto and Philadelphia, winning two Stanley Cups with the Flyers and a pair of Vezina Trophies. He was a first team all-star twice and racked up 55 shutouts.

Bernie Parent—the greatest stand-up goaltender of all time (Graphic Artists/Hockey Hall of Fame).

JACQUES PLANTE

I had the opportunity to talk with Jacques Plante, and realized that he and I were very different. For instance, he was into knitting, and I wasn't. However, the man changed goaltending significantly and I admired him because of that. He was tremendously quick on his feet with good puck anticipation and ability to read the play. He was good, if not great, at every aspect of the game. He was a student of the position, an intelligent, thinking goaltender who did so many things well. And the sum of those "wells" made him great. And of course, he popularized the use of face masks. He was not afraid to

Jacques Plante—great at every aspect of the game (Imperial Oil-Turofsky/Hockey Hall of Fame).

challenge—to come out and play the angle—or to play the puck behind the net, taking some of the heat off his defencemen. In doing so, he introduced the "offensive" aspect to the position. Plante played for some exceptional hockey teams in Montreal with extraordinary team and individual accomplishments. He played on six Cup winners and placed his name on the Vezina Trophy seven times. He was a first team all-star three times, making the second team on another four occasions. The years of Jacques Plante, Terry Sawchuk, Glenn Hall, Johnny Bower and Gump Worsley have been referred to as the Golden Era of Goaltending. For years, clubs from the six-team era carried just one goaltender. Eventually, they all took to carrying a back-up on the bench, but it wouldn't have been hard to argue that NHL fans were watching the six best goaltenders in the world! Today, there are more than fifty goalies on NHL rosters. If we boiled that number down to six—with your Roys and McLeans and Belfours—there's no doubt we'd rediscover the same level of greatness between the pipes.

TERRY SAWCHUK

If you think of the Ken Danby print, "At the Crease", that's Terry Sawchuk's stance. He had his legs a little wider apart than most goalies of the day, even up above the knees. Instead of an inverted "V", his legs were straight up and down, very similar to the goalie in Danby's work. He didn't challenged shooters; he was content to stay close to home at the top of the crease like most other goalies of his era. Sawchuk had great feet, relying on the skate save rather than the butterfly for low shots. His feet were so quick that he was able to nail shots with them all the time, and any goaltender today who's tried to make skate saves from the crease knows how difficult that is. He'd drop one knee down and throw out the other skate. And he had a great trapper, even on shots coming from close in. He was an immense talent with great concentration and tremendous quickness, and who can

argue the point after checking out his playing statistics? Terry Sawchuk holds NHL regular season career records for most games played (971), most wins (435), and most shutouts (103). He won four Vezina Trophies and four Stanley Cups, and was named to the first all-star team three times, making the second team on four other occasions.

GUMP WORSLEY

Gump Worsley was a short goaltender with small pads who played within his crease all the time. He was a bit of an enigma because, on the one hand, he had a

Terry Sawchuk still holds 3 NHL career records (Imperial Oil-Turofsky/Hockey Hall of Fame).

standup style with a very small opening between the pads, a stance that precluded the butterfly move. On the other hand, he wasn't a classic angle goalie who would stand up, take away the net and stay on his feet. Instead, he was a standup goalie who would kick pucks out like Sawchuk did, or dive at pucks, or do the two-pad slide. He played with a lot of guts and would do anything he had to do to stop the puck. He was a smart goalie who knew how to angle off pucks. But he was also a diver and a flopper who stayed in his crease, and you can't do that with any degree of success if you don't understand positioning, read the play well, and have good reflexes. When he played for the Rangers, I used to wonder how he could play good, consistent goal for so many years on such a poor hockey team. But he did. (Once, in the midst of yet another New York losing streak, a writer asked Gump which team gave him the most trouble. He answered, "The Rangers.") In his later playing years, he continued to play well with the Canadiens and the Minnesota North Stars. Worsley rode his playing style to a 21-year NHL career that produced four Stanley Cups, two Vezina Trophies, one first team all-star selection and one second team berth.

Gump Worsley and Johnny Bower, acknowledging each other's greatness (Imperial Oil-Turofsky/Hockey Hall of Fame).

Kirk McLean keeps an eye on the game (Relke).

RANDOM THOUGHTS FROM THE CREASE

While discussing the position one day, a goalie friend told me that he didn't think he ever played a game in which he didn't see something new. He was talking about goaltending's wonderful complexity, and the countless passing, shooting, deflection, rebound, clearing and collision possibilities around the net. If we recognize that to be true, then we also have to admit it's virtually impossible to cover in this book every occurrence that could conceivably transpire over the course of a game. You may find yourself instinctively doing certain things a mere handful of times in all the years you play the game; it's a case of considering your options and acting accordingly.

Some aspects of playing goal are definitely matters of personal preference, such as how you hold your stick while clearing the puck. It's a simple matter of evaluating your strengths and weaknesses. Do you have a backhand shot, or are you a lot stronger on your forehand? And how do you hold the stick when you shoot? Do you shoot with your blocker at the top of the shaft, or on the bottom of the shaft? It's a matter of personal preference, and like all goalies, I have my own opinion. I feel that when you shoot a puck, the strength comes from the lower hand. And since goalies tend to hold their stick with their dominant—or stronger—hand, the lower part of the shaft is where the blocker should be when you're shooting. You'll have more strength, and therefore more control over the stick, with the blocker hand down low, just above the point at which the shaft of your stick widens. For a lot of goalies, this will mean turning the stick around before shooting the puck. Such a move becomes automatic after awhile. And besides, in most cases you'll be retrieving the puck off the boards before you shoot it. That will give you the time you need to turn the stick. But like I said, this is one of those areas where personal preference comes into play.

BEHIND THE NET

Staying with the play when an opposition player has the puck behind your net is another area in which goalies have their individual preferences. There are general guidelines every goalie should keep in mind.

First and foremost, *find* the puck behind the net. If it means crouching down a bit and looking through the back of the net, fine.

A famous goaltending story is the one that has 44-year-old manager/coach Lester Patrick putting on the pads and leading his New York Rangers to victory in a 1928 Stanley Cup game against the Montreal Maroons. It is usually presumed that Patrick had never before played the position. But six years earlier—on January 9, 1922—Patrick played ten minutes in goal for Victoria of the Pacific Coast Hockey Association when regular goalie Norman Fowler was sent off for fighting. Patrick even stopped a penalty shot by Jack Adams in that game, although he did give up a goal. Ten days later, he filled in for three minutes of a game against the Vancouver Millionaires. So technically speaking, Patrick wasn't a goaltending rookie when he took to the ice on behalf of the Rangers in that historic Stanley Cup matchup.

You've got to be prepared to be intense during those plays and always follow the puck, no matter how long the player has it behind the net. Some players—like Wayne Gretzky and Doug Gilmour—can wear you down when they get the puck back there. But when they're about to put it out front, your aim is always the same: *Get the skate to the post, and get the stick out.* The skate on the post will prevent the easy wraparound goal (there's nothing worse than the wraparound play that goes off the outside of your skate blade and into the net), and the stick held outside the goalpost and as close as possible to the goal line will take away the pass or force the passer to carry the puck a little wider than he wants to. If the puck-handler does decide to carry the puck a little

---

At The Crease

When you combine great artistic talent with a subject matter of major significance, the result can be impressive. That's what happened when Ken Danby applied his skills to the world of goaltending. The result? "At the Crease", arguably the most famous hockey-related work from the artistic world.

I doubt that Danby considered whether or not his work would be subjected to critical technical analysis, however that doesn't change the fact that, technically, there's very little that's sound in the painting. For example, the goalie is bent too far forward, the stick blade isn't flat on the ice, and the trapper isn't open with the palm facing the puck. As a result, "At the Crease" makes an unintentional statement about the inadequate state of goalie coaching in minor hockey!

Having said that, however, I have a confession to make: I love it. "At the Crease" brings back childhood days in those old, cold, classic arenas in Woodbridge and Newmarket and Goderich, where parents drank coffee or hot chocolate to keep the blood flowing, and you'd put your trapper on the one little radiator in the dressing room to warm it up before you hit the ice. Danby's net—with a rectangular rather than a circular shape on top—is an old country arena cage you used to find in those ancient rinks. The love of the game was thick in the air in those small-town arenas. And when I look at the Danby print, that's what I see—by-gone days when I couldn't wait to get to the rinks where the game was just pure fun.

wider to get outside your stick, that will give you time to get your whole body across to the post, and from there you can begin to move out and challenge the shot. *Under no circumstances should you be happy with falling or diving along the goal line.* That's cheating yourself. The shot *may* hit you, but that has more to do with good luck than good goaltending.

It comes back to skating. If you're strong on your feet and you can go post-to-post with the puck, automatically getting the stick outside the post each time, you'll be in good shape, no matter who has the puck behind the net. And you'll be in even better shape if you can go post-to-post and then advance on the puck to take away the angle if it's passed or carried out front. Unfortunately, far too many goaltenders don't use the strength in their feet. Instead, they cop out and drop to the ice, hoping the puck hits

them. How many times have you seen a player carry the puck out from behind the net, or pass it to a teammate, and have the quick shot go up under the crossbar? Good goal, right? Well, not necessarily. If the goaltender was strong enough on his feet to go post-to-post and then move out a couple of feet to take the angle, there's a good chance the shooter would be sent skulking back to his bench rather than taking bows at centre ice.

As in all other aspects of the game, just remember: If you're on a roll, really playing well, then you're going to make the save doing it my way. But if you're having a tough time, and the puck doesn't seem to be bouncing your way, it shouldn't change the way you approach things. The best way to get out of that tough stretch is to play it technically solid. Use your foot strength, stay with the play and take away the net.

A COMPREHENSIVE REVIEW OF GOALTENDING FUNDAMENTALS

The following chapters assume that Ian Young's previous two books on goaltenidng, **Behind The Mask: The Ian Young Goaltending Method** and **Beyond The Mask: The Ian Young Goaltending Method, Book 2—Advanced Techniques,** have been read. **Behind The Mask** details the fundamentals of playing goal, while **Beyond The Mask** introduces drillwork to develop these fundamentals. While this book provides a comprehensive overview of goaltending basics, it would be advantageous to refer to the relevant sections in the earlier books for diagrams and details. With this in mind, read on and review the elements of technically competent goaltending:

- stance
- angles
- skating and motion
- ice shots
- rebounds
- deflections
- screen shots
- breakaways
- two-on-ones
- two-on-nones

Ed Belfour shows perfect stance (Relke).

STANCE

Through the decades, for the most part, goaltenders were self-taught. They developed their own stances and, theoretically, those who were able to best maximize movement, maintain balance and recover for the second or third shot were the ones who advanced farthest up the hockey ladder.

Those of us brought up in the era of the six-team NHL, watching the likes of Glenn Hall, Jacques Plante, Terry Sawchuk, Johnny Bower, Gump Worsley and others, remember them for their excellent work between the pipes. All were accomplished professional goaltenders, and yet each had his own distinctive style and a stance that complemented that style.

Today, although most young goaltenders work out on their own—figuring out the position and developing a style that "works"—there are more and more goalie coaches in minor hockey. On the surface, this would appear to be a major advancement. But it has its pitfalls.

Just as Johnny Bower—the classic example of the traditional stand-up puck-stopper—never tried to turn himself into a butterfly-style goaltender, goalie coaches should not attempt to radically disrupt whatever style works for an individual. As the saying goes, if it ain't broke, don't fix it.

Rather than initiating major overhauls, the role of the goalie coach should be to administer minor tuneups and the odd modification to produce a smoother-running puck-stopping machine. And don't forget—the "machine" may have a long way to go in its development, and many of the original parts may have yet to be broken in. So tread softly, and above all, don't get frustrated! After all, Patrick Roy wasn't built in a day.

Each individual will develop a stance that, generally speaking, best fits his or her build and experience. On the other hand, that doesn't mean we can't offer that individual a model stance—or the ideal crouch, if you will—that allows for maximum protection of the net, a universal model from which all other stances can be evaluated and, presumably, improved.

Before we begin this little journey through the crease, keep in mind that I never claim that the stance I teach is the only way to play the position. Just as there's not one style of goaltender—there's the stand-up style; there's the butterfly style—there is a range of comfortable stances as well. (*Behind The Mask*, pp. 23-29)

MODEL STANCE

In my own case, the development of a "model stance" goes back to something that happened to me when I first joined the Oshawa Generals as a 15-year-old in 1963. In fact, it was the major turning point in my goaltending career, and the genesis of my present goaltending theory.

It occurred in my first game against the Montreal Junior Canadiens, at the Bowmanville Arena. Their big star was a young Yvan Cournoyer, who went on to play on ten Stanley Cup winners in 16 years with the Montreal Canadiens. In that first meeting—to make a long and painful story as short as possible—he beat me three times. All three shots went along the ice and off a goalpost.

I had played all-star hockey all the way through my minor hockey days, and I wasn't used to being beaten so badly. But I knew one thing in my heart—I didn't have a prayer on those shots. I had no idea how to stop them. I couldn't move fast enough to reach the shots.

Now, Yvan Cournoyer was a great player. But I wasn't so naive as to think that he was the only accurate shooter I'd ever have to face. For every Yvan Cournoyer, there will be another sniper on another team, and maybe two on the next. By the time you reach NHL level, there could be as many as ten on any one roster. So I was sure of one thing: If I wanted my goaltending career to advance much further, I had to learn how to meet those situations head on.

I decided that for me, the most efficient way of handling low shots to either side was by using the butterfly.

Easier said than done.

At first, it felt clumsy, uncomfortable. I stood in my old stance, legs together, and while teammates came in and fired shots during practice, I concentrated on the butterfly move. It didn't take long for me to realize that everything the butterfly implies—going down and getting up easily, with no awkwardness—can't be done if the legs are kept closed. It's just not possible. I was going down too slowly, tripping over my knees on the way. Not only that, but with the legs closed, I was negating the fluidity of my movement in all directions— forwards, backwards and laterally.

My conclusion was an obvious one: I had to open up my stance a few inches, so my legs were in an inverted "V" position where

Mike Fountain (Martin Oravec).

I kept the knees together and opened up a little at the bottom. That gave me fluidity in my motion, and comfort while moving in any direction.

I can hear what you're saying: If you open the legs, then you're asking for trouble…how about the 5-hole?"

True, the odd shot will find that opening, and there will always be misguided people who think you can play the game with your pads closed. But the negative effects of the inverted "V" are far outweighed by the advantages. For every shot that slipped through that opening, I probably stopped 20 drives to the low corners, or I had the comfort—and therefore the mobility—to move with the play. Increased mobility alone makes the inverted "V" a high-percentage move, allowing a full complement of actions that will help you respond to virtually all situations around the net.

On November 29th, 1990, Buffalo Sabres goaltender Clint Malarchuk stopped thirty shots in a 2-1 victory over the Montreal Canadiens at the Forum. The only shot that beat him came off the stick of Tom Chorske early in the second period. Chorske skated down the right side, wound up and rifled a shot that went between Malarchuk's pads. The television commentators called it a bad goal; the sportswriters called it a bad goal. What did Malarchuk say about it?: "The guy shot a cannon. People think that's a bad goal, but the guy hit the five-hole. Unless you're a goalie, you don't know how hard that is."

And yet, 99% of the coaches out there will still say, "No, you've got to squeeze those legs together!" They'll always blame the goalie for a 5-hole goal because it's the worst-looking goal imaginable. But the same shot that finds the five-hole can move at half the speed and go in off the lower post, and people will say, "That's a great shot, right off the post. What's the poor goalie going to do about those?"

Well, there's a lot the "poor goalie" can do about those...as long as he's playing with the inverted "V" as part of his stance.

In my own case, I discovered that by advancing on the puck-carrier, then backing up, I was able to handle shots low to the corners by using the butterfly. If I'd known that before my first encounter with Cournoyer, I would have had a much better chance of stopping those shots. In retrospect, I owe him so much. He set me on the path to goaltending cognizance by forcing me to recognize the importance of motion, the butterfly, and the inverted "V".

Everyone's heard the story of the goalie who tried to commit suicide by jumping in front of a train. It didn't work, goes the story, because the train went between his legs. The basis for the humour is a common, yet incorrect perception that goals between the pads are "bad" goals. Let's see if we can come up with an improvement:

Did you hear about the goalie who tried to commit suicide by jumping in front of an airplane? It didn't work because he went down too soon and it flew over his shoulder.

It might not be funny, but at least it makes sense from a goaltending point of view.

COMFORT ZONE

When I first begin working with any goaltender, I say, "Just stand there in your stance. Now go down and up with the butterfly. Okay, now do it five times in a row."

The result looks okay, but it's not really impressive. So next, I tell him to skate towards me, and then start going back. At that point, I tell him to go down and up, down and up. He finds that it's a little easier. With this simple example, I've introduced him to the concept of incorporating motion into his stance.

But another difficulty rears its ugly head at this point: The goalie discovers that certain aspects of the stance—certain moves—run counter to his most comfortable spot. It might be an awkwardness moving laterally or forward to challenge a shooter. So I stress that the stance has to be so comfortable and natural for every move he makes that he doesn't even know he's IN a stance. If he's going out, coming back, or moving laterally, he's got to flow like a ballerina, dancing on his feet. When he gets that comfortable feeling where fluidity is part of his play whenever he moves, chances are he's achieved the most comfortable stance. That leaves one less thing to think about during a game. And let's face it — when you're playing goal, the less you've got to think about, the better off you'll be.

In order to achieve that fluidity, the goalie must realize his perfect "comfort zone". In general, this can be achieved by keeping the following in mind:

Imagine a line that runs straight up and down, flowing from your shoulders through your knees, and extending down to ice level to the balls of your feet. That imaginary line should be a constant, whether you're standing still, or moving forwards, backwards or laterally (*Behind The Mask*, pp. 23-28).

If the line goes to the toes instead of the balls of the feet, then you're too far forward. If it leads to the heels, you're too far back. In either case, you'll be off-balance. If the line is straight to the balls of the feet, you'll discover a couple of things:

First, all the weight should be on the muscles just above the knees. You'll feel it there and on the balls of the feet. Secondly, you'll find that you can make a lot of moves comfortably and naturally.

And for the discerning goalkeeper, there are a couple of definite "DON'TS" to keep in mind:

1) *don't lean forward with your shoulders ahead of your knees*. Why? Because not only will this make it difficult to react to quick, high shots, but with the least bit of bad luck, you could fall flat on your face mask. This is called a mistake, and usually results in great embarrassment.

2) *don't stand too tall by straightening out the knees too much*. This hinders foot speed, leaving you susceptible to low shots to the corners. This, too, is called a mistake.

One of the first things I do when I begin working with a goaltender is to ask him to go into his stance and bounce up and down. Then I'll ask him to move his shoulders about while he's bouncing. If he says, "I feel really good, I feel really comfortable," then he's got it! That's the way he should feel in game situations.

Anything else demands too much work and is too mechanical. The goalie becomes too rigid, too static in his play, and his game takes on a staccato-like appearance: "boom-boom-boom; boom-boom-boom." We don't want "boom-boom-boom." We want a natural flow to the play, and you can't do that if you're not comfortable with the way you've positioned yourself.

Although this might not be what most coaches want to hear, goalies aren't computerized robots that, once programmed, will maintain the perfect stance until the end of their playing days—or at least, until their computer chip goes defective. All too often, goaltenders will break that comfort-zone stance and lose what was once their most comfortable and fluid position. They'll concentrate too much on the puck, and a number of things—all of them bad—can occur. The shoulders will drop, automatically causing the trapper to drop; the blocker hand will go down as well so that, although the heel of the stick may be touching the ice, the blade will be tilted up and off the ice; and the five-hole will open too wide because the legs will spread.

Suddenly, the stance has been altered drastically.

That's why there's a clear message the coach has to instil in his goalies: *retain the stance that gives you your most comfortable position.*

Of course, Mr. Coach, you may be just too busy with other things to afford your goalie even this minimal amount of on-going attention. If that's the case, just replace that computer chip and re-programme the necessary information into his memory banks.

STANCE BREAKDOWN

Often, the breakdown of a goalie's stance is the reason behind a goal because of the extra inches of space he'll give the shooter. A lot of coaches don't consider the stance when they evaluate performances. They'll say, "You gave up a rebound," or "You went down." But there's more to most situations than that. It's one thing to position your goalies and get them comfortable in a stance, but subsequent to that, when you're analyzing their play, remember the stance.

This breakdown in stance occurs everywhere the game is played, even at the NHL level. When I coached Kelly Hrudey in New York, the Maple Leafs beat the Islanders 4-3 at Maple Leaf Gardens. I used to get the game tapes from the Islanders after every game, study them, then converse with Hrudey. When I looked at the tape of that game, I noticed three of the goals beat Kelly on his trapper side, up high. They all came from a fair distance—at least thirty feet out and on the wing.

I began by checking out his angles and positioning, things like that. But when I slowed down the video, I discovered the problem was more basic than that: His stance had broken down at the point of the shot. That is, as the forward's stick connected with the puck, Kelly fell into a lower crouch and his trapper dropped 8 or 10 inches. There was no way he could recover with the trapper, because in the NHL, they fire bullets.

If he'd maintained his proper stance, he would have had the glove at the proper level to handle those high shots.

TRAPPER POSITIONING

Some goaltenders have a tendency to forget about—even abuse—the poor old trapper. This is a most unhappy circumstance, since the position of the trapper is one of the most important things to remember about a stance.

In general, the trapper must be kept to the side of your knee, equidistant between the crossbar and the ice (in other words, at knee level); and with the catching pocket of the trapper facing the shooter.

That may sound simple enough, but it's not so easy to remember.

When Oshawa went to the 1983 Memorial Cup in Oregon, we picked up Allan Bester as our third goaltender, in case of injury. I was on the ice doing a few things with the goaltenders, and I mentioned to Allan that I thought he carried his trapper too high. He responded that he was coached

that way, so I asked him the principle behind the positioning. He responded, "Well, if I have to drop it down, the trapper simply goes with my body. But if I have to lift it up, it has to go against gravity. So I keep it up."

Some goalie coach along the way had theorized—and relayed that theory to Allan—that this is the perfect trapper position. But it's dead wrong.

For one thing, there's no point to having to drop your arm three feet to make a save— or lift it three feet, for that matter. Put it equidistant between the ice and the crossbar and you've got just two feet to cover in either direction.

When I joined the Maple Leafs as Goalie Consultant part way through the 1990-91 season, I reminded Bester of that 1983 discussion. All he said was, "Oh, I forgot about that...I don't do that any more." Indeed, he didn't. In fact, he'd gone too far the other way, and instead of holding his trapper up high, he had it down low. Now, Allan's a short goaltender, and with his catching glove sometimes a foot off the ice he looks like a prime candidate to get beaten high on shots from in close. But his comeback was that he has great confidence in his trapper. He felt it was the quickest part of his game and he could nail those rising shots from short range. I don't agree with that, but Allan did and, after all, he's the guy who had to go out there and make the stops.

One of the more bizarre theories of trapper positioning is the one that has goalies holding their catching hand out front. The theory seems to be that this will eliminate that occasional goal that sneaks its way between the body and the arm. To this I say: Why in the world would you put your trapper in front of a part of the body that's already blocking a part of the net? Although thoroughness is an admirable trait, there's no need to, in essence, "waste" the trapper. Why have two pieces of equipment blocking one part of the net when you can have two pieces of equipment blocking two parts of the net?

Play the percentages! After all, a large part of goaltending is the ability to cover as much of the net as possible. Your trapper is your friend—better-looking, much more polite, twice as useful and at least three times as intelligent as most forwards. It won't mind one little bit if you consider it an extension of your pads.

When I'm confronted by any of these problems—trapper too high, too low, or in front of the body—I ask my goalies, "When you catch the puck, where do you catch it? Out to the side of your body, of course. So does it make sense that on every shot you should have to move the trapper too far up, too far down, or too far away from your body in order to catch it?"

I also point out the number of times a guy comes with a point-blank shot that hits the middle of the trapper. Just because it's *there and open*! And even though you know it's mostly luck, people in the rink put their hands together and say, "Oh, what a great save!"

Accept the compliments. After all, if people can be wrong about five-holes and so many other things related to goaltending, I figure they owe you at least that much.

BLOCKER & STICK POSITION

Regardless of your size, you should have a stick that complements your stance. I tell my goalies to get into their stance with the stick blade in front of the feet, equidistant between them, and then just bounce, going back and forth in a comfortable manner. When they do this the size and lie of the stick should be such that:

1) the blocker is at about knee level, just outside your pad;

2) the bottom edge of the stick blade is flat on the ice; and

3) the blade is kept in front of the body, flat on the ice.

The first point addresses the need to cover as much of the net as possible. As with the trapper, the blocker can be considered an extension of the body. Years ago, I knew one young goaltender who used a wholly unsuitable goal stick. The wide or paddle portion of the stick extended so far up the shaft that he was forced to hold it too high. His blocker was up just under the crossbar. Of course, it threw his stance out of kilter and made it extremely awkward to make any kind of a move to his right, or stick side. When the problem was explained to his parents, the boy's father didn't buy a new stick. He merely attacked the old one with a hand saw. The result was a far more suitable stance.

The second point—having the stick blade flat on the ice—is something that should be driven home time and again. After all, while some five-hole goals can be excused—even expected—the shot along the ice and between the legs doesn't fall into that category. Not only is it embarrassing, but too many of them can earn you a lengthy stay at the end of the bench.

In general, almost any skating drill can help in this regard if the goaltender concentrates on keeping his stick blade flat on the ice. And just as the proper stance and stick size can help keep that blade on the ice, concentrating on keeping it there will help define your stance by maintaining a proper shoulder height. Result? Your comfort-zone stance is reinforced.

The third point—keeping the blade straight up and down, or at right angles to the ice—is another of those contentious points you'll run up against in some coaching circles.

Every now and then I run into a young goaltender who tells me that he was taught to position the stick blade well in front of his body, and on an angle. The theory seems to be that if the stick is on an angle, it's easier to deflect pucks. Well, you don't have to do

that to deflect pucks to the corners—unless the point is to deflect pucks into the upper corners of the net!

Even on low shots when you go to the butterfly—hopefully with the knees coming together on the ice—the blade of the stick should be at the point where the knees come together. That removes the infamous five-hole along the ice. And because the blade of the stick is flat, with both the toe and the heel touching the ice, it automatically positions your blocker and stick shaft in the upper corner, where they can handle high shots or deflections. Almost everything is accounted for. The only thing that's not natural in this scenario is the position of the trapper. It's the only piece of equipment you have to condition yourself to get into the open area.

Sound difficult? Not really. It's a matter of mental discipline and repetition through practice.

SUMMARY

Watch the goalie as he goes into his crouch: A comfortable stance, complete with the inverted "V" with the pads slightly apart, offering mobility; the trapper is equidistant between the ice and the crossbar, beside the knee; the stick blade is in front, but flat on the ice, straight up and down between the feet, positioning the blocker naturally at the side of the knee.

That's what we want to see all the time! If you're comfortable, don't change it.

This is the stance that gives you the greatest advantage — your shoulders aren't down low; your legs aren't too far apart; your stick isn't on its heel; your trapper isn't in front of your body or turned down and out of the play. In short, it's a stance that will maximize your ability to stop pucks.

And when you go down for the low shots, the pads are extended, meeting at the knees; the stick is still flat on the ice, covering whatever "five-hole" might exist; the blocker and trapper are out to the sides, covering the high corners.

If you can do all of this, and do it consistently, you'll enjoy great success as a goaltender.

Ian Young displays a perfect stance (Ian Young files).

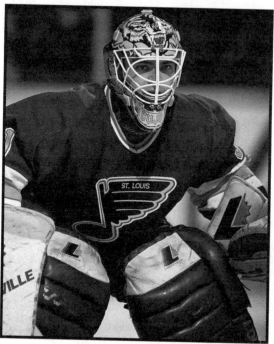

Curtis Joseph (Relke).

ANGLES

When I first coached Peter Sidorkiewicz in Oshawa back in 1983, he had a rigid, mechanical, stationary game. I knew changes were in order so I put Peter on a training program that included angles, motion and skating. I told him that I didn't care if he came 15 feet out of the net because, assuming he didn't lose his relationship to the net, it would help create a positive aggressiveness in his play. I told him that I'd rather see a goal go in because he was being aggressive, than a goal go in because he was sitting back in the crease, giving the shooter fat corners to pick. I don't know many coaches who get upset when a goaltender plays the shooter aggressively.

We played Peterborough in the OHL semi-finals that year, and they had us down 3 games to 2. The next game in their rink was a tough one. In the third period, a Peterborough player came down the wing and all of a sudden, Peter's challenging the shooter! My reaction was one of immediate panic: "Oh my God...he's really doing it!"

The guy fired a slapshot and Peter, still moving forward, did the splits and made a tremendous trapper save. That's the moment—and he agrees with this—that Peter Sidorkiewicz realized he had to aggressively come out of the net and play high on shooters. It was also the play that turned the game around. We won the series and went to the Memorial Cup.

Now, I don't encourage goalies to go 20 feet out of the net on every one-on-one situation. But I do promote angles work based on something called "telescoping".

Telescoping theory, or the principle of playing angles, is something that came to me when I was doing some coaching at the University of Waterloo. It's based on the premise that everything done by a goalie is related to angles, and that all other aspects of the position are negated if you don't block off the net from the shooters.

The theory is based on three parts of the net—the two posts and the centre of the crossbar. Here's how it works:

Place a puck exactly between the hash marks, about 45 feet from the net. Now imagine that you're above the ice surface, staring down at the play that's about to unfold. If that puck is shot straight to the net, it would cross the goal line at the crossbar's mid-point. In other words, the path travelled by the puck would run exactly perpendicular to the crossbar.

Now take that same puck and draw two more straight lines—one to each goalpost. Looking down from our lofty perch, we've now got something that resembles a teepee, or two isosceles triangles side-by-side. Or, if you prefer, a telescope (*Behind The Mask*, pp. 45-6).

If we put a goalkeeper in the crease, we'll see that there's scoring space between the outer parts of his body and the two lines going from the puck to the posts. Our task is to remove that space by having the goalie move towards the puck. But now comes a key point that so many goalkeepers tend to ignore: *The line from the puck to the middle of the net must always run through the goalie's body and extend through the middle of his back, straight to the crossbar's mid-point.*

As our hero advances on the puck, he eventually hits the point at which his body is touching those imaginary puck-to-post lines on both sides. Once done, a shot will either hit the goalie, or simply go wide. And as we all know, if you force a shooter to fire wide, that's just as good as a save. So that's the ideal angle for the centre-angle scenario; anything past that point is essentially inefficient because it's not necessary.

Now let's start over, but this time we'll move the puck to one side—say, between the hash mark and the dot. Our lines remain the same: We still have two of them extending from puck to posts, and the centre-line from the puck to the middle of the crossbar. However, there's not as much net to worry about because the puck is over on the wing. Instead of six feet of net to cover, there's perhaps five-and-a-half feet. So it stands to reason that if the goalie moves out to take the angle—keeping the puck-through-the-body-to-the-crossbar line in mind—he won't have to move out as far to meet the puck-to-post lines, *because the goal isn't as wide from this angle.*

Now move the puck five feet closer to the net. The puck-to-post lines are squeezed tighter so you don't have to be out as far in order to take the angle. Again, the puck either hits you, goes wide, or the shooter is forced to try something else. So remember: Don't do yourself the disservice of not giving yourself the angle.

Sometimes that's not as easy as it sounds. I recall one game in St. Catharines when Ken Hodge came in on me. He had a laser beam for a shot, so if you didn't have your angle, you were in real trouble. I remember thinking as I moved out on him that I wanted him to put the puck two or three feet off the ice. That's because really high shots and really low shots make you move, whereas pucks up in the mid-zone, no matter how quick, are easier to block.

Well, Hodge came in, shot, and did just what I wanted. The only problem was, it got by me and the crowd went nuts. He did just what I wanted him to do and he still scored. And when I took a peek behind me, I saw why. He had all kinds of net to look at because I'd lost my centre-line angle.

One of the most severe cases I've ever heard of a goalie losing an angle was relayed to me by a friend who played college hockey in the U.S. He was on the bench at the time and had a perfect view of the puck's trajectory when it was fired from the blueline near the left boards. The goalie's body, so goes the story, was so far off line that the shot went past him on the short side and *caught the far corner of the net!* It was a particularly bad moment for the goalie who, by all accounts, was a good athlete with experience at the Junior "A" level.

To avoid such embarrassing moments, I have a little something that helps a coach check on his goalie's relationship to the centre line. I'll drop a puck on the ice—just about anywhere will do—and tell the goalie to take his angle. Give him time to be convinced that's he's positioned himself properly, then tell him to stay there. Then, place something—a pylon or a pile of pucks will do—on top of the net at that middle point of the crossbar. Now skate back out, stand behind the puck, and take a look. **If your goalie is positioned properly on his angle, that pylon, or pile of pucks, will line up with the top of his helmet.**

LOSS OF ANGLE

I'm not a big believer of the landmark theory that some use as a way of reading angles. The thinking is that if a goalie can keep tabs on his relationship to various landmarks on the ice surface—such as hash marks, faceoff dots, the other net, or the point at which the blue line meets the boards—he can instantly re-affirm his relationship with the net.

While that would make for a direct pipeline to Angles Heaven, I don't like to rely in using these landmarks because I don't want goalies to think too much about angles when the play is hot and heavy. I want it to be instinctive.

That doesn't mean that thinking doesn't play an important role in playing the position. On the contrary, goaltending is all cerebral. Stance, angles, skating, reflexes— all of those things play a role in the development of a goaltender. But if you're not thinking about the game, evaluating situations as they evolve, you'll pay the price.

Think of it this way:

A parent or friend can drive you to the rink.

A trainer can sharpen your skates.

A coach can warn you about the other team's sharpshooters.

But once the game begins, you're on your own. *You have to be your own coach for three straight periods, while using reactions that have become automatic.*

Even so, your most diligent pre-game preparations can fall apart when the play fails to unfold to your liking. A quick turnaround play, for instance, when you're caught out of your goal. You haven't got time to glance around and check your angle to the net, and you certainly don't have time to check out the landmarks.

The shooter is coming, and he's coming quickly.

You're caught beyond the point of the ideal angle. You've lost the centre line.

Your coach has begun to construct a gallows—monogrammed with your initials—behind the bench.

Your parents discuss plans to rent out your room.

And your fans are searching their game programs, trying to familiarize themselves with your understudy.

In short, things don't look good.

But all is not lost if you know that the closer you get to the puck, the better your chance of making up for the fact that you're OFF the centre line. You can still cover a large chunk of the net by getting close to the play.

Simply speaking, if you're out of the net and slightly off angle, the fact that you're out high can take away some of the net from the shooter. At the same time, you're forcing a shot. Hopefully, the shooter will sacrifice some accuracy in order to get off a quick shot, and hand the advantage back to the good guy.

ANGLES ON FACEOFFS

From a spectator's point of view, it's a relatively innocent situation. Whether caused by an icing, a deflection into the stands, or by your freezing of the puck, the result is the same—a faceoff in your end.

The drop of the puck means little to the fans; it happens all the time. For coaches, it could mean little more than an opportunity to replace tired legs with fresh ones.

But for the goalie, it's a potentially dangerous situation. All five opposition skaters are in your end of the rink, a possible goal just seconds away.

How do you handle it?

First of all, recognize the fact that every faceoff situation is different. Let's say the faceoff is on the dot to your left. Before the puck is dropped, stand back and assess the alignment of the offence you're facing; judge the offensive possibilities, the potential danger plays.

If the opposition has a player on the boards, forget him. He's negated.

If they have two players in the middle of the ice—one on the hash mark, the other on the faceoff circle—forget the man on the hash mark. He's negated by your two teammates in the middle. That leaves you with a couple of dangerous scenarios—a pass to the man on the circle, or a pass to the point.

And that brings us to the man taking the draw.

Is he a right-handed or a left-handed shooter? If he's right-handed, he's on his forehand. And if that's the case, he has three options: pulling the draw back to the point, passing to the man on the circle, or taking a shot directly off the faceoff. Of those options, the forehand shot is your first priority. In this case, I recommend playing higher, on the outer edge of the crease. Your initial responsibility is the shot, so play the angle.

But if the man taking the draw is a left-handed shooter—and therefore on his backhand—the situation is different. The initial shot off the playoff dot isn't your main concern. Instead, you're facing two other initial responsibilities: a draw to the man on the faceoff circle, or a draw to the point. Obviously, the one that poses the most immediate danger to you is the short draw to the man on the faceoff circle. Your intial concern should be a pass off the faceoff, and the shot that might result.

In this situation, you don't have to play the faceoff dot angle as much. You can position yourself slightly away from the short side post, anticipating a draw to another player.

TAPPING POSTS

Something rather unpleasant happens to me when I hear a goalie say, "I don't want to come out too far because I don't want to lose my net." I lose my *mind*.

The only reason for a goaltender to experience this fear—one that will hold back his development—is because he hasn't been taught how to take the angle and maximize his chance of retaining it. But it can be done, with the help of the goal posts.

A shooter is racing down the wing. As you prepare to take the angle, tap the short side post to help get your bearings.

If that happens to be your trapper side, tap the post with the catching glove.

If it's on your blocker side, get used to slapping the post with the top of your stick.

These simple moves will help you locate *both* posts and in so doing, allow you to find the all-important mid-point of the crossbar.

Forget about trying to hit the far side post. It's too far away. Besides, in most cases you won't have the time to check out both goalposts. But if you can't reach the near-side post you'll know right away that you're off the centre-line.

I encourage my goalies to constantly tap those posts; it should be an automatic move.

ANGLES RE-DEFINED

There's a new style afloat in hockey circles these days, one introduced to the professional ranks by the likes of Ed Belfour, Curtis Joseph and Felix Potvin. That style is prompting a re-definition—or an expansion—of our understanding of angles work. The style I teach has the goalie coming out and using the telescoping theory to take away the net, then flowing back with the play to handle cross-ice passes and the deke. You're continually taking the angle, and then ready to move left or right if the play doesn't come directly to you. The three goalies I've just mentioned tend to go down a lot, and the common wisdom in some hockey circles is that they can be beaten high. But when you consider that Belfour's been in Vezina Trophy territory for several years now, and Potvin is one of the league's up-and-coming stars, and Curtis Joseph played absolutely outstanding goal for St. Louis in the 1993 playoffs, maybe it's time to re-evaluate that position. Who's beating them upstairs on a consistent basis? It's easy to say, "Go high," but when it's not done with a lot of regularity, that's a pretty good indication that there's something wrong with that strategy. Take a look at this new style, and what it means.

In its most general terms, taking the angle means taking away the net from the puck. When the puck gets close to Potvin, for instance, he goes down in such a way that he's blocking off the net. He'll go to a kind of distorted butterfly, and lay the shaft of the stick flat on the ice. For a loose puck situation right out front, or for an opposition player who's in close—say, with the puck inside or just at the top of the crease—there's little chance of the puck finding a path to the back of the net. He's on top of the puck, taking the net away by simply boarding it up, and being close enough to the point of the shot that when he goes down, the shooter will hit him with the puck.

Potvin and others are saying, "If you're going to score on me, you're going to have to make the perfect shot." With all the congestion at the top of the crease these days, that's not going to happen too often. If you've got a good angle on a guy, and he beats you low, stick side, in off the post, it doesn't mean that your angles stink, or that they've discovered your weakness. It just means they made a great shot. Let's face it — if they do put one upstairs, just under the crossbar, it's time to give the shooter some credit.

That doesn't mean I'm sold on the style. The puck can change direction very quickly out there, and although I don't mean to put down Potvin, he's actually committing his shoulders to that play when he puts the shaft of his stick on the ice. And once that's happened, if the puck hits a skate and is redirected to one side or the other, his reaction time to that deflection isn't going to be great because he's not in position to get up and over to the puck. But the style I teach—butterfly to the knees with the body upright, trapper out and the stick in the five-hole, forcing the blocker to the upper corner—would also work in the situations that led to Potvin's style. What's more, if the puck does change direction after you've dropped for the shot, you can be right back on your feet and moving in that direction.

SUMMARY

In general, when addressing the question of angles, all right-thinking goalies should keep the following in mind:

Learn your angles and play them aggressively through the use of telescoping;

If you're caught out of the net without time to check your angle, put pressure on the shooter by forcing the play;

Remember to check out the opposition player taking faceoffs in your end of the ice to determine if he's taking them on his forehand or his backhand; and,

Get accustomed to tapping the short side post to quickly re-establish your angles.

And remember: The goalie who covers the angles correctly, is correctly covering all the angles.

Kirk McLean—quick and mobile (Relke).

SKATING AND MOTION

It's an old story.

A group of youngsters get together on the local pond, pick sides, and get ready for a few hours of shinny. This one might lay claim to the name Wayne Gretzky, while that one becomes Mario Lemieux. It's a typical Canadian winter experience.

Of course, the better players are soon gobbled up, "signed" to long-term contracts that won't expire until young legs are exhausted and it's time to go home for dinner. And as each team swells in numbers, the available pool of "talent" diminishes in kind. Finally, only a couple are left—the weakest players because, usually, they're the weakest skaters.

Often, the solution is easy: put them in goal. We've heard stories about the goaltender who got his start for precisely that reason: he was weak on his feet. Sadly, in many cases, such stories are only too true.

Unfortunately, the scenario is not only absurd, but this tradition of weak-ankled goalies has tended to mask one of hockey's best-kept secrets: If you aren't strong on your feet, you *can't play goal!*

When they're young, most goalies—and their coaches—ignore this basic hockey truth. Eventually, they pay for it. It might be at the bantam level, or perhaps when they reach midget age. Some might make it as far as junior hockey before the truth becomes painfully clear. But when you have to make two or three quick moves around the crease area—moves that require changes in direction—you'll find out. When you have to go down and then regain your feet in goalmouth scrambles, you'll find out a second time. And when you have to go post to post, or angle to post, and must do so in a hurry, there will be no more doubt in your mind.

SKATING

Balance, quickness and mobility—three excellent reasons for working on your skating. Without them, you severely limit your chances of becoming an NHL goaltender.

Besides, it's what makes goalies such wonderful dancers.

It's unfortunate that when people think of goaltenders, chances are the last thing they consider is skating ability. In fact, unless there happens to be a shot on net, most fans don't even look at the goalie during games. Instead, most eyes will follow the puck. Some might notice a forward without the puck as he moves to an open spot. And a few may even glance at the defence, to see if one of them will follow up on a play, sneaking into the slot for a quick pass or a rebound.

But until a shot is launched, few, if any, bother to watch the goaltender.

If they did, they might be surprised to see how much work—how much motion—is involved. The goalie cruises through the crease, moving forward, backward and laterally, going down for a low shot and regaining his feet immediately — all with heavy pads and other equipment strapped to legs, arms and torso. Indeed, many goalkeepers claim some of their most physically demanding game sequences are pressure situations during which the opposition doesn't manage even a single shot!

At my goalie school, I try to create a scenario that kids will understand. The more I use this example, the more I believe coaches and all hockey adults can also benefit from the lesson it teaches: That skating is essential to goaltending.

Picture Wayne Gretzky, number 99 himself, coming in on net from the wing at full speed. He carries the puck, and looks up. There's no opening because the goalie has advanced, cutting down the angle. The Great One is forced to carry the puck across the net to the far side, hoping to force the goalie to go down, or lose his position in relation to the net.

But our goalie is well prepared. He stays on his feet, moving with the play, and continues to block the net. The result? An "easy" save. Number 99, reduced to one final option, takes a shot that's blocked by our hero with the mobile pads.

When you think of it, hasn't the goalie, in fact, *outskated Wayne Gretzky?* Not only that, but *he's done so while moving backwards and sideways!*

On the other hand, disaster awaits the goalie who, for whatever reason, fails to develop strength and speed in the feet. I see it all the time, not only in minor hockey, but even at the junior and—believe it or not—the professional level.

Here's what it looks like:

Goalie goes for the fake, and falls down.

Goalie tries to move forward to cut down the angle, and doesn't get there in time.

Goalie tries to shift from backward to lateral motion, and can't keep up with the play.

Goalie gets bombed. Goalie gets cut.

Why? Because he thought that stopping pucks was all he had to work on. Sooner or later a lack of skating skills will catch up with you, so *keep those feet moving!*

In practices, even if the coach doesn't insist on it, participate in all skating drills. In fact, there's not a skating drill for forwards or defence that goalies shouldn't do. Every drill promoting forward skating, backward skating, and lateral movement is beneficial to the goalkeeper.

When I played at Oshawa, I was convinced that the mobility drills I put myself through, day in and day out, were helping me become a better goalie by improving my skating ability, and I derived great satisfaction from performing well in drills being done by the rest of the team.

One of those drills was a basic one—everybody lines up at one end of the ice and the coaches call players by position: "Forwards...defence...goalies." Wave after wave of churning legs powered their way from goal line to goal line. When my turn came, I would skate as hard as I could. Every time. Before long, I was taking on other guys on the team, and I took great personal pride in the fact that I could outskate some of my defencemen! In full equipment! The bottom line is this: I developed into a good skater.

I even beat Bobby Orr a couple of times. Of course, it would have been a lot tougher if he hadn't fallen down on those occasions.

How important is skating to a goalkeeper? Well, just about everything you read in this section, whether it's drills or game situations, has to do with strength in the feet—in other words, with skating.

If you're faced with a centre breakaway and you go down early, you're not skating well enough.

If the shooter moves in on the wing and cuts in front, and you can't keep up with the play by moving laterally, you're not a good enough skater.

If the puck comes from the corner to the slot and you can't move quickly enough from the post to the high angle, you're not a good enough skater.

And if you go down for one shot but you're too slow getting back up for a rebound, you're not a good enough skater.

From a goaltender's point of view, that's skating. And with every play that's made, if you don't get there quickly, you're not a good enough skater. I defy anyone to present a situation around the net that doesn't require the goalkeeper to be strong on his feet.

I'll go even further than that. Most people consider quick reflexes a necessary tool for the successful goaltender. But if you have a weak-skating goalie with the world's best reflexes, he won't make it to the National Hockey League. On the other hand, if you take a kid with strong skating abilities and average reflex action, you've got a different situation. My money would be on the kid who's stronger on his feet. On the subject of reflexes and their relative importance to goaltending, Ken Dryden has written of the time he and his wife tested their eye-hand reactions at a science museum. Hers were slightly faster.

So even if a skating drill is a little uncomfortable at first, stick with it. The fact that it's difficult is all the proof you need that the drill is for you. If you can overcome the initial lack of comfort, you will reap benefits down the road. Only through hard work and repetition will you find the strength and the training to automatically make the correct moves in game situations.

One word of caution: if the coach asks you to perform a triple axel or a double toe loop, leave the ice. It seems you've gone to the wrong rink and accidentally joined a figure skating club.

MOTION

Now that you're ready to challenge Elvis Stoiko for skating supremacy, you're also prepared to address the basic skating motions necessary to build your game.

Foreward:

In most cases, when a forward advances on goal, the last thing the goaltender should do is stay deep in his net. That leaves large targets for the shooter. It's necessary to move forward to "challenge" the shooter in order to achieve the high angle.

Backward:

Of course, you can't get caught too far out of the net or the shooters will simply skate around you. This is bound to create some miserable moments and prompt less sensitive teammates to avoid you in public. Therefore, skating backwards while maintaining the angle is essential to the position. It has the added advantage of making it easier to move left or right.

Lateral Motion (Left or Right):

Moving side to side is important for a number of reasons: going post to post, reacting to dekes, executing the two-pad slide, following the puck behind the net, etc. There are two methods for moving side to side, and each should be used in particular situations. The SHUFFLE is used to follow the flow of plays that develop high in the deep slot or near the blueline; the T-PUSH permits rapid lateral movement while also offering a diminished five-hole.

Up-Down:

What goes up must come down. And vice versa. This is true for airplanes, birds, tempers, Goodyear blimps and goaltenders. In fact, goaltenders should be placed at the head of the list because of the frequency of the down-up move. Strength in the feet is crucial here. Without it, you'll be too slow and clumsy going from ice to stance.

Seldom are any of these moves performed in isolation. The goalie who's trying to achieve the angle is constantly in motion as the puck moves around his end of the ice. You're moving out, backing in, going down, getting up, moving post to post, moving out again to take the angle. One move flows into the next, and the next, and the next.

Bobby Orr used to help me work on my mobility at the Oshawa Civic Auditorium.

Bobby would come in and fire the puck as hard as he could, keeping the puck low. I knew I'd be using my butterfly, so I was able to condition myself to drop quickly.

I'll stress that this is a drill, and shouldn't be interpreted as promoting the butterfly in response to anticipation. When you're facing a shooter, it's a cardinal sin to go down early. Instead, watch the shot; if it's low, then the butterfly is an appropriate move.

When Bobby skated in on me during that drill, I'd move out to take the angle, then back in on goal as he advanced, telescoping all the way. When he fired the puck, I'd go to the butterfly. Because I was moving backwards at the time, something happened to the puck when it hit my pads: It stopped dead. In effect, I *absorbed the puck into my pads*. The force of the puck was cushioned. As a result, I wasn't giving up many big rebounds.

Often a goaltender goes into the butterfly from a stationary position. You may not have an option in certain situations, but when you do that, and then extend your pad to block the shot, you'll be presenting the opposition with fat, juicy rebounds.

Even if the puck does pop in front of you by a foot or so, it's simple to get to it and freeze it or clear it off the side, if you remember the principle of bouncing right back onto your feet.

Seldom will a goaltender be faced with a situation where he's forced to the butterfly while moving forward. It can happen, of course, but usually only if the shot comes sooner than you think it will and you haven't had time to achieve your high angle. It's a rare situation, but because it's a possibility, it's not a bad idea to work on going to the butterfly while moving both backward *and* forward.

I put my goaltenders through a lot of gruelling skating drills. In one, they skate the length of the ice and every time I blow the whistle, they drop down, get back up, and keep moving. They do it moving both forward and backward so that if the forward butterfly becomes necessary in a game, they're ready for it.

In one of my favourite drills—the Butterfly Drill—I'll put a goalie ten feet inside the blueline, and line up 8 or 9 shooters near centre ice, each with a puck. On the whistle, the goalie will start backing up while the shooters, one after one, move in and fire low shots to either side.

The goalie's aim is to get back to his net. He's skating back, going down in the butterfly, getting up, back, down, up, back, down, up...until he's used to automatically doing the butterfly. *Motion is retained throughout the drill.*

T-PUSH

When I began working at Maple Leaf Gardens with Peter Ing and Jeff Reese, I told them that on shots from the point, I wanted them to play a foot in front of the crease, to cut down the angle. They said, "I should be able to stop a shot from there! There's no reason for me to come out so far."

They're right. If an NHL goaltender standing inside his crease can't stop a slapshot from just inside the blueline, then he shouldn't be at that level of competition.

But next I asked, "What do you do if that guy comes in on you now?" Light bulbs of revelation began to flicker as they realized that they've got to begin outside the crease in order to have the backward motion they'll require to move laterally. If the forward passes, or cuts across the front of the net, a goalie will look pretty silly trying to keep up with the play if he's standing flat-footed.

This is where your motion comes in, and why it's so important to your game.

If the puck moves laterally while it's still well in front of the net, a simple *shuffle motion* will allow you to stay with it while maintaining your angle. But if the play is right in front of the net, and there's no time to shuffle, we have to rely on the *T-push.*

"I could move. I could get there. I was a good skater, which is the most important element of goaltending."
—Hall of Famer Glenn Hall, one of the first butterfly goaltenders.

Many goalies turn and move laterally with the play in a situation like that. But then the side of the body is facing the puck. And a lot of goalies will try a poke-check — a low percentage move, as far as I'm concerned. Nevertheless, poke-checking is part of a goaltender's instinct, so I don't wholeheartedly discourage it.

But I strongly suggest the T-push.

The T-push is based on motion: Coming back with the play and being able to move laterally with your body facing the puck while retaining the stance. Its intent, quite simply, is to keep you on your feet while minimizing the five-hole.

The T-push has your feet placed in the shape of a "T". The foot closest to the direction in which you want to travel points outwards; the other leg is bent slightly at the knee with the knee tucked in, removing the five-hole. With short, quick moves across the top of the crease, you not only stay with the play, you're blocking the five-hole with your pads...*while you retain your stance.*

The integrity of your stance is protected: Your shoulders stay at the same height, squared to the puck, with the basic shoulders-through-knees-to-balls-of-the-feet line intact.

Keep the following in mind: When a player comes off the wing, drives for the net and cuts in front, your first move will give him some an opening in the five-hole. That's normal. After all, when you take that first big step with one leg and push off with the other, you can't help but leave an opening. But if the puck-carrier continues to move across the net, and you decide just to shuffle across, there will be a gaping five-hole every time you take a step with the lead foot.

When I coached with the Islanders, I discovered that Kelly Hrudey had very little motion in his game when he got to the NHL. So he had developed his own unique way of handling players who broke in and cut across the crease. Kelly was a lunger. Instead of using the T-push and doing a series of quick little shuffles from side-to-side, Kelly would stand still, a foot outside the crease on a breakaway. If the shooter deked to his blocker side, Kelly would lunge to his right, throwing his blocker to the puck. He theo-

The goaltending thoughts of the great Russian coach Anatoli Tarasov were based largely on his observations of Jacques Plante, whose method was to skate out of the net and challenge the shooter. Tarasov said, "I came to the conclusion that it was necessary to make the goalie more manoeuvrable, and ready for all surprises. He would have to be an acrobat! He would have to have the ability to skate in the open ice along with our forwards."

rized that by getting the blocker close to the puck, he was angling off—the blocker became another pad.

Unorthodox? Sure, but Kelly had confidence in that move. And after all, he's the guy who had to do it.

A goalie will go down on 99% of the dekes he faces on breakaways. It might be a two-pad slide, a one-pad slide, a butterfly, or Kelly and his diving lunges. But whatever the move, in most cases he'll go down automatically, without thinking. But I ask my goalies to consider the benefits of staying on their feet as long as possible.

Sometimes I'll ask my goalies to stay up during a particular drill, just to see if they can do it. In most cases they can, but they just don't know it. Still, I coach from the point of view that they'll more than likely go down on a deke. So my first question is: When and under what circumstances *should* you go down? Do you go down immedi-

ately? Do you go down halfway across the crease? Or do you go down at the far post?

The answer is simple: *use the T-push and hold your feet as long as possible.* The longer you can do that, retaining the angle, the tougher it will be for the shooter to lift one into the upper corner.

There isn't a situation—rebounds, screen shots, deflections, two-on-ones, or whatever—that doesn't stress the importance of the three major goaltending aspects: 1) stance, 2) angles, and 3) skating and motion. In fact, these three aspects make up 90% of the position.

If you've got a comfortable, flexible and fluid stance; if you have an appreciation and understanding of angles; and if you're strong on your feet and able to flow forwards, backwards, left and right and up and down, the rest of the game is a stroll in the royal garden.

You've got a game fit for a king!

"I wasn't that strong a skater when I played minor hockey, but it didn't take me long to figure out that I had to take power skating courses. Skating is probably the most important thing about goaltending. If you're not strong on your feet, you won't be able to keep up with a lot of those guys. Like Russ Courtnall. You can't believe how fast he is. As goalies, we've got to be able to follow him across the net. We have to move as fast as he does. That'll give you an idea of how fast you have to go, whether you're using the T-push or the shuffle. Mike Gartner's another one. If you can't keep up with guys like Courtnall and Gartner, they'll make you feel silly."
— Jeff Hackett

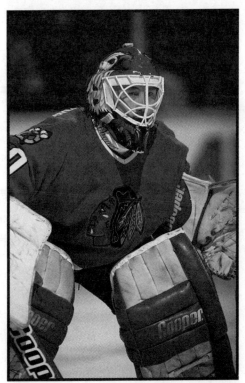

Belfour waits for a shot along the ice (Relke).

ICE SHOTS

There are several types of stops that can bring a crowd to its feet. Just about any save on a breakaway will do. And the trapper save from point-blank range never fails to generate a few "Ooohs" and "Ahhhs". Even the low-percentage poke check, and the desperation fish-out-of-water sprawl, will have people calling your name and making comparisons with goaltending greats from the past.

But most goalies—being the honest, trustworthy people we are—will admit that the most difficult stops to make are the ones right along the ice.

Earlier, I related the story of three Yvan Cournoyer shots that beat me along the ice in my first junior game and prompted me to re-evaluate my stance. That led to a number of changes in my game, including the introduction of the butterfly. But the butterfly isn't the only weapon a well-trained goalie can use to confront those ice-skimming pucks.

What makes these stops so difficult is the quickness required, and the fact that there's more to making the save than just turning the skate blade. All parts of the body have to move in unison, reacting automatically with a precision developed through hard work and repetition in practice sessions.

Here's what I mean: stand in your basic stance. Not on the ice, necessarily; you can do this in your living room. Now imagine a shot going to your right, along the ice. If you turn your right foot to deflect the imaginary puck while staying erect in your stance, you'll only be able to extend that foot about a foot-and-a-half or so. Any shot beyond that range will get past you.

Now let's try it again. But this time, as the right foot turns out, drop the left knee down toward the ground, or ice surface. What you'll find is that your right-foot extension is greatly increased to three feet, four feet, maybe more.

Lowering the left or back knee closer to the ice has an added advantage: It allows you to turn the right skate blade more than you could from an erect, standing stance.

And that helps to achieve your immediate aim of deflecting the puck away from the net, towards the corner of the rink.

Of course, you have at your disposal more than a skate blade to stop such a shot. Let's not forget our instrument of good deeds, that great defender of the just cause; yes, I'm referring to the Loyal Lumber of the Lords of the Rink, the goal stick!

Ideally, in the above-mentioned situation, the stick should be placed to the front of your right skate, between the puck and the skate blade. Due to your unerring concentration and timing, the skate acts as support for the stick as the puck is deflected out of harm's way.

I'm not talking about anything difficult here. Once the manoeuvre is practiced, you'll find that 99.9% of the time, the stick will automatically go to the strong point, the point of the skate. *And it's the skate that kicks the stick, re-directing the puck.*

There are four aspects to the move:

1) The skate moving to the puck is turned perpendicular to the other skate, and shoots out to the side to intercept the shot;

2) The other leg should be bent down close to the ice surface, allowing for greater extension of the foot making the save;

3) Get the stick in front of the skate. With the stick supported by the toe of the skate, it's a simple matter to kick the puck away from the danger areas; and

4) Keep your eye on the puck to the point of the kick.

The skate save demands reaction time and so should be reserved for shots that come from a distance—30 feet or so. Anything closer makes it too difficult to turn the skate in time. For shots coming from close range, we're left with two options:

1) Your first option on an ice shot from close range is to have the technically correct position on the puck. That is, you're out on the angle taking the net away by using your telescoping theory. Remember, if you're out far enough, the shooter has nothing to shoot at, no corners to pick. Assuming your stick is flat on the ice, the puck should hit it.

2) Your second option for an ice shot from close range is the butterfly. It's the ideal move on a puck that's released quickly where you don't have the opportunity to move to the optimum telescoping angle.

But when it comes to the butterfly, there are a few points to keep in mind. In general, drop immediately to your knees, extending your pads in both directions to reach the puck-to-post lines. Remember, the first point of contact on the ice is your knees.

At the same time, the blade of the stick should come to the inevitable five-hole that will appear along the ice between the tops of the pads. If a shot happens to hit that area, you've got it covered with a stick that's supported by your pads. As long as those pads aren't spread too far apart when you go to the butterfly, a shot along the ice has no chance to force its way under the stick blade and reach the net. Instead, the stick will be forced back against your pads, giving you better control of possible rebounds.

Now consider a shot from your right or left. If it comes from directly in front, theoretically, you'll be positioned dead centre in the middle of the net, extending your pads to both sides. But if a shot should come from the wing, the *least* important extension is to the short side, just on the general theory that your basic stance before the shot is taken should cover the short side of the net. In other words, the need for a lot of pad extension on a short side shot along the ice is minimal.

Shots to the far side are a very different matter. Quickness is of utmost importance, but getting to the puck is only part of your problem. Let's face it: the further you extend your pad, the more you open the five-hole, and the less support you're giving your stick. Not even proper stick placement will save you if an 85 M.P.H. ice-level shot hits a stick held by only one hand, with no pad to lend support in cushioning the blow. The puck can force its way under the stick, find the back of the net, and seriously affect membership drives initiated by the president of your fan club.

Knowing your relation to the net is crucial here; that should tell you exactly how far you have to extend the leg. *If your pad has to extend one foot to reach the shot, but you extend your pad two feet, then you've gone too far and opened up the five-hole too much.*

Again, it comes down to angles. Ideally, you'd like to have the time and be in position to flow back with the play, absorbing the puck with a butterfly. Without that time and motion, a butterfly move can lead to a rigid "thrust" of the pad, resulting in those rebounds we'd just as soon avoid. Instead, we prefer positioning that allows a butterfly move that not only covers the puck-to-post relationship, but angles the pads back towards the net in a "V" formation, deflecting pucks away from the danger zone.

This is as good a time as any to remind you of one of Ian Young's most important goaltending tips. Regardless of whether you give up a rebound that goes right back into the danger zone for a secondary shot, or manage to deflect the puck into a corner, *get right back up on your feet.* If you're not able to freeze the puck, you have to be mentally conditioned to regain your feet in every live situation. Don't ever say to yourself, "Oh, there's no need to get up in a hurry." Eventually, that kind of attitude, that kind of laziness, will cost you.

Don't cheat your teammates.

Don't cheat *yourself.*

After all, we goalies clothe ourselves in the garb of the modern gladiator. If we're to successfully do battle on the side of good, and survive to take pride in our accomplishments, we can't rest until the fight is done. Or at least, until the whistle blows.

Patrick Roy is one of the best goaltenders in hockey. When he's on his game, Roy has a great butterfly move that gives him an edge on ice-level shots. Not only is he quick, but he gets that stick flat on the ice between his knees with both hands high, covering the upper corners. He uses the move a lot, and usually gets away with it. Why? Because he's always "on" the puck with a focus that's second to none. He's also got tremendous puck sense, and a combination of reflexes and technical positioning— or blocking off—that makes the save.

But Roy gets himself in trouble occasionally by going down a little too soon—a lot of goalies will do that—and that's really a case of lost concentration. I blame it on practice sessions and how they're conducted, even at the NHL level.

Let's face it: Who cares about the poor old goalie? Not most forwards and coaches, that's for sure. Take a look at the goalie's involvement with practices at just about any level of the game. It's a simple case of shots, shots, and more shots. And when are forwards most happy? Why, when they're scoring, of course.

But if coaches would spend more time working with goalies, using drills that develop their play while eliminating weaknesses, the results would be dramatic.

It's the same in any sport. In baseball, for example, if a player doesn't see a fastball for three games and all of a sudden the first pitch in the fourth game is a 100 M.P.H. fastball, do you think he's going to hit it out of the ball park?

Probably not.

But if he's seeing fastballs all the time, his perception and anticipation will allow him to pick up the ball and make an appropriate response with his swing.

And that's why I don't cheat my goalies by sitting in the stands and watching them practice. I get on the ice and push them! When we work on shots along the ice, I make it a natural progression. First, the skate save without the use of a stick. Pucks are lined up at the hash marks and shot, rapid fire, to one side only. Then there's a similar series of shots to the other side. Remember, these are strictly skate saves.

Now, alternate shots…left side, right side, left side, right side, all at a high pace.

Then run through the entire procedure again, this time with a stick.

Next, it's the same scenario, only this time use the butterfly.

This basic progression in skill development is something that made a lot of difference in the play of Peter Sidorkiewicz, Kirk McLean, Jeff Hackett, Mike Fountain and Fred Brathwaite when they played for me at Oshawa. By the end of a season, boy, could they move. I can only hope that as their pro careers continue, they're given the attention at practice that you need to reach, and then maintain, a high level of proficiency in these moves.

But whether it's Peter, Kirk, or a 12-year-old between the pipes, just remember this: The drill has to be done at a quicker pace than the goalie is used to handling. *Always push yourself to the limits of your speed.* The result will be an entire realm of development—skate saves and butterfly—that will not only make you comfortable with the moves, but increase your confidence and puck-sense for a wide variety of game situations.

Paying even a minimal amount of attention to a goalie's ability to handle ice shots can make all the difference in the world. A goalkeeper friend who played in Europe tells the story of his Czechoslovakian coach who used the morning-of-a-game skate for more than just loosening up and target practice for the forwards. The coach would spend ten or fifteen minutes with my friend, firing shots along the ice. The grateful goalie claims it helped his concentration on the puck, and made a big difference in the game later that evening, when it really counted.

Sean Burke is a great goaltender, not just because of his size and anticipation, but because of his ability to read shots and go down well with the puck. Goalies like Burke and Roy can go down just a little bit earlier than most goalies and usually get away with it because of a puck sense that helps them react to situations. But for goalies without that puck sense—and the confidence that goes with it—terrible things can happen.

I've always claimed that a lot of goalies over-compensate for a lack of confidence by going down too soon. It's an unfortunate part of the game's psychology, really, but if you think about it, a goal doesn't look as bad if a goalie at least appears to be doing his best to stop it.

If a guy skates in and scores on a 25-foot shot along the ice and you're just standing there, you're going to look pretty stupid.

And who wants to look stupid?

A goalie who's standing erect when a shot eludes him looks weaker than the goalie who's beaten while in the butterfly—even if the latter went down *before the shot was taken.* At least it *looks* like he's making a stab at it. But if truth be known, it's a premeditated attempt to avoid embarrassment and has nothing to do with good goaltending.

The vast majority of goaltenders are consumed by the desire to learn and improve. And with that in mind, I'd like to reinforce something mentioned earlier in this book: There's no one style of goaltending that *has* to be played, and that applies to ice shots as much as to breakaways or any other part of the game. When it comes down to playing goal, it's a case of "to each his own". We shouldn't be coaching goaltenders at any level of the game by saying, "You have to stay on your feet," or "You have to bend that leg more to extend the skate properly," or "You should use the butterfly." Instead, let's give them the options. They will discover for themselves what is most comfortable...and what works for them.

Isn't the bottom line making the save? Who cares what they look like as long as they stop the puck? We know that the enemy will do his best to beat you, and that the shot along the ice is one of the toughest to handle. We've given you some options to use, try them out. Then settle on the ones that work best.

In other words, for the great battles to come, choose your own weapons.

Felix Potvin eliminates the possibility of a rebound (Relke).

REBOUNDS

There are two important strategies to remember when it comes to handling rebounds. The first—and I have to admit, this is a personal favourite—is to avoid them. The second is to be aware of the possibility of a rebound.

Both points are covered by a drill I use. It sounds stupid in its simplicity because it doesn't really deal with rebounds. You see, some coaches utilize goalie drills that are based on the existence of a rebound. But as I said, I prefer to *avoid* them. In a practice situation, isn't it better to concentrate on ways to avoid rebounds? And that's where my "stupid" drill comes in.

When I worked with my Leaf goalies, I commandeered the help of a few players to execute the drill. Guys like Daniel Marois, Vincent Damphousse, Tom Fergus, Mike Foligno and Darryl Shannon—to name a few—came out for my rebound drill. For them, it was a chance to work on certain shots. For the goalies, it was an opportunity to prepare themselves to control rebounds.

Here's what happened:

A shot came at the blocker.

A shot came to the trapper side.

A shot came to the five-hole.

A shot came to the belly.

In short, shots went everywhere. And in every case, the goalie's objective was the same: *control the rebound.*

There's no great secret here. Just get used to controlling those shots, thereby preventing rebounds. That's the drill I prefer to conduct. Here comes the shot, and what are you prepared to do about it? I ask my goalies to control it. What I found was that every shot—whether it was directed straight at the goalie, or high or low to a corner— was either smothered or directed out of harm's way. My goalies stopped being sloppy with the puck, and very few pucks found their way back into the danger zones.

Rebounds? What rebounds?

It comes down to concentration. I've heard of tennis coaches who tell their students to pick up the ball, fondle it, stare at the seams—more or less become its good buddy. I wouldn't go that far, but I do have a little advice that can help you get your concentration level to the point where you can't help but focus on the job at hand. When you're in a game, *the only thing in the building is that little black disk.* Whenever a shot is taken, all you've got to do is concentrate on that black disk. Being focussed to that extent makes saves easier because you're picking up the *puck faster.* If you're only half-focussed, your reaction time is diminished.

And if you're properly focussed, truly concentrating on your job, you'll be that much closer to satisfying the terms of Ian Young's Compulsory Rule of Rebound Recovery: If you had to go down to make one stop, get back on your feet immediately. I insist that the moment your knees hit the ice, you should be on your way back up again. After one save you should immediately get back up, focus on the puck, move to the angle and shut 'em down all over again.

You can save yourself a lot of trouble by either absorbing the initial shot, or at least deflecting the rebound away from the front of the net. If you're flowing back with the play, your pads should deaden the puck, preventing those rebounds that look so good to the attacking forwards. And if those pads are angled slightly back in a "V" formation when you go to the butterfly, instead of sitting parallel to the goal line, any rebounds that do escape your vigilance will end up at the side of the net, and not directly in front. So make that an aim of your workouts: any rebound that occurs should not end up between the two faceoff dots; if the puck's going anywhere, let's make sure it's not up the middle.

Again, it's a simple case of focussing, working hard at practice, and conditioning yourself so that any time a shot comes low to the stick side, it'll go to the corner; if it's low to the glove side, we'll make it go to the other corner. If you do that, you've already beaten most rebound possibilities with the result that the only *legitimate* rebound is the result of a quick, hard shot from fairly close range that doesn't give you time to react. And then of course, you're right back on your feet.

CLEARING THE PUCK

Despite your best training and intentions, rebounds are going to occur. You'll get a piece of the shot and watch the puck bounce in front. Assuming you're not far from a prospective trouble-maker, you have a couple of options: freeze the puck, or clear it.

It's a never-ending quandary: To freeze or not to freeze, that is the question.

If you do, you're giving in to a natural tendency to stop the action before something awful happens. If we're talking about heavy duty action, the freeze is your play. Too many things can go wrong if you attempt to clear it in crowded conditions. Better safe than sorry.

But if you have the time and the room to manoeuvre, you might want to reject the freezing option and clear the puck instead. Often, choosing this course of action is based on an evaluation of your team's faceoff effectiveness against a certain opponent. In 1991, Oshawa played Sault Ste. Marie for the OHL championship and we lost almost every faceoff in the series. Freezing the puck was just about the same as conceding an instant turnover inside our zone. If we're not winning draws, the goalie should avoid holding pucks for faceoffs. The prudent thing is to clear the puck.

Here's a drill that helps build wrist strength while you work on clearing the puck cleanly. It involves having pucks fired in along the boards behind the net. Your job is to 1) control it; and 2) practice different ways of clearing it (*Behind The Mask*, p. 64).

The first part of the drill involves fielding the puck smoothly. That involves keeping the blade flat on the ice with the toe of the stick against the end boards while angling your stick so there's no danger of the puck deflecting back in front of the net.

The second part of the drill includes a number of options. You can work on ways of leaving the puck for your defence in a way that doesn't create confusion between you and them. You can "soft" it into the corner, or rifle it high along the boards and out to centre. You might even try to perfect a high, clearing "pass" over the boards.

The drill can be turned into a more realistic "game" situation by positioning a skater at or near the playoff dot, and having him chase the puck as it's fired behind the net. For the goalie, it's some added pressure and increases the tempo of the clearing attempt. After all, I'm the guy who always wants to see things done at a faster pace than my goalies are used to performing them.

But no degree of quickness will ensure 100% success at clearing the puck if there's a communication gap between you and your teammates. Defencemen and forwards alike should be giving you a verbal hand with simple commands: "Leave it", "Into the corner", "Up the wing"...*anything that helps you make the quick play.*

It doesn't matter if you've got the strongest wrists in the world — if no one's helping you, and there's a guy on your tail getting ready to strip you of the puck, it can only mean trouble. You've got to have people yelling at each other out there.

In a certain sense, we can think of goaltending in football terms. In some situations—like clearing pucks off a rebound—I consider the goalie a team's quarterback. Like a Q.B., he's got to know the opposition's "defensive alignments". When they forecheck, how do they get into your zone? What do they do with their defence? Where are their forwards? Are they high on the boards, or coming in deep? Are the defencemen pinching, or staying back? Should you "soft" it into the corner, or put

it high around the glass?

Unfortunately, a lot of goalies don't think in terms of the opponent's forechecking pattern. But knowing the answers makes a big difference in a quickly developing situation. For example, if you know their forwards are pinching deep along the boards but the defenceman is laying back, then you also know you can shoot high along the boards from, say, the net area to about five feet inside the blueline. Nobody's going to pick it off.

Or, if their forwards are pinching deep, and the off-side winger is coming down the middle, flooding one side of the ice, why would you throw the puck that way? If you know that's their forechecking pattern, and you've got to make the quick decision, you can play the puck to the weak side, giving your second defenceman not only the puck, but a little less pressure. Knowing *immediately what to do with the puck in a given situation should become part of your game.*

But whether he considers himself King of the Kick-Save, Prince of the Poke-Check, Duke of Deflections, Baron of Breakaways or Viscount Vezina, there's something else our regal hero already knows: Handling rebounds properly—and being successful in most other aspects of the position, for that matter—are dependent on whether or not our Lord of the Rink is given enough time to work at his royal trade during practice sessions.

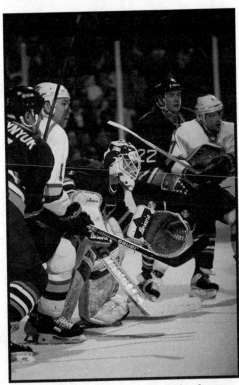

Sean Burke's defenders help eliminate the deflection (Relke).

DEFLECTIONS

Most goalies will tell you that there are certain incidents that stick in the minds forever. It could be something not directly connected to the game, like the look of anxiety on a face in the crowd following a scramble in your crease. But more than likely it's a great save on an unusual play, or a particularly embarrassing goal.

When I was 13 years old and playing for the Scarborough Lions at Toronto's Ted Reeve Arena, a Ted Reeve player came across centre ice and hammered a slapshot. My defenceman deflected the shot at the blueline, and the puck took off in another direction. I ended up diving two feet off the ice, across the crease, to catch the puck. This is on a deflection from the blueline! I learned then that deflections are nasty critters that don't give us much time to react.

Two years later I was with the Oshawa Generals. My first game was against the Montreal Junior Canadiens, and boy was I nervous! When I stepped onto the ice for the warmup, I looked up and saw Rogie Vachon in goal. They also had Serge Savard, Jacques Lemaire, Yvan Cournoyer, Rejean Houle, Andre Boudrias—all on one junior team!

For a rookie goalie, it was a scary sight.

It was tied 4-4 in the final minutes of the game when Andre Boudrias came down the ice and wound up for a shot from just inside the blueline. Bobby Orr was my defenceman on the play, backing up about ten feet away from Boudrias and maybe 30 feet in front of me. Boudrias took a wicked slapshot, Bobby went down, and the puck hit his shoulder. I moved for the initial shot, and the puck took off in another direction and caught the corner of the net. They added an empty net goal and beat us 6-4.

There's a graphic illustration of the fact that you don't have a lot of time to react to a deflection. You have a split second to make your move, so you'd better have a plan mapped out ahead of time.

There are two basic yet crucial points to handling deflections:

1) Read the deflection possibilities! If you've got an opposition player five feet outside the crease, you should realize automatically that there's a deflection or re-direct situation plotting your downfall. The villain could be a deflection from directly in front, from the side, or from the guy who breaks from the wing and alters a puck's flight to the net. For proper anticipation, *you need to be aware of all these situations.*

2) The second point to keep in mind—at the risk of sounding repetitive—is *angles.* If an opponent deflects the puck ten feet in front of the net, where's your best chance of making the save? On the goal line? No. On the edge of the crease? No. *It's in front of the puck.* Therefore, your aim is to get as close as you can to the *point of deflection* as quickly as possible, while staying on your telescoping centre line, maintaining your angle to the net. This is intricately connected to the first point since you won't get there quickly if you don't recognize the existence of a deflection possibility. Instead, you could find yourself too deep in the net. You won't be playing the deflection—it will be playing you! Once the initial shot is taken, you've got to position yourself as close to the puck as possible (*Behind The Mask*, p. 92).

It's important to note that we're talking about deflection possibilities in the general vicinity of the net. For deflections that occur from far out, you shouldn't be moving to the point of the deflection. Instead, you should be counting on your reflexes to react to the puck.

The proper way of playing deflections means that you have to deal with two angles: First, there's the angle on the initial shot; secondly, the angle on the possible deflection. Which angle is the most important? In this case, it's the second angle—keep in mind that we're discussing deflections here. Often, you'll see a defenceman wind up for a shot but instead of shooting, he'll pass to a teammate standing at the side of the net and go for the tip-in.

Unfortunately, in those situations I see too many goalies moving out to take the angle on the shot from the point, moving beyond the two or three players cruising just outside the crease area. If you can't stop a shot from the blueline that you can see all the way—and let's not even worry about having the angle on that shot—then you might want to consider taking up another sport that doesn't rely so heavily on basic reflex ability. Why not stay deeper in the net and make it easier to play a secondary situation, whether it be a deflection, a re-direct, or *a screen shot?*

A classic example was a big goal scored by Toronto's Nikolai Borchevsky against Red Wings' goalie Tim Cheveldae in over-time of game seven of a Norris Division semi-final in 1993. It was, quite simply, a case of a goaltender eliminating his options. Doug Gilmour passed to Toronto defenceman Bob Rouse, who was racing in from the point. Cheveldae moved well out to take the angle on the shot, reducing his involvement in the play to facing the shot. Rather than shoot, however, Rouse slipped a pass that slid out of Cheveldae's reach to Borchevsky, who had skated out of the corner behind Cheveldae. Borchevsky's deflection found the net, the Leafs found themselves in a divisional final, and the Red Wings found themselves on the golf course. Even if Rouse had shot, what would Cheveldae's chances be if the puck went off the end boards and back out front? He would have been tap dancing in the slot with the puck sliding back in front for an easy tap-in.

Realizing possible deflection situations is just one of the things a technically competent goalie will do automatically. Sure, he'll also take the occasional gamble and challenge the shooter at the point, but by and large, he'll size up the situation and act accordingly.

Another thing about deflections: when a situation dictates that you move to the point of the deflection, stay on your feet. Staying up allows you not only to make the save, but also to move for the rebound. Why would you move to take the angle on a deflection, and then go down? What would that achieve? Once again, the goalie who goes down when it's not necessary is over-compensating. Maybe he's just trying to extend more than the standing position permits. But if you're reading the play well and moving to the point of the deflection, in most cases there's no need to leave your feet.

So far we've dealt with shots deflected by opposition players. But occassionally your own defenceman pulls a practical joke and helps out the enemy by re-directing the puck in your direction. In that long-ago situation where the puck went off Bobby Orr's shoulder and beat me, at least he was far from the net, trying to block the puck with his body. But that's a different story than a defender who waves his stick at a shot, somehow thinking that's a better move than letting the goalie handle it. If this becomes a chronic problem, an off-ice discussion becomes necessary. It's time to sit down and have a little heart-to-heart with your best on-ice buddy, and the message should go something like this:

"A defenceman's job is to protect the goalie, and that should be more than enough to keep you busy. You've got to take the man in front of the net, neutralizing his stick and cutting down on the deflection possibility. If possible, clear him out so I'm not faced with a screen shot or a forward driving for a rebound. When that puck's coming from the point, you should be taking out the forward, removing him from the situation. That's your job...to protect the goalie.

But leave the puck alone! Don't start throwing your stick at the shot, trying to deflect it away. More often than not you're going to re-direct it to an uncovered portion of my net. And I won't like it very much..."

In summing up deflections, we have three points to remember: 1) Be aware of the deflection possibilities; 2) move to the point of the deflection; and 3) make sure your defencemen stick to *their* job.

Number 3) is up to the defencemen. If they do their jobs properly, you can take care of numbers 1) and 2).

IT EVEN HAPPENS TO *THEM*

We know that playing goal can be one of life's more frustrating afflictions. Think of it: Twenty legs churning this way and that, a small black disk that can travel at mind-boggling speed, and 10 sticks that can, at any given time, re-direct the flight of that disk. The chances of being caught off-guard are readily apparent.

It's part of the game, a part you have to learn not only to live with, but to anticipate. But even when you do expect the unexpected, strange things can happen. Peter Sidorkiewicz knows all about it. When he was with Hartford in a playoff game against Boston, the Whalers led by a goal early in the third period. Ray Bourque tried to fire the puck along the boards from centre ice, into the Hartford zone. Says Peter, "He goes to shoot it around the boards and I started to move out of my net. But at about the blueline it hit (teammate) Paul Cyr's skate, and deflected straight at my net. I'm 10 feet out of the net by this time so it's too late, see ya later, it's in. We were in total control at the time, but when that happened, we folded.

The next thing you know, it's 6-1. A stupid deflection like that turned it around."

That wasn't the first time Peter and the Bruins found themselves on opposite sides of an embarrassing moment. "In my first year in the league," says Peter, "Michael Thelven dumped it into the cross corner. I wanted to get to it before their guy, who was racing down the wing, so I left the net. But Joel Quenneville, my defenceman, gives it a high stick at the blueline, gets a piece of it, and it's in. I'm waiting for the puck in the corner, the puck's in the net, and I'm standing there looking like an idiot!

"But you can't get too upset about it. Your defencemen save you so many times by deflecting pucks away that they make up for the odd one that beats you. It puts you off when they deflect one by you, but things happen so fast that sometimes it's just a natural reaction on their part."

Kirk McLean agrees with that: "A guy comes down the wing on a 2-on-1 and winds up for a shot, and one of your guys throws out his stick. It throws you off balance. But it's a natural thing for them to do."

Kirk also remembers deflections of a different kind. These ones won't happen as frequently, but they're immensely embarrassing when they do occur.

"We were playing Winnipeg," he says, "and it was tied in the last minute of play. The puck came to our end and I went out to play it. Ed Olczyk was coming down the wing as I went to clear it up the boards. I

shot, it hit him on the shin pads on a really weird angle, and went right in the net. All I can remember thinking was, how did that thing go in? Luckily, we came back to tie it with about two seconds left."

It was just one of those things…a flukey set of circumstances that registered high on the frustration scale. But McLean's not alone in that department. Here's how Sidorkiewicz described one of his NHL encounters with the hockey fates.

"One year, I gave up just two goals at home in two games against Chicago. Both goals were stupid. The second time they came to town, we're winning something like 3-0 halfway through the third period and I went out to field the puck. I think it was Jeremy Roenick coming down one way, and my defenceman Alain Cote was coming down the other side. I shot the puck, Cote peeled off, it hit his skate, went right to Roenick, and he had an empty net. The fans gave it to me pretty good."

Although the last couple of examples are about as common as a full lunar eclipse, they can happen—even to the pros. But we're more concerned with the every-day occurrences — the shots that deflect off a defenceman or opposition forward from close range. And for those situations, my recommendation is to play the percentages: Read the situation, move to the point of deflection, and the Gods of Goaltending Probability will be with you over the long haul.

Kay Whitmore clears his crease (Relke).

SCREEN SHOTS

Handling screen shots is one of the most difficult things to teach a young goaltender. But it can also be one of the most rewarding when you help your goalie develop the necessary quickness and positioning.

There are two distinctly different screen shots: the shot from the point when the front of the net is clogged with attackers and defenders; and the play that develops on the wing before the shooter cuts in front and takes a shot after the puck has disappeared from the goalie's view (*Behind The Mask,* p. 88).

SCREEN SHOTS FROM THE POINT

I know a lot of hockey people who say that the goalie should come right out into the crowd. The theory is that you can cover the angle somewhat, and when you hear the stick slapping the puck from the point, drop down into your butterfly, cover the lower corners, and hope it hits you. Part of the reasoning behind the theory—and it has some legitimacy —is that there's a better chance a low shot can make its way past some legs than there is for a high shot to sneak through the much thicker upper bodies that plug the front of the net.

It sounds good, but this covers only one situation. By handling screen shots in this manner, you're precluding yourself from any other option.

Let's look at it.

First of all, by going into the crowd you're losing the puck. You're *giving* them the screen! And what happens if the shot doesn't make it to the net, but merely makes it to the slot? Or what if it goes to the *side* of the net and you're trapped in the traffic out front, down on the ice, looking for nickels? And of course, if there's a rebound, you're still facing the same traffic-related problems.

Another thing: At the 1990 NHL All-Star Game in Pittsburgh, Al Iafrate won the hardest shot contest. He let one rip that wasn't far off the 100 M.P.H. mark. Take that speed and point it at the net. If you

move into the crowd in front of the net and lose your angle just slightly, you've got little chance on a shot that heads for a wide-open corner.

To make matters worse, whenever you head into a crowd you run the risk of being blocked out of the play. In short, you're putting all your eggs in one basket when you skate into a crowd in front of the net. Stay in the crease, where you're somewhat protected.

I believe the goalie's primary concern is to find the puck! You do that by crouching low. And if you have to, go right back to the goal line. By crouching low, you're almost automatically in the butterfly position for the shot. And wherever that puck goes, you're picking it up at some point on its flight to the net.

If it turns out to be a pass to the short side of the net, you can use your incredible foot strength and proximity to the goal line to move to the short side post. If it's a pass to the far side, those dancing feet will again get you over there in time. If it comes to the crowd in front, *then* you can move out and take away not only the angle, but the possibility of a deflection as well. And if this happens, *aren't you right where a lot of coaches are telling you to be in the first place?* The only difference is, by picking up the puck as soon as possible you've given yourself a whole list of other options.

Let's run through it again:

1) *Find the puck!* Get back in the net and

crouch low, legs apart, automatically cutting off the lower corners. Since your legs are spread so wide, just inches away from the ice, you're in great shape to go into a quick, full butterfly extension, if you have to.

2) Since you've found the puck, by sizing up the situation around the net you'll be in a position to react to the shot and go to the point of the re-direct or the one-time shot. Again, it's about angles.

Remember: The opposition has four simple options: a shot on net from the point; a shot to the crowd in front for a deflection or a secondary shot; a shot to the short side for a re-direct; and a shot to the far side for a re-direct. Your job is to pick up the puck and make the appropriate move.

THE SUDDEN SCREEN

It happens all the time. The winger barrels down the ice and you've got him all the way. You've achieved the correct telescoping angle, and a backward motion maintains it as he approaches the net. But he doesn't want to play fair. Suddenly, he cuts into the middle. Just as the puck disappears behind a defender's leg, he lets it go, and you catch a faint glimpse of galvanized rubber as the black disk whizzes past. With a little luck, it could hit you or go wide. But too often it finds the back of the net.

Nobody blames you, really. After all, it was screened. But deep in your soul, you're frustrated. You could have had that one, and you know it.

There's a major problem for goalies and those who coach them. Screen shots have been very difficult to simulate in practice situations. Stance, mobility and knowledge of angles can be taught, but how do we deal with the Phantom Shot from the Slot?

I agonized over this problem for several years. How could I simulate this all-too-common game situation without crippling every defenceman on the roster? Let's face it: There isn't a defender in all of hockey who relishes the thought of standing in front of a series of hard shots just so his goalie can practice screen shots. Besides, only a small percentage of drills done in this manner will actually result in a drive that's well-hidden until it clears the defenceman's legs.

After considerable thought, I designed the Screen Shot Apparatus. After a little factory construction, I was the proud owner of something that some people might consider a rather suicidal device, but that without question increases reflex abilities and lateral motion in the butterfly. With this goaltending aid, you know the shot is coming—you just don't know where or when.

The concept is simple. The device has two posts and a cross beam, and suspended from the beam is a canvas-like screen that can be raised to whatever level you desire —six inches, one foot, two feet, whatever. The screen is placed twenty feet in front of the net and is raised a foot off the ice. The goalie stands in the net while one or more shooters line up on the other side of the apparatus taking shots. When the puck is fired under the screen, the goalie's task is to react quickly, picking up the puck in mid-flight, relying on reflexes to make the save.

If you don't develop quickness in a hurry, it can be a humbling experience.

But the beautiful thing about the screen is its versatility. Shots can come from any distance while the screen can be moved from side to side, placed anywhere from 15 to 40 feet in front of the net. I can move the screen closer to the goalie, I can move the puck further back, I can arrange the puck and the screen anyplace that will give the goalie a chance to react.

As a coach, I'm not looking for saves. Instead, I'm watching movement, quickness and development. And for the move that comes in off the wing to a screen shot from the slot, it's perfect!

For example, place the screen out as far as the hash marks, set a foot-and-a-half off the ice. As the shooter advances from the wing, the goalie goes out high to take the angle. When the shooter cuts across behind the screen, the goalie moves laterally with the play. All of a sudden, the puck is hidden and the shot is taken. You can imagine how disconcerting that is for the goalie. And yet, it's a situation that occurs in every game!

Reaction time is extremely important — move left, move right, butterfly. It's sink or swim time for the big guy with the bigger pads. The scenario can include a pass from the wing to the slot for a one-time shot, but the result will always be the same: there's a point where you're going to lose the puck. In too many cases, that's when a goalie loses his motion as well. But with the apparatus, you can develop the ability to maintain the motion and pick up the shot when it's launched.

The screen shot is a standard part of today's game. But at one point, the NHL did its best to do away with it. At a league meeting of October 19, 1931, a new rule was put in place: "If a player on the attacking side, not in possession of the puck, takes up any position at or near the goal of the defending side in such a way as to obscure or interfere with the vision or movements of a goalkeeper, while the latter is in his net, the referee shall at once stop the play and order a face-off (outside the blueline)...A goal scored while the vision or the movements of a goalkeeper, in his net, are being interfered with by a player of the attacking side, shall not be allowed."

When you watch the crease encroachments that are permitted these days, it's almost as if there isn't such a thing as a goal crease any more. Skaters play inside the crease on a regular basis, driving to the net and through the goaltender. That's no different than defencemen being allowed to use the blade of the stick to hold back offensive players. When did this become part of our game? The old give-and-go pass play seldom happens anymore because you're going to get three or four slashes in the belly or the face before you get through to take the return pass. And they wonder why highly-skilled European teams challenge and beat us at our own game! To a large extent, it's because we're slowing down our own game by permitting tactics that would have been routinely penalized years ago.

More and more, goalies are forced to retreat deep in the net because defencemen and forwards are whacking each other to death in front. There's nothing wrong with screening a goaltender—that's a legitimate part of the game—but there is something wrong with making goalies fair game by permitting all the movement inside the crease. If penalties for unforced entry into the goal crease were called on every occasion, it would give the goaltender a lot more breathing room.

So let's assume that certain rules were implemented and rigidly enforced: First of all, the crease is the goalie's exclusive domain, and encroachment by opposition forwards is absolutely forbidden; and secondly, nobody's allowed to use his stick to hammer guys to the ice in front of the net. What does that leave us with? *The true screen situation.*

Not only does that give the noble goaltender a fighting chance to make the save, but it also provides a less hazardous environment around his net. In recent years the NHL has said it wants to restrict contact between forwards and goalies. But enforcement of the rules is inconsistent at best, and somehow, I doubt that they will totally eliminate the skater with screening intentions from encroaching on the good guy's crease.

Another goalie coach used to tell his players that if a forward was crowding them, backing into the crease and freezing them on the goal line, they should jump past him, leaving the screen behind, and play the shot. I've done that myself, although only on those occasions when I knew I could get away with it since I was convinced the shot was on its way to the net. But strange things can happen on a puck's journey from point A to point B. It can get re-directed to points C or D while you're dancing with the group out front, so it's not something I teach.

It's like the poke-check. I don't support it, but I know it's going to happen in game situations. And, technically-speaking, if everybody played every situation the way they're supposed to be played, there would be shutouts every night.

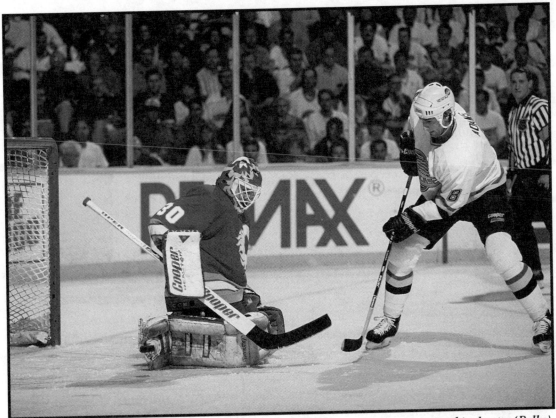

Mike Vernon comes out to meet his shooter (Relke).

BREAKAWAYS

The forward curls in the neutral zone, a long clearing pass streaking towards the blade of his stick. The defencemen, caught by surprise, scramble to recover.

But it's too late.

Accelerating quickly, the forward splits the defence. The spectators rise in anticipation, the intensified noise of the crowd deafening. Why? Because one of the most dramatic and exciting moments in sports is unfolding.

The breakaway.

More than sixty feet away, the goalkeeper has seen the play unfold, knowing before anyone else in the building that the threat of a breakaway pass was very much a real one. Senses alerted immediately, he began his preparations.

He was going one-on-one.

In essence, there are two types of breakaway. The *centre* breakaway, as the name implies, sees the shooter moving straight at the goal down the centre of the ice. A penalty shot is the classic example.

The *angle* breakaway occurs when the shooter drives at the net from the wing, having cleared all defenders.

In both situations, the forward has the option of shooting, or deking to either side. And in some ways, the goalie's responses are the same. As we'll see, these two breakaway types are different enough to warrant distinct methods of countering them.

CENTRE BREAKAWAY

When a player comes straight in on goal, unimpeded, he has five basic shot opportunities: The two upper corners, the two lower corners, and the inevitable five-hole. As a result, your first responsibility is to remove those openings. Whatever you do, don't give the shooter the opportunity to look up, see all kinds of net, and break into a grin.

Instead, come out high and take away as much of the net as possible by using your telescoping theory. If you're foot-strong and comfortable with your ability to move backwards—there's that motion again—you can come as high as the hash marks, if you want.

The higher you come, the more net you're taking away.

Now draw two lines from the posts to the puck and see where your body is in relation to them. If you're out high, on the ideal telescopic angle with your body, skates and shoulders touching the lines, you'll probably find yourself very close to the hash marks. But as the puck approaches, it's obvious that the puck-to-posts lines will change. This is a crucial consideration because it tells us not only that you have to move back with the play, but also that *you'll lose the angle if you move back at the same speed as the puck.*

This is where basic geometry enters the picture. Just because the puck comes in two feet doesn't mean the goalie should move back two feet. In fact, you may have to move back only *one* foot. After all, maintaining the same speed as the approaching puck will have you crashing into the back of the net by the time the shooter hits the hash marks.

This will make it exceedingly difficult to make the save, and almost impossible to take out life insurance.

Once you've attained the maximum angle on the puck, remember that the rate at which you approach the net is less than that at which the *shooter* approaches the net. You should maintain the proper angle to the puck throughout the forward's invasion.

An early caution: we've talked about stance and the need to avoid a breakdown. But often goalies will concentrate on the deke scenario so much that a low crouch will develop as the play approaches the net. We already know that's not a very good idea. The stance will open too much, exposing a larger five-hole; the shoulders will drop, causing the trapper to drop and open the upper corner on that side; the blocker will drop, not only exposing the upper corner but causing the stick blade to lift, leaving just the heel on the ice. In short, you'll concede the upper corners and the five hole, both on and off the ice. To avoid this, you require a high level of concentration to ensure a normal, comfortable stance before you address a breakaway shot or deke.

If you can do that while moving back and maintaining the angle, you've already presented the forward with a bit of a dilemma. He'll look up, not see very much net, and have to make a decision. Suddenly, at the high pace of a breakaway, he has to ask himself, "What are my options…what am I going to do?" And remember—the more you make a shooter think, the higher the likelihood that his accuracy will suffer.

A goalie friend told me of a goal he allowed that he hasn't been able to forget. He prided himself on the motion he incor-porated into his play, and his success on breakaways. One day he faced a penalty shot with seven minutes to play in a score-less game. But by the time the shot was taken, he'd lost his concentration. Instead of moving high to take the angle, he stayed in the crease, relying on reflexes. The shooter came in, saw a corner and picked it cleanly for the only goal of the game. It was a nothing game really, an exhibition match. But to this day that's the only shot that still haunts him, the only one he'd like to play again. Why? Because he didn't give himself a chance on the play. And as we know, goalies don't get a second chance.

Keep in mind that if the shooter holds the puck out to one side of his body, he still has the option of shooting. Occasionally, a goalie will tend to go with the movement of the shooter's body, losing the angle in the process. But if you stay centred on the puck, you won't leave much to shoot at. Not seeing any net to go for, he might panic, giving you an easy save.

On the other hand, if the shooter moves the puck in front of his body and starts to coast with the play, straddling the puck, chances are he'll end up trying a deke.

But what happens when a goalie, moving backwards in the inverted "V" stance, starts to move one way or the other with the deke? On the first step, as the lead foot moves with the play, the five-hole is temporarily wid-ened. Remember, there's no T-push on a centre breakaway. The T-push is used to move long distances across the net when the puck-carrier cuts in front, and should be reserved for plays breaking in on the wing.

So here's our situation: A skater coming in on a centre breakaway and denied a corner of the net is forced to go to the deke. As he moves to the right or the left, the five-hole will be widened momentarily. (And believe me, a good shooter will take advantage of that, ruining your moment on centre stage.) At this point a lot of goalies put themselves at a disadvantage by lifting out of their stance when they make that first move, pulling their stick off the ice in the process, and enhancing the five-hole danger. But that's a matter of concentration, really. I find that goalies tend to forget about stick placement in a situation like that because they're in such a hurry to get the body across.

However, if you remember to retain your stance and keep the stick flat on the ice and between your feet as you move across, you'll find yourself stopping 50% of those five-hole attempts by denying the goal along the ice. Don't forget that the five-hole is a legitimate target for a quality shooter, and as with any other part of the net, it has to be a source of concern.

Another common mistake is the one that has goalies lunging with the first deke, either feet or head first, taking themselves out of the play. Even if they manage to make the first stop, they're too busy break-dancing to get in position for the rebound. This can be the result of poor skating, but as often as not it's another case of loss of angles through inadequate concentration.

Look at it this way: Skates don't deke goalies—hips and shoulders do. If you find yourself being deked badly by the first move, you're too preoccupied with peripheral activity. Instead of concentrating on the puck and your angles, you're paying too much attention to the shooter's body. You should be concentrating on that puck so much that your focal point narrows to the feet and the puck area, the feet being the outside of the periphery. Those feet, of course, enter into the equation because if they straddle the puck, they can tip you off to the deke situation.

Continue to construct the centre breakaway scenario. You're coming back in the inverted "V", maintaining your angle all the way. If the puck carrier decides to deke to one side or the other, your first move in that direction will momentarily widen the five-hole, but proper stance with the stick flat on the ice between the feet will minimize the five-hole danger along the ice. But let's say the shooter decides to make his deke, then hold onto the puck. That puts you in a position that might require you to go down.

You have to get to the post. And here, as in most cases, there's a right way and a wrong way.

First of all, *don't* get your pads to the post by dropping deep in the crease and throwing your legs parallel to the goal line. This kind of manoeuvre could leave you inside the goal line; even if the puck hits you, it could be a goal.

Your aim is to force that shooter to make a commitment on the deke *while you're still at the top of the crease.* Your motion, your backward flow, will take you back to the post. At this point you have to decide whether to use a one-pad slide, or a two-pad slide.

On the one-pad slide, you go down and extend the short side pad to the post. Your body is upright; your blocker is out, stick at the knees to cover the five-hole; and your trapper is up and out, covering as much of the net as possible.

With the two-pad slide, too many goalies try to thrust their legs at the post, momentarily suspending their pads above ice level. It's important to do the two-pad slide properly, with the bottom pad going along the ice, skates directed to the post or just outside the post. If the skates should happen to end up inside the net, you've defeated your purpose. Again, even if you block it, the puck can end up across the goal line.

Whichever way you go, your "ice" arm— the one that goes to the playing surface— should be *flat* on the ice to block a comeback shot. If the ice arm happens to be the stick arm, it should be lying along the ice with the stick extended, also flat on the ice with the toe pointing upwards. The trapper arm has to be above the pads, covering as much of the upper net as possible.

If the trapper arm is the one that's flat on the ice because of a deke to the stick side, the blocker and stick must be positioned above the pads, again to cover as much of the upper net as possible. Some people instruct their goalies to turn their blocker so the palm is facing the play. They feel—and I can see their point—that this helps block more of the upper net by positioning the stick blade *above* the pads. But I don't teach goalies to turn the stick and expose the hand to the shot because I've seen broken fingers result. The leather around the fingers on the blocker hand isn't meant to stop pucks going 80 miles an hour!

Regardless of the way you do it and the way it looks, that extra piece of equipment has to be covering a part of the net. An arm, a blocker, a trapper, a stick—whatever it happens to be, use it! Don't get lazy and find yourself with two pieces of equipment covering the same area.

Once you've made the move, get right back on your feet. Too many goalies stay down once they get there, playing rebounds from their hips. Whether it's from laziness, poor conditioning or lack of concentration, it's a bad and often fatal mistake.

We've covered the one-pad slide and the two-pad slide—two ways of going down and dealing with dekes off centre breakaways. Unfortunately, both can have negative repercussions because every time you go down, you leave part of the upper net uncovered. A shooter deking to his backhand will almost invariably go high under the crossbar. The only real way to prevent that is to *be on your feet when he shoots!*

There's no reason for a goalie to feel he has to go down on a centre breakaway that ends in a deke. After all, you'll face forwards who are slower than others, and stickhandlers not that quick with their dekes. Often, you can hold your feet, go with the deke, and be in position to block those shots heading for the roof of the net.

Saying that is a simple matter, but it's not always easy to execute the move under game conditions. In fact, dekes can happen so quickly that you might find yourself hitting the ice most of the time. Still, the option of holding your feet should be there, and the best way to provide yourself with that option is to practice a very simple drill.

While facing centre breakaways in practice, stay on your feet at all costs. Don't worry about the pucks that get by you because, before you know it, your increased foot strength and improved concentration will help minimize the need to go down.

That's the ultimate way to play a deke off a centre breakaway.

ANGLE BREAKAWAY

On an angle, or wing breakaway, you don't have quite as much net to cover. In order to establish the proper telescopic angle, there's no need to come out as far as you would on

a centre breakaway. Still, the general theory is the same.

Starting with your short side post (a little tap should do), come high on the angle, at least to the maximum telescopic point, taking that puck-to-body-to-net centre line. In effect, you cut off the net and retain your stance, taking away the initial shot. The shooter might take an early drive at the five-hole if he sees a little daylight, but your work on the five-point drill (*Beyond*, p. 47) should take care of that: Go to the butterfly—stick between the pads, using your backward motion to help cushion the shot. If a rebound does get out of reach, you should be right back up on your feet for the next shot.

SHORT SIDE DEKE

The response to a deke to the short side should never be a two-pad slide. The two-pad slide is essentially a "last resort" move by goalies who aren't using motion properly. In most cases, they're standing still at the time and have no other recourse than to lunge at the play. However, using superior motion and coming back while retaining the angle, you realize that it's a relatively simple matter to flow to the short side and stay on your feet.

Remember, the shooter has just three short side options at this point. He can go high with the shot, try for the five-hole, or simply jam the puck straight at you. If you're on your feet, closing the five-hole, he hasn't much of a chance to score. Especially since, by moving to the post, your pads will come together automatically, eliminating his five-hole opportunity. But if the shooter has an exceptionally quick move to the short side and forces you to the ice, you still have the option of going to the one-pad butterfly with the short side pad to the post, body upright with the stick on the ice and the trapper and blocker held high.

Here's a situation you'll come across from time to time. Even if you've played the one-pad slide perfectly, the forward might hold onto the puck just a little longer than usual—or maybe they'll get a second scoring chance because they fanned on their initial shot. At any rate, you're down with one pad extended and the puck is still out front. My advice is this: Immediately move the pad to the puck. Don't sit there expecting the worst, because if you do, that's exactly what will happen.

If you're still concentrating on the puck—as you should be—then close that gap between the puck and the pad. Even six inches can make a difference. There's nothing unusual here—it's playing the angles. Only in this case, you're taking away a part of the upper net by closing the angle that exists between the puck and the crossbar, and the puck and the top of the pad.

Angles—if you forget them, you may as well give up the position.

DRIVING ACROSS THE NET

If the shooter sees no shot possibility and rejects the short side deke, he'll drive across the net. Here again, as with the centre breakaway, your first move with the leading leg will leave a large five-hole. But your initial glide, even with the stick covering the ice-level five-hole, won't be enough. That sin-

In 1941, the NHL decided on two classifications of penalty shots, a minor and a major. The minor penalty shot was called when a player, other than a goaltender, fell on the puck within ten feet of the goal. For this offence, the opposition was granted a penalty shot from a line that was 28 feet from the goal. The major shot, awarded when a player was tripped on a clear breakaway, permitted the shooter to skate right in on goal, "and fire from point-blank range." Today, of course, whether a penalty shot is called because a player is tripped on a clear breakaway, or because a defender grabs the puck with his hand in the crease, the shooter is allowed to skate right in on goal and shoot or deke.

gle push across the crease won't get you there. The shooter will keep moving until he outflanks you, and scores. Even the "desperation" two-pad slide won't get you all the way across the net, assuming you've started high enough to eliminate his shooting opportunity coming in from the wing.

Instead, we have to employ the T-push!

At first, people were sceptical of the T-push. It's not a normal recommendation from goalie coaches because it's not something you can do if you're weak on your feet. But if you put in the time and the work to develop it, you're chances of climbing hockey's goaltending ladder will be greatly increased (*Behind The Mask*, pp. 35-6).

Let's go through the T-push again.

The moment the shooter makes his move to cut across the net from your right to left, you turn your left skate parallel to the goalline. Since your right skate is still at right angles to the goalline, your feet have developed a "T" shape. The left knee is bent slightly while the right one is bent into the back of the left knee, cutting off the five-hole. With a series of short, choppy steps you shuffle across the crease.

You've kept the high angle, staying on your feet, shoulders squared to the shooter. The net, including the five-hole, is still blocked off. No matter how long he holds onto the puck, at some point the shooter is going to panic. He'll shoot, you'll be in position to stop him, and the reporters will want to talk to you, not him, after the game.

Throughout the T-push, your stance is the same as always except the pads will turn a bit with your feet. Once you get comfortable with the move, you'll find that you'll be facing the puck directly. The trapper will be out, the blocker will be out, the stick will be flat on the ice, and you'll be flowing with the puck.

Think about it, going back to our one-on-one with Wayne Gretzky. If the Great One comes in from the wing, what's he looking for? The open net, of course. And if your superior skating ability and unmatched understanding of angles has taken that away and convinced him that a deke to the short side is an exercise in futility, he'll cut across the net, looking for the five-hole or holding onto the puck until you've gone down. But the T-push not only allows you to remove that five-hole, it also keeps you on your feet as you move across the net. Number 99 is not only thwarted, he's demoted—to at least a 98.

Of course, most goalies will still insist on using the poke check whenever a shooter crosses in front of the net. Unfortunately, a lot of goalies don't know how to use it. They'll telegraph the move and take themselves out of the play. Even if you're well-trained in the technique, it's a dangerous play because if you miss, you're like a fish out of water. And even if you do get it, where's the puck going? In a lot of cases, right back out front. So by using the poke-check, you're running the risk of being down and at the mercy of forwards following up on the play.

I don't encourage the poke-check. Most goalies will continue to use it instinctively and, unfortunately, it will always be part of the game. But I prefer playing the percentages.

I'll take stance, angles and motion anytime.

And the advantage on that most dramatic of all hockey plays—the one-on-one confrontation between a goalie and the forward on a breakaway—will shift decidedly to the man between the pipes.

PARTY TIME!

Canadians enjoy a good party. Realizing that, this country's best players went out and provided a pretty good excuse for another big bash by winning the 1991 Canada Cup tournament — our fourth Cup victory in five tries.

Again, goaltending was a big part of the story. Bill Ranford stopped 27 shots in the final game, a 4-2 win over the United States. He was superb — a real battler with quick hands, fast feet, and the mental toughness to come up big in that high-pressure situation. It didn't surprise anyone when Ranford was chosen tournament MVP.

But the Americans had a pretty good one of their own at the other end of the ice. In fact, Mike Richter of the New York Rangers was a big part of the Yankee drive for the final, and stood tall as the Canadians poured 40 shots at his net in the tournament finale. But with 7:47 to play, he gave up the winning goal.

On a breakaway.

It was a classic one-on-one confrontation, Steve Larmer breaking free after stealing the puck at the Canadian blueline. Richter should have had plenty of time to move out, take the angle, and maintain it by skating backwards as Larmer advanced on the goal. But for some reason he didn't play it that way, and Larmer scored. After the game, Richter admitted, "I didn't get a good start coming out of the net. I couldn't get out fast enough as the play developed."

Richter found himself frozen closer to the net than he wanted to be. "Because of that," he said, "I had to open my pads a little more than I would have liked. He made a move and put it between my legs."

There were those who faulted the American goalie because it was a five-hole goal. But his real problem was that he didn't get out on the play.

Richter certainly isn't the only goalie who's made a mistake on a breakaway in a big game. While viewing old Stanley Cup highlight films, I came across several examples of Jacques Plante playing centre breakaways in a rather unorthodox fashion. For at least part of his career, Plante had a habit of moving out on the puck-carrier and then falling down—always to his left. The films provided a number of examples of the shooter waiting for the move before lifting the puck over the fallen goalie.

But Jacques Plante—quite correctly—will always be remembered as one of the "all-time greats". He was a six-time Stanley Cup winner who captured the Vezina Trophy on seven occasions, and still ranks second in career wins with 434, just one less than Terry Sawchuk. You don't accumulate that kind of track record without knowing what you're doing out there. However, the game has changed. I grew up admiring all of the guys in that era—Jacques Plante, Terry Sawchuk, Johnny Bower, Glenn Hall, Gump Worsley—but I'm convinced that today they wouldn't get away with some of the manoeuvres they used back then. In my opinion, the quickness of today's game alone makes sound and consistent technique an absolute necessity.

On the other hand, we have to keep in mind that deviation from sound technique is not only possible, but inevitable. People make mistakes, and coaches should keep that in mind. One day at my goalie school, we were working on centre breakaways and I chastised one of my students for sloppy leg work. "Wait a second," I yelled. "Your pad wasn't on the ice." Then I remembered my own playing days and had to admit to him that I had made the same mistakes.

It's important to me that my students realize that even Ian Young made mistakes out there once in awhile. Hard to believe, but it's true. The position carries enough pressure without expecting perfection all the time. Besides, let's not forget that once you reach a certain level of competition, the opposition has some pretty good moves of their own. Jeff Hackett found out about that when he was with the Islanders. It was an experience he won't soon forget.

"One night we were playing St. Louis," recalls Jeff, "and they had us down something like 5-1 after two periods. I started the game on the bench, but went in for the third period. In the first minute, Adam Oates came in on an angle breakaway and cut across in front. I stayed with him real well and made a pretty good stop. Now I was really into the game, feeling good about things, and ready to stone them. Well, on the same shift some other guy—I didn't know who it was at the time—came in on a centre breakaway. I just know I'm going to stop him. But then he winds up...and BOOM! I never even saw it! Upper shelf, glove side. Without even looking, I knew who it was. Brett Hull! You know, guys like that can ruin your day."

Kirk McLean points out that the most special of all athletes have an extra advantage. He names two of the best-ever players as examples: "Lemieux and Gretzky. They have such good hand-eye co-ordination. Those guys get breakaways while playing two men short. They read the play so well for one thing, and for another they pick it out of the air. They gamble, and if they don't get it, they're in trouble. But nobody's going to care because they're still going to get their four or five points a game. But they just knock everything down. It's unbelievable. You cannot throw a cross-ice pass when one of those two guys is out there."

Peter Sidorkiewicz has his own selection as Man I'd Least Like to Meet on a Breakaway. "One on one, nobody's more dangerous than Lemieux. I played an exhibition game against him a few years ago and he had something like five breakaways against me. Just unbelievable moves. He came down one time—he's got that big long reach—and gave me a big move, then another, then pulled it back. By this time I'm about six feet out of my net, and it's in. Goal.

"Later, we had a two-man advantage and somehow he got another bloody breakaway. I know he's going glove side, so I'm cheating like crazy. I'm getting ready to make my best glove move—which isn't very good, by the way. So here he comes down the middle of the ice with the puck held out to his side. You know how most guys have to bring the puck back to snap it? Well, he doesn't. He just came down, hit the hash mark, and BING—in off the crossbar. All the guys were coming down to me and saying, 'Wow, did you see that?' They couldn't believe it."

Remember: On breakaways, the shooter has the initial advantage over the noble goaltender. Not only does he have the puck, but he knows what he's planning to do with it. There's nothing we can do about that part of the equation. But we do have some pretty effective weapons of our own—the technically correct way to take the angle, for one thing, and the ability to maintain it with motion, quickness and determination.

Wield these weapons with consistency and confidence, and the world will continue to unfold as it should.

Felix Potvin (Relke).

NO FAIR— THEY'RE USING TWO-ON-ONES!

Like just about everything else in goaltending, two-on-ones are a matter of angles. We've talked about telescoping, coming high to take the angle and moving back to maintain it. We've talked about goalies moving laterally across the top of the crease, trying to retain body positioning and thus keep the angle. We've discussed moving a pad to a loose puck to remove the upper part of the net. We've even addressed the case of the NHL goaltender who thrusts his blocker to the puck because he's trying to achieve the angle on the play.

What all these situations have in common is a goalie using his body and parts of his equipment to block the puck's path to the net. In short, playing the angles.

It's the same thing on a two-on-one, the only difference being that *angles on a two-on-one are two-fold:* 1) The goalie's position in relation to the puck; and 2) the defenceman's position in relation to the attacking forwards. And without a doubt, this latter point is the most crucial consideration of a two-on-one.

When the puck-carrier crosses the blueline, that's the widest point of a two-man rush. But you know your defenceman isn't going to be on the blueline when the two onrushing forwards reach it. He's got to be closer to the net, skating backwards and moving towards the goal. And like you, he can't be moving back at the same speed as the onrushing forwards or he'll end up in your lap.

Instead, the two attackers and the defenceman have to form a triangle that undergoes what I call a reverse telescoping effect as the play approaches the net.

If we draw a line that runs from one forward to the other, then by the time they reach the blueline, our defenceman might be, say, ten feet away from that line. As the forwards approach the goal, the difference between the defender and that line should be reduced to, say, four feet. And at a certain point—hopefully, just inside the hash marks—the defenceman is between the puck-carrier and the off-side winger. When that happens, the pass option has been removed. The goalie is handed puck responsibility and must make a commitment to the puck-carrier.

Chalk one up for the loyal defenceman. By playing *his* angles properly, getting on that line between the two enemy forwards, he's eliminated the pass option and earned an honoured spot in the House of Goalie.

Of course, when the puck was high at the blueline, the goalie had to move back and forth to follow passes between the two attackers. That's because both options— the shot and the deke—were still there. But at some point—and it was just a matter of time—you had to make your commitment. Ideally, it was when the defenceman eliminated the pass.

If the forward hits his point of commitment and decides to drive to the net, he has three options:

1) He can take a shot. But if you've made your commitment to the shooter, you should have the angle well in hand.

2) He can make a move to the short side. But if you're starting high and moving back, you should be able to get to the post on your feet. If not, the one-pad slide is the next best thing.

3) He can drive straight to the net. And when he does, your job is to stay with the puck and make sure it doesn't get jammed into the net. Your defenceman's responsibility is to take out that forward. Although

this does reintroduce the pass option to a certain extent, the defenceman can't just stand back and let the winger drive through unimpeded. He has to get a piece of him. If he doesn't, it's like conceding a breakaway! But with all these things happening—goalie coming high, defenceman playing the reverse telescope and getting on that line between the two attackers—it's very difficult for that puck to be passed successfully to the off-winger. It will seldom happen. But because it's a possibility, the goalie has to recede deeper into his crease than usual, so he has the option of reacting to the pass by moving to the other side of the net.

In essence, that's the way to play a two-on-one. It's a very simple, very basic play, but it won't be executed properly if the goalie and the defenceman don't understand each other's role.

It comes down to communication.

COMMUNICATION & THE TWO-ON-ONE

To explain the reverse telescoping theory at Oshawa, I called the defencemen and the two goalies together for an old fashioned chalk-talk. Everyone agreed with the theory, but there was an interesting by-product of our little talk. I also managed to bridge the communication gap between the goalies and the defenders. Next game, all of a sudden, every defenceman knew what the goalie was thinking, and the goalkeeper was aware of what his defencemen were trying to do.

On two-on-ones, they were working together. True teamwork had been introduced.

As a goalie coach, however, I never instruct defencemen and goaltenders on two-on-ones without first clearing it with the head coach. I have to make sure that the coach appreciates what I'm saying and agrees with the theory. It's no good for me to tell his defence one thing, and then have him yelling at them during the next game because they're not playing the two-on-one to his liking. There has to be unanimity on the coaching staff so the application—shift-by-shift, game-by-game—is consistent.

Mike Vernon (Relke).

EVEN MORE UNFAIR. . . THEY'RE USING TWO-ON-NONES!

The two-on-none isn't one of hockey's more common plays, and you certainly won't see it as often as two-on-one or three-on-two breaks. But it's a situation that can, if worked on regularly in a practice environment, help make a goaltender strong on his feet.

Think about it: Instead of facing one guy breaking in on you, you've got two of them. You've *still* got to get high on the angle, but because there's a possibility of one or more passes, you've got to move laterally.

Now, just as you shouldn't use the T-push on a centre breakaway, you should stay away from it on two-on-none situations as well. Instead, since the opposition is moving on you from the point, if not farther out, I recommend the shuffle.

And remember: Each time you do the shuffle, you're trying to go across with the play while maintaining the puck-to-body-to-net relationship, and being aware of the non-puck-carrying forward.

As the play comes across the blueline, you take the angle. If the puck is passed, you've got to move with it. Why? Because not doing so will leave the shooter with a large target, of course. And that's not going to win you very many MVP awards.

But moving laterally isn't the only motion employed on the two-on-none. Just as our telescoping theory tells us that you have to move back as a shooter advances, then every pass from shooter to shooter on the two-on-none requires you to reduce your distance from the net so you don't get caught out of position.

In short, as you get to the point where each pass hits a stick, you have to stop moving laterally and begin flowing back with the play. If a return pass heads suddenly in the other direction, again you have to shuffle laterally to maintain the puck-to-body-to-net relationship, and then flow back with the play.

The key word here is "flow". By moving high and coming back, you're initiating the motion that allows you to develop a smooth flow in your game. This is preferable to the staccato-like movements that plague a goalie who's just standing still. Instead of a *lunge across, stop—lunge across, stop* response, you want to be *flowing* with the play.

Having said that, if the approaching skaters continue to pass the puck even when they're practically on your doorstep, you have to reach into your bag of goaltending tricks to find a way to move quickly from one side of the net to the other. This is where the hop-over comes into play. The hop-over is a quick lateral hop, crossing one leg over the other, and can be the quickest way to get from point "A" to point "B". It may not always be the prettiest move, but it can help you cover several feet in a hurry. After all, isn't the whole idea to get to point "B"? Besides, if it's performed with enough flair and grace, it could earn you an audition with the National Ballet.

At a certain point on the two-on-none—after one, two or three passes—the forwards are forced to make a commitment. Will the man with the puck shoot, or deke? And how should you respond?

If it's a shot, the picture I've painted still has you high enough on the puck to take the angle.

If it's a deke, your motion—laterally and backwards—should allow you to flow back to the post with the appropriate move.

It all comes down to strength on your feet, and goalies who can't skate, *can't do this.* If a coach wants to see how good a goalie is on his feet, just send in a couple of shooters on a series of two-on-none's. If you've got a guy who's not good on his feet, he won't be able to challenge, he won't be able to stay high, and he won't be able to move laterally. Before the shooters are even close to the net, he'll be lunging, diving, flopping all over the place on his belly or back, trying to make the kind of save that falls under the "Hail Mary" category.

If that's the case, you're in trouble.

But if a goalie can successfully stop a two-on-none scenario—or even if they score but he's able to flow with the play to the point of a commitment by the shooters— then you've probably got a good goaltender, one who's strong on his feet.

TWO-PAD SLIDE

I know there are times when you tell yourself, "I'm going to use the two-pad slide." You've determined that this guy is going to deke you, so the use of the two-pad slide is fully pre-meditated. If it's done properly— and used sparingly—it can be an effective goaltending tool. Unfortunately, the two-pad slide can also be used to cover a weakness — perhaps a lack of concentration, or insufficient strength on the feet. (*Behind The Mask*, pp. 70-73)

Generally speaking, the two-pad slide should only be used in extreme emergencies. And normally, that emergency is when you've been caught out of the play. Instead of flowing with a puck that's going one way, you're heading in the other direction. Or, you're caught flat-footed, and the shooter skates by you.

You're beaten, you panic, and out go the pads.

But if you're with a two-on-none as it develops—out high to take the angle and then using your lateral and backward flow to maintain the puck-to-body-to-net relationship—then you shouldn't have to suddenly throw both pads to one side or the other.

Put it in perspective: A two-on-none is not a common scenario for a goaltender, and you won't see more than a handful of them during your entire career. However, it can still be used as a valuable drill for developing angles, motion, and strength on your feet. In other words, two-on-nones are a "must" for practice purposes.

And believe me, they'll drive your feet crazy.

AWARD-WINNING GOALIES

HART MEMORIAL TROPHY

The Hart Trophy is awarded annually "to the player adjudged to be the most valuable to his team". The winner is selected in a poll by the Professional Hockey Writers' Association in the 24 NHL cities at the end of the regular schedule. The Hart Memorial Trophy was presented by the National Hockey League in 1960 after the original Hart Trophy was retired to the Hockey Hall of Fame. The originial Hart Trophy was donated to the NHL in 1923 by Dr. David A. Hart, father of Cecil Hart, former manager-coach of the Montreal Canadiens.

HART TROPHY WINNERS:

1929—Roy Worters, New York Americans
1950—Charlie Rayner, New York Rangers
1954—Al Rollins, Chicago Blackhawks.
1962—Jacques Plante, Montreal Canadiens.

CALDER MEMORIAL TROPHY

The Calder Trophy is awarded annually "to the player selected as the most proficient in his first year of competition in the National Hockey League". The winner is selected in a poll by the Professional Hockey Writers' Association at the end of the regular schedule. From 1936-37 until his death in 1943, Frank Calder, NHL President, bought a trophy each year to be given permanently to the outstanding rookie. After Calder's death, the NHL presented the Calder Memorial Trophy in his memory and the trophy is to be kept in perpetuity.

CALDER TROPHY WINNERS:

1936—Mike Karakas, Chicago Blackhawks
1939—Frank Brimsek, Boston Bruins
1945—Frank McCool, Toronto Maple Leafs
1950—Jack Gelineau, Boston Bruins
1951—Terry Sawchuk, Detroit Red Wings
1953—Lorne Worsley, New York Rangers
1956—Glenn Hall, Detroit Red Wings
1965—Roger Crozier, Detroit Red Wings
1970—Tony Esposito, Chicago Blackhawks
1972—Ken Dryden, Montreal Canadiens
1984—Tom Barrasso, Buffalo Sabres
1991—Ed Belfour, Chicago Blackhawks
1994—Martin Brodeur, New Jersey Devils

VEZINA TROPHY

An annual award "to the goalkeeper adjudged to be the best at his position" as voted by the general managers of each of the 24 clubs. Leo Dandurand, Louis Letourneau and Joe Cattarinich, former owners of the Montreal Canadiens, presented the trophy to the National Hockey League in 1926-27 in memory of Georges Vezina, outstanding goalkeeper of the Canadiens who collapsed during an NHL game November 28, 1925, and died of tuberculosis a few months later. Until the 1981-82 season, the goalkeeper(s) of the team allowing the fewest number of goals during the regular-season were awarded the Vezina Trophy.

VEZINA TROPHY WINNERS:

1927—George Hainsworth, Mtl Canadiens
1928—George Hainsworth, Mtl Canadiens
1929—George Hainsworth, Mtl Canadiens
1930—Tiny Thompson, Boston Bruins
1931—Roy Worters, New York Americans
1932—Charlie Gardner, Chicago Blackhawks
1933—Tiny Thompson, Boston Bruins
1934—Charlie Gardiner, Chicago Blackhawks
1935—Lorne Chabot, Chicago Blackhawks
1936—Tiny Thompson, Boston Bruins
1937—Normie Smith, Detroit Red Wings
1938—Tiny Thompson, Boston Bruins
1939—Frank Brimsek, Boston Bruins
1940—Dave Kerr, New York Rangers
1941—Turk Broda, Toronto Maple Leafs
1942—Frank Brimsek, Boston Bruins
1943—Johnny Mowers, Detroit Red Wings
1944—Bill Durnan, Montreal Canadiens
1945—Bill Durnan, Montreal Canadiens

1946—Bill Durnan, Montreal Canadiens
1947—Bill Durnan, Montreal Canadiens
1948—Turk Broda, Toronto Maple Leafs
1949—Bill Durnan, Montreal Canadiens
1950—Bill Durnan, Montreal Canadiens
1951—Al Rollins, Toronto Maple Leafs
1952—Terry Sawchuk, Detroit Red Wings
1953—Terry Sawchuk, Detroit Red Wings
1954—Harry Lumley, Toronto Maple Leafs
1955—Terry Sawchuk, Detroit Red Wings
1956—Jacques Plante, Montreal Canadiens
1957—Jacques Plante, Montreal Canadiens
1958—Jacques Plante, Montreal Canadiens
1959—Jacques Plante, Montreal Canadiens
1960—Jacques Plante, Montreal Canadiens
1961—Johnny Bower, Toronto Maple Leafs
1962—Jacques Plante, Montreal Canadiens
1963—Glenn Hall, Chicago Blackhawks
1964—Charlie Hodge, Montreal Canadiens
1965—Terry Sawchuk, Johnny Bower
        Toronto Maple Leafs
1966—Lorne Worsley, Charlie Hodge
        Montreal Canadiens
1967—Glenn Hall, Denis Dejordy
        Chicago Blackhawks
1968—Lorne Worsley, Rogatien Vachon
        Montreal Canadiens
1969—Jacques Plante, Glenn Hall
        St. Louis Blues
1970—Tony Esposito, Chicago Blackhawks
1971—Ed Giacomin, Gilles Villemure
        New York Rangers
1972—Tony Esposito, Gary Smith
        Chicago Blackhawks
1973—Ken Dryden, Montreal Canadiens
1974—Bernie Parent, Tony Esposito
        Chicago Blackhawks
1975—Bernie Parent, Philadelphia Flyers

1976—Ken Dryden, Montreal Canadiens
1977—Ken Dryden, Michel Larocque
Montreal Canadiens
1978—Ken Dryden, Michel Larocque
Montreal Canadiens
1979—Ken Dryden, Michel Larocque
Montreal Canadiens
1980—Bob Sauve, Don Edwards
Buffalo Sabres
1981—Richard Sevigny, Denis Herron, Michel
Larocque—Montreal Canadiens
1982—Bill Smith, New York Islanders
1983—Pete Peeters, Boston Bruins
1984—Tom Barrasso, Buffao Sabres
1985—Pelle Lindbergh, Philadelphia
1986—John Vanbiesbrouck, NY Rangers
1987—Ron Hextall, Philadelphia Flyers
1988—Grant Fuhr, Edmonton Oilers
1989—Patrick Roy, Montreal Canadiens
1990—Patrick Roy, Montreal Canadiens
1991—Ed Belfour, Chicago Blackhawks
1992—Patrick Roy, Montreal Canadiens
1993—Ed Belfour, Chicago Blackhawks
1994—Dominic Hasek, Buffalo Sabres

CONN SMYTHE TROPHY

An annual award given "to the most valuable player for his team in the playoffs." The winner is selected by the Professional Hockey Writers' Association at the conclusion of the final game in the Stanley Cup Finals. Presented by Maple Leaf Gardens Limited in 1964 to honor Conn Smythe, the former coach, manager, president and owner-governor of the Toronto Maple Leafs.

CONN SMYTHE WINNERS:

1966—Roger Crozier, Detroit Red Wings
1968—Glenn Hall, St. Louis Blues
1971—Ken Dryden, Montreal Canadiens
1974—Bernie Parent, Philadelphia Flyers
1975—Bernie Parent, Philadelphia Flyers
1983—Bill Smith, New York Islanders
1986—Patrick Roy, Montreal Canadiens
1987—Ron Hextall, Philadelphia Flyers
1990—Bill Ranford, Edmonton Oilers
1993—Patrick Roy, Montreal Canadiens

WILLIAM M. JENNINGS TROPHY

An annual award given "to the goalkeeper(s) having played a minimum of 25 games on the team with the fewest goals scored against it." Winners are selected on regular-season play. The Jennings Trophy was presented in 1981-82 by the National Hockey League's Board of Governors to honour the late William M. Jennings, longtime governor and president of the New York Rangers and one of the great builders of hockey in the United States.

WILLIAM M. JENNINGS WINNERS:

1982—Rick Wamsley, Denis Herron
Montreal Canadiens
1983—Roland Melanson, Bill Smith
New York Islanders
1984—Al Jensen, Pat Riggen
Washington Capitals
1985—Tom Barrasso, Bob Sauve
Buffalo Sabres
1986—Bob Froese, Darren Jensen
Philadelphia Flyers
1987—Patrick Roy, Brian Hayward
Montreal Canadiens
1988—Patrick Roy, Brian Hayward
Montreal Canadiens
1989—Patrick Roy, Brian Hayward
Montreal Canadiens
1990—Andy Moog, Rejean Lemelin
Boston Bruins
1991—Ed Belfour, Chicago Blackhawks
1992—Patrick Roy, Montreal Canadiens
1993—Ed Belfour, Chicago Blackhawks

THE HOCKEY HALL OF FAME:

The Hockey Hall of Fame was established in 1943. Its permanent home is at BCE Place in downtwon Toronto. The Hall was officially opened to the public on August 26, 1961 at its original home on the grounds of the Canadian National Exhibition. It opened at its present location on June 18, 1993. Following is a list of goalies who have been inducted in to The Hockey Hall of Fame. The date in brackets indicates the year in which the player was inducted.

Francis Charles Brimsek (1966)
Walter Edward "Turk" Broda (1967)
William Ronald Durnan (1964)
Anthony James "Tony" Esposito (1988)
Charles Robert "Chuck" Gardiner (1945)
Edward "Eddie" Giacomin (1987)
George Hainsworth (1961)
Glenn Henry Hall (1975)
Harry Lumley (1980)
Bernard Marcel Parent (1984)
Joseph Jacques Plante (1978)
Claude Earl "Chuck" Rayner (1973)
Terrance Gordon "Terry" Sawchuk (1971)
William John "Billy" Smith (1993)
Cecil "Tiny" Thompson (1959)
Vladislav Tretiak (1989)
Georges Vezina (1945)
Lorne "Gump" Worsley (1980)
Roy Worters (1969)

ALL-STAR GOALTENDERS:

The First and Second All-Star Team game was introduced in the 1930-31 season. Voting for the team is conducted among the representatives of the Professional Hockey Writers' Association at the end of the season.

1992-93—First Team: Ed Belfour, Chi.
Second Team: Tom Barrasso, Pit.
1991-92—First Team: Patrick Roy, Mtl.
Second Team: Kirk McLean, Van.
1990-91—First Team: Ed Belfour, Chi.
Second Team: Patrick Roy, Mtl.
1989-90—First Team: Patrick Roy, Mtl.
Second Team: Daren Puppa, Buf.
1988-89—First Team: Patrick Roy, Mtl.
Second Team: Mike Vernon, Cgy.
1987-88—First Team: Grant Fuhr, Edm.
Second Team: Patrick Roy, Mtl.
1986-87—First Team: Ron Hextall, Phi.
Second Team: Mike Liut, Hfd.
1985-86—First Team: J. Vanbiesbrouck, NYR.
Second Team: Bob Froese, Phi.
1984-85—First Team: Pelle Lindbergh, Phi.
Second Team: Tom Barrasso, Buf.
1983-84—First Team: Tom Barrasso, Buf.
Second Team: Pat Riggin, Wsh.
1982-83—First Team: Pete Peters, Bos.
Second Team: Roland Melanson, NYI
1981-82—First Team: Bill Smith, NYI.
Second Team: Grant Fuhr, Edm.
1980-81—First Team: Mike Liut, St. L.
Second Team: Mario Lessard, L.A.
1979-80—First Team: Tony Esposito, Chi.
Second Team: Don Edwards, Buf.
1978-79—First Team: Ken Dryden, Mtl.
Second Team: Glenn Resch, NYI.

1977-78—First Team: Ken Dryden, Mtl.
Second Team: Don Edwards, Buf.
1976-77—First Team: Ken Dryden, Mtl.
Second Team: Rogatien Vachon, L.A.
1975-76—First Team: Ken Dryden, Mtl.
Second Team: Glenn Resch, NYI.
1974-75—First Team: Bernie Parent, Phi.
Second Team: Rogatien Vachon, L.A.
1973-74—First Team: Bernie Parent, Phi.
Second Team: Tony Esposito, Chi.
1972-73—First Team: Ken Dryden, Mtl.
Second Team: Tony Esposito, Chi.
1971-72—First Team: Tony Esposito, Chi.
Second Team: Ken Dryden, Mtl.
1970-71—First Team: Ed Giacomin, NYR.
Second Team: Jacques Plante, Tor.
1969-70—First Team: Tony Esposito, Chi.
Second Team: Ed Giacomin, NYR.
1968-69—First Team: Glenn Hall, St. L.
Second Team: Ed Giacomin NYR
1967-68—First Team: Lorne Worsley, Mtl.
Second Team: Ed Giacomin NYR
1966-67—First Team: Ed Giacomin, NYR.
Second Team: Glenn Hall, Chi.
1965-66—First Team: Glenn Hall, Chi.
Second Team: Lorne Worsley, Mtl.
1964-65—First Team: Roger Crozier, Det.
Second Team: Charlie Hodge, Mtl.
1963-64—First Team: Glenn Hall, Chi.
Second Team: Charlie Hodge, Mtl.
1962-63—First Team: Glenn Hall, Chi.
Second Team: Terry Sawchuk, Det.
1961-62—First Team: Jacques Plante, Mtl.
Second Team: Glenn Hall, Chi.
1960-61—First Team: Johnny Bower, Tor.
Second Team: Glenn Hall, Chi.
1959-60—First Team: Glenn Hall, Chi.
Second Team: Jacques Plante, Mtl.

1958-59—First Team: Jacques Plante,Mtl.
Second Team: Terry Sawchuk, Det.
1957-58—First Team: Glenn Hall, Chi.
Second Team: Jacques Plante, Mtl.
1956-57—First Team: Glenn Hall, Det.
Second Team: Jacques Plante, Mtl.
1955-56—First Team: Jacques Plante, Mtl.
Second Team: Glenn Hall, Det.
1954-55—First Team: Harry Lumley, Tor.
Second Team: Terry Sawchuck, Det.
1953-54—First Team: Harry Lumley, Tor.
Second Team: Terry Sawchuk, Det.
1952-53—First Team: Terry Sawchuk, Det.
Second Team: Gerry McNeil Mtl.
1951-52—First Team: Terry Sawchuk, Det.
Second Team: Jim Henry, Bos.
1950-51—First Team: Terry Sawchuck, Det.
Second Team: Chuck Rayner, NYR
1949-50—First Team: Bill Durnan, Mtl.
Second Team: Chuck Rayner, NYR
1948-49—First Team: Bill Durnan, Mtl.
Second Team: Chuck Rayner, NYR
1947-48—First Team: Turk Broda, Tor.
Second Team: Frank Brimsek, Bos.
1946-47—First Team: Bill Durnan, Mtl.
Second Team: Frank Brimsek, Bos.
1945-46—First Team: Bill Durnan, Mtl.
Second Team: Frank Brimsek, Bos.
1944-45—First Team: Bill Durnan, Mtl.
Second Team: Mike Karakas, Chi.

1943-44—First Team: Bill Durnan, Mtl.
Second Team: Paul Bibeault, Tor.
1942-43—First Team: Johnny Mowers, Det.
Second Team: Frank Brimsek, Bos.
1941-42—First Team: Frank Brimsek, Bos.
Second Team: Turk Broda, Tor.
1940-41—First Team: Turk Broda, Tor.
Second Team: Frank Brimsek, Bos.
1939-40—First Team: Dave Kerr, NYR
Second Team: Frank Brimsek, Bos.
1938-39—First Team: Frank Brimsek, Bos.
Second Team: Earl Robertson, NYA
1937-38—First Team: Tiny Thompson, Bos.
Second Team: Dave Kerr, NYR.
1936-37—First Team: Norm Smith, Det.
Second Team: Wilf Cude, Mtl.
1935-36—First Team: Tiny Thompson, Bos.
Second Team: Wilf Cude, Mtl.
1934-35—First Team: Lorne Chabot, Chi.
Second Team: Tiny Thompson, Bos.
1933-34—First Team: Charlie Gardiner, Chi.
Second Team: Roy Worters, NYA
1932-33—First Team: John Ross Roach, Det.
Second Team: Charlie Gardiner, Chi
1931-32—First Team: Charlie Gardiner, Chi.
Second Team: Roy Worters, NYA
1930-31—First Team: Charlie Gardiner, Chi.
Second Team: Tiny Thompson, Bos.

GOALTENDING MILESTONES

1877

March 11

Hall of Famer Paddy Moran was born. Moran played 16 years from 1902 to 1917, winning two Stanley Cups with the Quebec Bulldogs of the National Hockey Association.

1885

October 27

Hall of Famer Hugh Lehman was born. Lehman had a 20-year career from 1909 to 1928. He played 12 seasons with Vancouver Millionaires, leading the Pacific Coast Hockey Association champions to a Stanley Cup victory in 1915.

1898

February 12

Ottawa goalie Fred Chittick staged a one-man strike, claiming he had not received his share of complimentary tickets to a game. Without him, the Senators lost 9-5 to the Montreal Victorias in Amateur Hockey Association play.

1900

June 23

John Roach was born in Port Perry, Ontario. Roach was one of hockey's smallest goalies at 5' 5", 130 pounds. He played 14 years with the Leafs, Rangers and Red Wings, winning the Stanley Cup with the 1922 Toronto St. Pats.

October 19

Roy Worters was born in Toronto. Worters, at just 5' 3" and 130 pounds, played 12 NHL seasons from 1925-26 to 1936-37. He never won a Stanley Cup, but he was the first goalie to win the Hart Trophy as the league's MVP. He also took the Vezina Trophy in 1931.

1903

December 30

The first goal line was painted on the ice from goalpost to goalpost. In a successful start to a Stanley Cup defence, the Ottawa Senators beat the Winnipeg Rowing Club 9-1.

1905

February 18

Fred Brophy, playing goal for Westmount in the Canadian Amateur Hockey League (one of several predecessors of the NHL), raced the length of the ice and scored a goal against Paddy Moran of the Quebec Bulldogs.

1906

March 7

Fred Brophy, playing goal for Montreal in the newly-formed Eastern Canada Amateur Hockey Association (another predecessor of the NHL), stickhandled his way up ice and scored a goal against the Montreal Victorias.

1910

February 23

Georges Vezina played for his hometown of Chicoutimi in an exhibition game against the barnstorming Montreal Canadiens. Vezina shocked the hockey world by shutting them out. The following fall he joined the Habs and stayed with them for the next 15 years.

December 31

Georges Vezina, the "Chicoutimi Cucumber", made his debut with the Montreal Canadiens. Vezina lost that game 5-3 to Percy Lesueur and the Ottawa Senators. Vezina played 328 consecutive games for the Canadiens before illness forced him to leave his final game on November 28, 1925.

1914

May 15

Walter "Turk" Broda was born in Brandon, Manitoba. Broda played 14 NHL seasons from 1936-37 to 1951-52, winning the Vezina Trophy as the League's top goalie twice, making the first All-Star team twice, and the second team once. A great playoff performer for Toronto, Broda played on five Stanley Cup winners and had 13 shutouts in 101 playoff games while posting a 1.98 GAA.

1915

January 13
Quebec's Paddy Moran got the win in National Hockey Association play as the Bulldogs beat Georges Vezina's Montreal Canadiens 3-2 in what was a record-length overtime game to that point. Jack McDonald beat Vezina for the winning goal at 50:28 of extra time.

January 22
Bill Durnan was born in Toronto. Durnan played seven years for the Montreal Canadiens from 1943-44 to 1949-50, winning the Vezina Trophy six times. He played on two Stanley Cup-winning teams.

March 26
Hugh Lehman was in goal for the Vancouver Millionaires as they beat the Ottawa Senators 12-3 at home to sweep the Stanley Cup final three games to none. It was the first Stanley Cup final to be played west of Winnipeg.

1917

March 25
Harry Holmes was in goal for the Seattle Mets when they became the first U.S.-based team to win the Stanley Cup. Bernie Morris scored six goals on Georges Vezina as Seattle beat the Canadiens 9-1 to take the series three games to one.

December 19
In the first games ever played in the National Hockey League, Montreal's Georges Vezina was in goal as the Montreal Canadiens beat Clint Benedict's Ottawa Senators 7-4, while the Montreal Wanderers' Bert Lindsay outlasted Toronto Arenas goalie Sammy Hebert 10-9. Both games were played in Montreal.

1918

February 18
Montreal's Georges Vezina got the first-ever shutout in NHL play. Vezina and his Canadiens teammates beat the hometown Toronto Arenas 9-0.

February 25
Clint Benedict got the second shutout in NHL history, and the last of the new league's first season, when his Ottawa Senators beat the visiting Montreal Canadiens 8-0.

March 30
The Toronto Arenas beat the Vancouver Millionaires 2-1 to take the Stanley Cup three games to two behind the goaltending of Harry "Hap" Holmes.

1920

January 31
Fred Brophy was in goal for the Toronto St. Pats when Joe Malone of the Quebec Bulldogs became the only player in NHL history to score seven goals in one game. Brophy and the St. Pats lost the game 10-6.

August 11
Claude "Chuck" Rayner was born in Sutherland, Saskatchewan. He played ten NHL seasons between 1940-41 and 1952-53. He won the Hart Trophy as the League MVP in 1949-50 with the Rangers.

December 25
In the first NHL game played on Christmas Day, Toronto beat the visiting Canadiens 5-4. Ivan Mitchell was in goal for the Maple Leafs, Georges Vezina for Montreal.

1922

February 11
John Roach was in goal for the Toronto St. Pats and Clint Benedict for Ottawa when the two teams tied 4-4 in Ottawa after 20 minutes of overtime. It was the first NHL game to end in a tie. This was also the first season that overtime was restricted to 20 minutes. Before then, teams continued to play until a goal was scored.

1923

October 18
At the annual meeting of the Pacific Coast Hockey League, a rule was passed restricting goalie pads to 12 inches in width. That same year, the rule was adopted by the Western Canada Hockey League. The NHL adopted the rule in the fall of 1925.

1924

November 8
Johnny Bower was born in Prince Albert, Saskatchewan. Bower played 552 regular season games in 15 seasons and posted a 2.52 GAA between 1953 and 1970. His GAA in 74 playoff games was 2.54. Bower

played on four Stanley Cup-winning teams and was a first team All-Star in the 1960-61 season. He was a two-time Vezina Trophy winner.

December 17

Jake Forbes of the Hamilton Tigers and Alex Connell of the Ottawa Senators shared the glory when those two teams played the first scoreless tie in the eight-year history of the NHL.

1925

November 28

Georges Vezina was in goal for the Canadiens against Pittsburgh at Montreal's Mount Royal Arena when he collapsed at the start of the second period. Four months later, he died of tuberculosis.

December 26

The New York Americans and the Pittsburgh Pirates combined for a record 141 shots, 73 by the Americans and 68 by Pittsburgh, before a crowd of 10,000 at Madison Square Garden in New York. Jake Forbes made 67 saves in leading the Americans to a 3-1 victory. Roy Worters blocked 70 shots for Pittsburgh.

1926

March 17

Ottawa Senators goalie Alex Connell finished a superb regular season with a 4-0 win over Toronto. It was his 15th shutout in 36 games. He finished the regular season with a remarkable 1.17 GAA.

March 24

The great Georges Vezina died of tuberculosis in his hometown of Chicoutimi at the age of 39. The next season, the first Vezina Trophy was presented in his honour.

April 1

Montreal Maroons goaltender Clint Benedict shut out Victoria 3-0 to set a record with his third consecutive playoff shutout.

November 11

Harry Lumley was born in Owen Sound, Ontario. He went on to play 16 NHL seasons from 1943-44 to 1959-60, spending time with five of the six clubs at that time, Detroit, the Rangers, Chicago, Toronto and Boston. He won the Vezina Trophy once, the Stanley Cup once, and was twice named first team All-Star.

November 16

In the New York Rangers' first-ever game, Hal Winkler got the shutout in a 1-0 victory over the Montreal Maroons at Madison Square Garden. Bill Cook got the only goal.

November 18

Charles Stewart got the shutout for Boston in the Bruins' 2-0 victory over the Detroit Cougars in the Cougars' NHL debut. Herb Stuart was in goal for Detroit. The game was played at the Border Cities Arena in Windsor, Ontario, where the team played its first season while the Detroit Olympia was being built. The Cougars changed their name to the Falcons in 1930, and became the Red Wings two years later.

November 23

Montreal Canadiens goalie George Hainsworth recorded the first of his 94 career shutouts, blanking the New York Americans 2-0. His mark for career shutouts was later broken by Terry Sawchuk, but his single-season mark of 22 in the 1928-29 season still stands.

1928

February 18

Ottawa Senators goalie Alex Connell beat the Montreal Canadiens 1-0 in Ottawa for his record sixth consecutive shutout. Three of those shutouts were scoreless ties.

February 22

Alex Connell gave up a goal to Duke Keats in Chicago, bringing his shutout streak to an end. Connell's run of perfection included six shutouts, three of them going to ten-minute overtime sessions. The streak amounted to 460 minutes, 49 seconds, the equivalent of more than seven games and two periods.

April 7

When New York Rangers goalie Lorne Chabot was hurt by a Nels Stewart shot in the second period of the second game of the finals against the Montreal Maroons, 44-year-old manager/coach Lester Patrick put on the pads and took his place. Patrick permitted just one goal as the Rangers went on to win the game 2-1 at 7:05 of overtime.

April 14

Joe Miller was in goal for the New York Rangers when they won their first Stanley Cup, beating the Montreal

Maroons 2-1. The Rangers took the best-of-five series three games to two, becoming only the second American-based team to win the Stanley Cup, and the first since the Seattle Mets in 1917. Miller, a former New York Americans goalie, played the last three games of the final after Lorne Chabot was injured in game two.

November 20

Canadiens goalie George Hainsworth got the shutout in Montreal's 1-0 win over the Bruins the first time Boston Garden opened its doors to hockey. It was Hainswoth's first of 22 shutouts that he recorded over a 44-game schedule that season.

1929

January 17

Jacques Plante was born in Shawinigan Falls, Quebec. The man who popularized the goalie facemask had a 2.37 GAA in 837 regular season games over an 18-year NHL career that lasted from the early '50s to the early '70s. His GAA was even more impressive in 112 playoff games at 2.17. Plante played on six Stanley Cup-winning teams with Montreal, won six Vezina Trophies, and shared a seventh with Glenn Hall in 1969. He was a first team All-Star three times, and made the second team four times.

March 14

The Montreal Canadiens beat the Montreal Maroons 1-0. It was George Hainsworth's 22nd shutout of the 44-game season, a league record. His GAA was a remarkable 0.98.

May 14

Lorne "Gump" Worsley was born in Montreal, Quebec. Worsley played 21 NHL seasons with the Rangers, Montreal and Minnesota from the early '50s to the early '70s. In 860 regular season games he had a 2.91 GAA, and in 70 playoff games it was 2.82. A four-time Stanley Cup winner, he shared two Vezina Trophies (with Charlie Hodge in 1966, and Rogie Vachon in 1968),and made the first and second All-Star teams once each.

December 28

Terry Sawchuk ws born in Winnipeg, Manitoba. Sawchuk is the all-time leader in NHL shutouts with 103 over a 21-year career with five different teams between the 1949-50 and the 1969-70 seasons. He had

a 2.52 GAA in 971 regular season games, and a 2.64 GAA in 106 playoff games. He made the first All-Star team three times and the second team four times and was a four-time Stanley Cup and Vezina Trophy winner.

1930

February 20

Clint Benedict, who led the NHL in goals-against average six times and played on four Stanley Cup-winning teams with the Ottawa Senators and the Montreal Maroons, was the first goalie to use face protection during a game. It was a leather mask he used to protect a broken nose while he played with the Maroons. When the mask became dislodged during a scramble and he broke his nose again, Benedict decided to retire.

1931

April 14

George Hainsworth got the shutout as Montreal beat Chicago 2-0 in the fifth and deciding game to win the Stanley Cup.

September 13

Don Simmons was born in Port Colborne, Ontario. Simmons played 247 games with Boston, Toronto and the Rangers during an 11-year career from the late '50s to the late '60s. He was on two Stanley Cup-winning teams with the Leafs.

October 3

Glenn Hall was born in Humboldt, Saskatchewan. Hall played 18 NHL seasons from the 1952-53 and the 1970-71 seasons. He was a seven-time first team All-Star and made the second All-Star team four times. He was a Vezina Trophy recipient on three occasions and was a member of Chicago's Stanley Cup-winning team in 1960-61. Hall's GAA was 2.51 for 906 regular season games, and 2.79 for 115 playoff matches.

1932

February 13

The Leafs beat the Canadiens 6-0 with the shutout going to Benny Grant, who was only playing because Lorne Chabot, the number one goalie, was serving a one-game suspension for punching a goal judge during a 3-1 loss in Detroit six days earlier.

1933

April 3

Lorne Chabot got the shutout when Ken Doraty's overtime goal against Tiny Thompson gave the Maple Leafs a 1-0 victory over the Bruins in a semi-final game. It was the second-longest game in NHL history. The goal was scored 104 minutes and 46 seconds into overtime—at 4:46 of the sixth overtime session.

April 13

Andy Aitkenhead got the shutout in New York's 1-0 win over Toronto at Maple Leaf Gardens as the Rangers won the best-of-five Stanley Cup final three games to one.

July 28

Charlie Hodge was born in Lachine, Quebec. In 13 years with Montreal, Oakland and Vancouver from the mid '50s to 1971, Hodge had a 2.70 GAA in 358 regular season games. He was on four Stanley Cup-winning teams with Montreal. Hodge won the Vezina Trophy in '64, and shared it with Gump Worsley in '66. Twice, he was a second team All-Star.

1934

February 14

Charles "Chuck" Gardiner, the Vezina Trophy winner for the Chicago Blackhawks that year, was the goalie for the first-ever All-Star team game. They played the Toronto Maple Leafs in a benefit game for the injured Ace Bailey. The Leafs beat the All-Stars 7-3.

April 8

Detroit goalie Wilf Cude led the Red Wings to a 5-2 playoff victory over the Blackhawks at Chicago Stadium despite playing with a broken nose suffered in the second period.

April 10

Chuck Gardiner, Chicago's captain, made 40 saves and got the shutout as the Blackhawks beat Detroit 1-0 in overtime to win their first Stanley Cup, capturing the best-of-five series three games to one. Harold "Mush" March scored the game's only goal against Wilf Cude at 10:05 of the second overtime period. Cude handled 53 shots.

June 13

Hall of Famer Chuck Gardiner, considered by some as the greatest goalie of all time, died after a brain operation. He was 28. Gardiner played seven years for Chicago and led the Black Hawks to their first Stanley Cup just two months before his death.

November 8

Bill Beveridge played goal for the hometown Eagles before 12,600 fans as NHL hockey made its debut in St. Louis. The visiting Chicago Blackhawks won the game 3-1. Beveridge finished the season with a 2.98 GAA and three shutouts while playing all 48 games. Unfortunately, the Eagles finished with the worst record in the nine-team league and folded after the season.

November 10

Maple Leaf goaltender George Hainsworth stopped the first penalty shot awarded in the NHL. The shot was taken by Armand Mondou of the Montreal Canadiens in a game won 2-1 by Toronto at Maple Leaf Gardens.

November 13

The first NHL goal from a penalty shot was scored by Ralph Bowman of the St. Louis Eagles against Montreal Maroons goalie Alex Connell. The Maroons won the game 2-1.

November 20

Bill Beveridge was the unfortunate goalie who gave up the first hat trick completed in one period. Toronto's Harvey "Busher" Jackson was the marksman. He actually scored four goals in the third period of the Leaf's 5-2 victory over Beveridge and the St. Louis Eagles.

1935

March 16

In a 5-3 win over the Canadiens in Toronto, Maple Leafs goalie George Hainsworth was cut and had to leave the ice for repairs. During his three minute absence, forward Charlie Conacher played goal, without pads, and using just a goalie stick. He did not give up a goal.

November 23

Ed Johnston was born in Montreal, Quebec. Johnston had a 3.25 GAA in 592 regular season games during a

16-year career in the '60s and '70s, and played 18 playoff games with a 3.34 GAA. He was a member of Boston's Stanley Cup-winners in 1970 and 1972.

1936

March 24

Detroit goalie Norm Smith got a shutout win in the longest overtime game ever played. Smith beat the Montreal Maroons 1-0 in a game that was settled after 116 minutes and 30 seconds of overtime—at the 16:30 mark of the sixth overtime period. Mud Bruneteau scored the winning goal for Detroit against Lorne Chabot. The game began at 8:34 p.m. and ended at 2:25 a.m. after five hours and 51 minutes.

March 26

Norm Smith continued his trek towards the record for the longest playoff shutout sequence with a 3-0 win over the Montreal Maroons. That extended his shutout streak to 236 minutes and 30 seconds.

March 29

Detroit goalie Norm Smith saw his playoff shutout streak come to an end when he was beaten by Montreal Maroon's Gus Marker at 12:02 of the first period. Smith's shutout sequence of 248 minutes, 32 seconds, remains a record. The Red Wings won the semi-final series three games to none, and went on to take the Stanley Cup over Toronto, three games to one.

April 11

Normie Smith was in goal for Detroit when the Red Wings won their first Stanley Cup with a 3-1 win over the Toronto Maple Leafs. Smith and his teammates took the series in four straight games. The Wings were the last team of the original six era to win an NHL championship.

1937

March 25

Boston goalie Tiny Thompson faced the first penalty shot ever taken in a Stanley Cup playoff game. Thompson stopped Lionel Conacher in the Bruins' 4-0 win at home in a quarter-final match.

April 15

The Detroit Red Wings won their second straight Stanley Cup with a 3-0 win over the New York Rangers. Wings' goalie Earl Robertson stopped Alex Shibicky on the first-ever penalty shot in a Stanley Cup final. Robertson had shutouts in the final two games of the series, allowing just three goals in four games.

1938

February 10

Paul Haynes of the Montreal Canadiens got credit for the winning goal after Louis Trudel threw his stick when Haynes had a breakaway on Chicago goalie Mike Karakas. At the time, an automatic goal was awarded in such a situation. It was the first time in a decade that the rule had been used.

March 17

Bill Beveridge was in goal for the Montreal Maroons in the team's last game before folding. The Maroons lost to the Canadiens 6-3 at the Montreal Forum.

April 12

Chicago won the Stanley Cup with a 4-1 win over Toronto. Their American goalie Mike Karakas played his second straight game of the final with a steel-toed skate protecting the big toe broken in a semi-final game. Karakas allowed two goals-against in the two games.

1939

January 13

Cesare Maniago was born in Trail, B.C. Maniago played 568 games over 15 years in the '60s and '70s with Toronto, Montreal, New York, Minnesota and Vancouver.

April 16

Rookie goalie Frank Brimsek beat Toronto 3-1 as Boston won the Stanely Cup. Brimsek had a shutout and allowed only six goals in five games.

June 6

Ed Giacomin was born in Sudbury, Ontario. Giacomin played 610 regular season games from the mid '60s to the late '70s. His GAA for those games was 2.82, as it was for his 65 playoff games. He was first team All-Star twice, a second team All-star three times, and shared the 1971 Vezina Trophy with Gilles Villemure.

1940

February 22
The Montreal Canadiens were forced to use right winger Charlie Sands in goal after Wilf Cude was injured, leaving Montreal without an NHL-calibre goalie.

April 13
Toronto goalie Turk Broda took the loss as the Rangers beat the Maple Leafs 3-2 and won the Stanley Cup. It was a record third straight year that Broda was in goal when his team lost the Cup.

May 30
Gilles Villemure was born in Trois-Rivieres, Quebec. In ten years with the Rangers and Blackhawks between the mid '60s and mid '70s, Villemure had a 2.81 GAA in 205 games. In 1971 he shared the Vezina Trophy with Ed Giacomin.

December 2
Gerry Cheevers was born in St. Catharines, Ontario. Cheevers played 13 NHL seasons, most with Boston between the 1961-62 and the 1979-80 seasons. In 418 regular season games he had a GAA of 2.89. His GAA was 3.30 in 88 playoff games. Cheevers won two Stanley Cups with the Bruins.

1941

February 28
This was the last time a forward or defenceman donned goaltending equipment to play in a regular NHL game. Forward Andy Brannigan of the New York Americans played the last 7 minutes and 13 seconds of a game against Detroit when regular goalie Chuck Rayner was injured. Detroit won the game 5-4, but did not score on Brannigan.

March 4
Chicago goalie Sam Lopresti faced a record 83 shots, 37 of them in the first period, in a game at Boston Garden. Lopresti stopped a record 80 shots, but the Bruins beat Chicago 3-2.

March 16
Chicago coach Paul Thompson made history when he pulled goalie Sam Lopresti in the dying moments of a

loss against Toronto. It was the first time the move was used as a tactic in an NHL game. The move had no impact on the final score.

April 12
Frank Brimsek was in goal for Boston when they won the 1941 Stanley Cup with a 3-1 win over Detroit. Brimsek was the first American-born player inducted into the Hockey Hall of Fame.

1942

March 16
Roger Crozier was born in Bracebridge, Ontario. Crozier played 14 NHL seasons in the '60s and '70s, posting a 3.04 GAA in 518 regular season games; in 31 playoff games, it was 2.75. He was a first team All-Star in 1964-65 and won the Conn Smythe Trophy in 1966.

April 18
Turk Broda allowed just seven goals in the final four games of the series as the Maple Leafs completed the greatest comeback in the history of the Stanley Cup finals. Detroit won the first three games of the series, but Broda's work in goal led Toronto to victories in the next four games.

1943

April 8
Goalie Johnny Mowers shut out the Boston Bruins 2-0 as the Detroit Red Wings completed a four-game sweep of the Stanley Cup finals. It was Mowers' second straight shutout and he led all playoff goalies with a GAA of 1.94.

October 30
New York Rangers goalie Ken McAuley was in goal when Toronto's Gus Bodnar scored the NHL's fastest goal by a rookie. Bodnar scored 15 seconds into a 5-2 Maple Leafs win.

1944

January 23
The Detroit Red Wings routed the New York Rangers 15-0. Goaltender Connie Dion recorded the shutout and the Wings set two offensive records: most consecutive goals scored in a game, and biggest margin of victory. Ken McAuley was in goal for New York.

February 4

Gary Smith was born in Ottawa, Ontario. Nicknamed "Suitcase", Smith played for more NHL teams than any other goaltender. His 14-year career from 1965-66 to 1979-80 saw him play 532 games for eight clubs, Toronto, Oakland, Calgary, Chicago, Vancouver, Washington, Minnesota and Winnipeg.

February 20

Toronto goalie Paul Bibeault and his Chicago counterpart, Mike Karakas, were perfect in Chicago as the Leafs and the Blackhawks played the only scoreless, penalty-free game in NHL history. Bill Chadwick refereed the one-hour and 55-minute game.

March 23

Paul Bibeault of Toronto was victimized by Montreal's Maurice "The Rocket" Richard, who set an NHL record with five goals in one playoff game. The Habs won 5-1 at the Montreal Forum. It was the most goals scored in Stanley Cup play since Bernie Morris of Seattle scored six against the Canadiens' Georges Vezina in 1917, the season before the formation of the NHL.

April 13

Montreal goalie Bill Durnan stopped the first penalty shot in the history of the Stanley Cup finals, the second in playoff action. Montreal won the game 5-4, sweeping the series in four straight games.

October 28

Frank McCool played his first NHL game with Toronto in a 2-1 victory over New York. McCool played all 50 games for Toronto that year and was second to Montreal's Bill Durnan in goals against average, winning the Calder Cup as the league's top rookie.

1945

February 25

In Montreal, Toronto's Frank McCool was in goal when Rocket Richard scored his 45th goal of the season in a 5-2 Canadiens victory. That surpassed the single-season record set by Joe Malone, also of the Habs, in the NHL's first season of 1917-18.

April 3

Bernie Parent was born in Montreal, Quebec. Parent played 13 NHL seasons in the '60s and '70s, compiling a 2.55 GAA in 608 regular season games, and a 2.43 GAA in 71 playoff matches. A two-time Stanley Cup winner with Philadelphia, Parent's name appeared on the Vezina Trophy twice, and he was named to the first team All-Stars twice. He won the Conn Smythe Trophy in 1974 and 1975.

April 6

Toronto's Frank McCool and Detroit's Harry Lumley faced each other in the Stanley Cup final, the first time two rookies took to the nets in a final series. The Leafs won 1-0 as McCool recorded the first of his three consecutive shutouts in the series.

April 12

The Leafs' Frank McCool recorded his third consecutive playoff shutout over Detroit in the finals, beating the Red Wings 1-0 at Maple Leaf Gardens. That tied the record for consecutive playoff shutouts set by Clint Benedict of the Montreal Maroons in 1926.

April 21

Detroit goalie Harry Lumley recorded his second shutout of the Stanley Cup finals against Toronto in a game played at Maple Leaf Gardens.

April 22

Frank McCool and his Toronto team-mates beat Harry Lumley's Red Wings 2-1, winning the Stanley Cup in seven games. McCool had three shutouts and gave up just nine goals in the series. Lumley accomplished two shutouts and also allowed only nine goals.

1946

October 10

Lorne Chabot, an outstanding goaltender of the 1927-37 era, died in Montreal at the age of 46 after a long illness. He was a Vezina Trophy winner and a two-time Stanley Cup winner with New York and Toronto.

October 16

Toronto's Turk Broda was in goal as Detroit's Gordie Howe scored his first NHL goal in his first game. Sid Abel and Adam Brown assisted on the goal at 13:39 of the second period of a 3-3 tie.

November 16

Turk Broda outduelled Bill Durnan to earn the shutout

in a 3-0 Maple Leaf win over the Canadiens at Toronto in front of the largest Canadian NHL crowd to that point: 16,315.

November 30

Turk Broda got the shutout and Paul Bibeault the embarrassment as the Maple Leafs beat the Blackhawks 11-0 at Maple Leaf Gardens.

1947

January 2

Rangers goalie Chuck Rayner tried something a little different in a game at Madison Square Garden. Trailing 5-4, he spent the last 35 seconds of the game standing at the Toronto blueline while his teammates stormed the Leaf net—unsuccessfully.

January 8

Chicago's Paul Bibeault was in goal when Toronto rookie Howie Meeker scored five goals in a 10-4 win over the Blackhawks.

February 1

Rangers goalie Chuck Rayner, who had a habit of taking part in his team's offensive thrusts, made 3 rushes into the Canadiens' zone trying to score the tying goal in a game which New York lost 2-1.

February 9

Emile "The Cat" Francis made his debut as an NHL goalie with the Blackhawks, beating Boston 6-4 in Chicago. He played just 95 games in six seasons with the Hawks and the Rangers, but his work as a long-time NHL executive put him in the Hall of Fame Builders Category in 1982.

August 8

Ken Dryden was born in Hamilton, Ontario. Dryden won six Stanley Cups during the 1970s in eight seasons with the Montreal Canadiens. He was a five-time first team All-Star, and was named to the second team twice. He won five Vezina Trophies, sharing three of them with Michel "Bunny" Larocque. His GAA was 2.24 for 397 regular season games, and 2.40 over 112 games. Dryden won the Conn Smythe Trophy in 1971.

November 12

Rangers goalie Chuck Rayner missed the second period of an 8-2 home loss to Boston after a shot broke his

cheek bone. (Bob Decourcy, his replacement, allowed six goals before Rayner returned for the third period.) New York coach Frank Boucher said all goalies should be forced to wear facemasks, and Rayner began using a plexiglass mask in practice after the incident.

1948

January 31

Three native sons were honoured during "Owen Sound Hockey Night" at Maple Leaf Gardens in Toronto: new Leaf coach Hap Day, referee Butch Keeling, and 22-year-old Detroit goalie Harry Lumley.

November 21

With one and a half minutes left in the first period of a game played in Detroit, Canadiens goalie Bill Durnan lost two teeth to a deflected puck. Nonetheless, he played the rest of the game and earned a shutout in a 3-0 win.

November 25

A then-league record ten major penalties were handed out in Toronto's 2-0 win over Montreal at The Forum. Turk Broda got the shutout, beating Bill Durnan.

1949

March 6

Montreal's Bill Durnan beat the Bruins 1-0 in Boston for his fourth consecutive shutout. He finished the season with a league-leading ten shutouts in 60 games and a 2.10 GAA winning the Vezina Trophy for the fifth time in six years.

March 9

In a 2-2 tie at Chicago, the scoreless streak of Montreal's Bill Durnan was snapped at 309 minutes, 21 seconds. It was the fourth longest scoreless streak in NHL history.

December 1

Gil Mayer was called up from Pittsburgh as a fill-in for Turk Broda, who was suspended by Leaf owner Conn Smythe for being overweight. Mayer and the Leafs lost 2-0 to the visiting Red Wings. It was Mayer's only NHL game of the season, and one of just nine in his career.

December 3

The Maple Leafs' Turk Broda stopped 22 shots in a 2-

0 shutout over the Rangers in Toronto. Broda had missed one game when Leaf owner Conn Smythe suspended him for being overweight. In the six days between starts, Broda dropped eight pounds to 189.

1950

January 15

All-time shutout leader Terry Sawchuk got his first NHL shutout while with Detroit, beating the Rangers 1-0 in New York.

April 9

Leo Reise scored on Toronto's Turk Broda at 8:39 of overtime as Detroit beat Toronto 1-0 in game seven of a semi-final series. Harry Lumley got the second shutout of the series, Broda had three.

April 23

Chuck Rayner of the Rangers gave up the winning goal to Detroit's Pete Babando at 8:31 of the second overtime period of game seven, giving the Red Wings a 4-3 win over New York and the Stanley Cup. It was the first Stanley Cup final to be decided in overtime of the seventh game. Rayner won the Hart Trophy as the league's most valuable player, the second goalie to win the Hart, joining Roy Worters of the 1928-29 New York Americans.

May 15

Turk Broda was beaten by Leo Reise in overtime of a scoreless seventh game of the semi-finals as Detroit eliminated the Maple Leafs. Broda had three shutouts earlier in the series.

1951

January 27

Chicago's Harry Lumley gave up Jean Beliveau's first NHL goal. Beliveau was an amateur playing in his second NHL game under the league's five-game tryout rule for non-professionals.

March 21

Detroit's Terry Sawchuk led the league with his 11th and final shutout of his first NHL season in a 5-0 win over Montreal at Detroit. He made the first All-Star team and won the Calder Trophy as the top rookie.

March 31

Boston's Jack Gelineau and Toronto's Turk Broda

were in goal when the last no-decision overtime playoff game ended in a 1-1 tie between the Bruins and the Maple Leafs at Maple Leaf Gardens. The game was called after one overtime period at 11:45 p.m. because of the city of Toronto's Sunday curfew.

April 21

Gerry McNeil was in goal for Montreal when Bill Barilko scored the Stanley Cup-winning goal at 2:53 of overtime, giving Toronto a 3-2 victory in game five of the finals. (It was Barilko's last game. In the off-season, he died in a plane crash.) Montreal led 2-1 late in the third period but Tod Sloan tied it after Leaf goalie Al Rollins was pulled from the net with 32 seconds left to play. Al Rollins and Turk Broda shared Toronto's goaltending duties in that series, the only one in Stanley Cup history in which each game was decided in overtime.

November 24

When Chicago goalie Harry Lumley twisted a knee at Detroit, Hawks' trainer Moe Roberts played the third period in goal. Roberts didn't allow a goal in Chicago's 6-2 win. Roberts was 46 at the time, two years older than Lester Patrick was when Patrick filled in for an injured Lorne Chabot in a Stanley Cup final game in 1928.

1952

March 23

New York Rangers goalie Lorne Anderson was in goal when Chicago's Bill Mosienko set a record for the fastest three goals by one player. Mosienko beat Anderson three times in 21 seconds, all of them scored at even strength and assisted by Gus Bodnar in the third period of Chicago's 7-6 win. Anderson never played another NHL game, leaving the league with a one-and-two record and a GAA of 6.00.

April 13

Terry Sawchuk recorded the shutout as Detroit beat Montreal 3-0 in game three of the Stanley Cup finals. Gordie Howe scored his first two playoff goals as the Red Wings won game four to sweep the Habs.

April 15

Terry Sawchuk got the shutout in Detroit's 3-0 Stanley Cup-winning victory over Montreal at the Detroit

Olympia. That was Sawchuk's fourth shutout of the playoffs that year, tying the record for most shutouts in one playoff year. It was the fifth time a goalie recorded four shutouts, but Sawchuk did it in just eight games, something that had only been achieved by Clint Benedict of the Montreal Maroons 26 years earlier. Sawchuk allowed only five goals in the eight games for a playoff GAA of 0.63.

October 9
Though Lorne Worsley, in goal for the Rangers, lost his first NHL game 5-3 in Detroit, he went on to win the Calder Trophy as the league's top rookie of the year.

October 29
Canadiens goalie Gerry McNeil took a shot in the face in the first period but played the rest of the game, which Toronto won. Afterwards, it was discovered that his cheekbone had been fractured and required surgery.

November 1
Jacques Plante played his first game for the Montreal Canadiens. Montreal beat the New York Rangers 4-1 at the Montreal Forum.

November 8
Al Rollins of Chicago was beaten on Rocket Richard's 325th career goal at the Montreal Forum.

December 6
Terry Sawchuk got the shutout for the Detroit Red Wings in a 2-0 win over Chicago's Al Rollins at Indianapolis. It was the first time an NHL regularly-scheduled game was played in that city and the first time since 1928 that a regular season game was played outside an NHL city.

1953

April 4
Jacques Plante recorded his first playoff shutout, a 3-0 win over the Blackhawks at Chicago.

April 16
Gerry McNeil was in goal to record the shutout as Montreal beat Boston 1-0 at 1:22 of overtime to clinch the Stanley Cup in five games. Elmer Lach got the winning goal against Sugar Jim Henry. McNeil played three of the games in the series, recording two shutouts.

October 8
Johnny Bower played his first NHL game. He and the Rangers were beaten 4-1 at Detroit.

December 18
Detroit's Terry Sawchuk and Al Rollins of Chicago played in a 3-1 Red Wings victory at Indianapolis. The game was played amidst rumours that the Chicago franchise might fold due to poor on-ice performance and attendance in Chicago. The Blackhawks averaged just over 6,500 fans per game at home for the season.

1954

February 17
The top two goalies in the league went head-to-head as Toronto's Harry Lumley and Detroit's Terry Sawchuk battled to a scoreless tie in Toronto. Eight days later, Lumley played in another scoreless tie, this one against Jacques Plante and the Canadiens in Montreal. Lumley went on to win the Vezina Trophy, make the first All-Star team, and led the league with 13 shutouts.

February 20
Hall of Fame goalie Jacques Plante, who finished his career fourth on the all-time shutout list, recorded the first shutout of his NHL career as Montreal blanked Detroit 2-0.

March 19
Hometown Chicago beat Boston 7-0, giving Al Rollins five shutouts for a team that won just 12 of 70 games all season. Two of his shutouts were scoreless ties. Rollins won the Hart Trophy as league MVP.

April 16
Early in overtime of game seven, a clearing shot by Detroit's Tony Leswick deflected off the glove of Montreal defenceman Doug Harvey and past Gerry McNeil for the Stanley Cup-winning goal.

November 19
Rejean Lemelin was born in Quebec City, Quebec.

1955

November 5
Boston Bruins goalie Terry Sawchuk was in goal when Montreal's Jean Beliveau scored three times in 44

seconds in the second period of a game played in Montreal. Montreal won the game 4-2.

December 29
Jacques Plante was in goal for Montreal and Harry Lumley was between the pipes for Toronto in an historic game at Maple Leaf Gardens. It was the first time offficials wore vertically-striped black and white sweaters. The earlier black and orange sweaters appeared only black on TV. The Habs won the game 5-2.

1956

January 7
Mike Liut was born in Weston, Ontario.

1957

March 10
Detroit beat Chicago 2-0 in Detroit for Terry Sawchuk's league-leading 12th and final shutout of the year. Hall won the Calder Trophy as the NHL's outstanding rookie.

March 16
Lorne "Gump" Worsley was pummelled in the Rangers' goal losing 14-1 to the Maple Leafs in Toronto.

June 25
Greg Millen was born in Toronto, Ontario.

October 19
Chicago's Glenn Hall allowed Rocket Richard's 500th regular season goal. Richard, who was playing in his 863rd game, became the first player to hit the 500 mark. Assists went to Jean Beliveau and Dickie Moore at 15:52 of the first period in a 3-1 Montreal win.

November 7
Hall of Famer Roy Worters died at the age of 57. Worters had been the smallest goalie in pro hockey during his 12 year career in the 1920s and 1930s. Although he never won a Stanley Cup, he became the first goalie to win the Hart Trophy as the NHL's most valuable player in 1929. He also won the Vezina Trophy in 1931.

November 9
Don Simmons was in goal for Boston when Montreal's Claude Provost set the NHL record for the fastest goal scored from the start of a period. Provost beat Simmons

four seconds into the second period of a 4-2 Canadiens win.

December 29
When Boston's Don Simmons dislocated his shoulder in the first period of a game at Detroit, Red Wings' assistant trainer Ross "Lefty" Wilson played the rest of the game in the Bruins' net. He allowed only one goal in a 2-2 tie.

1958

March 13
When Jacques Plante hit his head on the crossbar during the second period of a game in Boston, Bruins' practice goalie John Aiken got a chance to play for the Canadiens. In 34 minutes, he gave up six goals for a 7-3 Boston win.

June 30
Bob Froese was born in St. Catharines, Ontario.

1959

November 1
Jacques Plante decided to wear a protective facemask after being cut in the face for 13 stitches by a backhand shot during a game against the Rangers in New York.

November 5
Montreal's Jacques Plante wore a protective facemask at the Montreal Forum for the first time. The Canadiens beat the Rangers 8-2.

November 12
Jacques Plante got his first shutout while wearing a mask as the Canadiens beat Toronto 3-0 at the Forum.

December 2
The Leafs beat the visiting Canadiens 2-1 as Jacques Plante lost for the first time while wearing his facemask.

1960

January 10
Bruins goalie Don Simmons tried a facemask for the first time and shut out Toronto 4-0 in Boston.

February 18
Andy Moog was born in Penticton, B.C.

February 28
Jack McCartan was in goal for the U.S.when the

Americans won their first Olympic hockey gold medal with a 9-4 win over Czechoslovakia at Squaw Valley, California. The Americans scored six goals in the third period.

March 6

Jack McCartan, fresh from backstopping the U.S. Olympic team to a gold medal at Squaw Valley, played his first NHL game for the Rangers in a 3-1 win at home over Detroit. He stopped 33 shots, nine of them by Gordie Howe. McCartan played just 12 NHL games over two seasons.

March 8

Jacques Plante, who popularized the goalie facemask when he began wearing one in 1959, gave in to pressure from his coaches and played without it once again. The Habs lost 3-0 and Plante played with a mask for the rest of his career.

March 20

The Rangers beat Montreal 3-1 in New York on the final night of the season while Chicago tied Boston 5-5. As a result, Canadiens goalie Jacques Plante won the Vezina Trophy by two goals over Chicago's Glenn Hall. It was Plante's fifth consecutive Vezina Trophy.

April 14

Jacques Plante got the shutout for Montreal in a 4-0 win over Toronto as the Canadiens completed a four-game sweep in the Stanley Cup finals. It gave the Canadiens a record fifth straight Stanley Cup. It was also the last game for Maurice "The Rocket" Richard who retired after the series.

1961

January 13

Kelly Hrudey was born in Edmonton, Alberta.

September 19

Don Beaupre was born in Waterloo, Ontario.

December 2

Toronto goalie Gerry Cheevers played his first NHL game replacing injured Johnny Bower and leading the Leafs to a 6-4 win at home over Chicago.

1962

January 17

Chicago's Glenn Hall played his 500th consecutive game, losing 7-3 at home to Montreal. Hawk's president James Norris presented a car to Hall in recognition of his achievement.

January 28

Hall of Fame goalie Percy Lesueur died at age 79. He helped Ottawa win 2 Stanley Cups in pre-NHL days.

March 14

New York's Gump Worsley was in goal as Gordie Howe scored his 500th career goal. Worsley got the win as the Rangers beat Detroit 3-2 at New York.

April 22

Don Simmons was in goal for Toronto when the Leafs beat the Blackhawks 2-1 in Chicago to win the Stanley Cup four games to two.

August 29

Jon Casey was born in Grand Rapids, Michigan.

September 28

Grant Fuhr was born in Spruce Grove, Alberta.

October 25

Eddie Johnston played his first NHL game for Boston in a 3-3 tie at home against Detroit. He played on two Stanley Cup-winning teams in Boston during a 16-year career spent with the Bruins, Toronto, St. Louis and Chicago before moving into the coaching ranks.

November 7

A game at home against Boston was Chicago goalie Glenn Hall's 503rd consecutive game, a goaltending record, but Hall was lifted from the game because of a back injury. Hall's streak began at the start of the 1955-56 season. The injury kept him out of action for three games. Hall appeared in all 70 regular season games from the 1955-56 season through the 1961-62 season.

1963

January 27

Habs goalie Jacques Plante questioned the size of the nets in Chicago. He measured them and discovered the goal posts were two inches too short at just 3' 10". Montreal beat the Blackhawks 4-2.

February 14
Mike Vernon was born in Calgary, Alberta.

March 26
Toronto's Johnny Bower became the first goalie to get an assist in Stanley Cup play. Bower and Allan Stanley assisted on Bob Pulford's goal at 3:30 of the first period in a 3-1 win over the Canadiens at Maple Leaf Gardens in the first game of a semi-final.

March 30
Montreal outshot Toronto 32-22, but the Leafs' Johnny Bower had his first playoff shutout in 38 tries as Toronto won 2-0. Bower added one more five days later as Toronto won the semi-final series.

June 29
Peter Sidorkiewicz was born in Dabrowa Bialostocka, Poland.

September 4
John Vanbiesbrouck was born in Detroit, Michigan.

1964

January 4
Toronto's Johnny Bower recorded a third consecutive shutout with a 3-0 win over Chicago at Maple Leaf Gardens.

January 18
Detroit's Terry Sawchuk shut out the Canadiens 2-0 at the Forum for his 95th regular season career shutout, that broke the record of 94 held by George Hainsworth during ten seasons with Montreal and Toronto from the mid '20s to the mid '30s.

January 25
Detroit's Terry Sawchuk was the winning goalie in a 5-3 decision over the Chicago Blackhawks, but he also gave up the first NHL goal scored by Phil Esposito who went on to score 717 during his career.

April 5
Chicago's Glenn Hall was the unfortunate goalie who gave up a goal by Gordie Howe that gave the Detroit star his 127th playoff point which broke Rocket Richard's record. Hall and the Hawks won the game 3-2 in Chicago.

April 25
Johnny Bower shut out Detroit 4-0 in Toronto to give the Leafs their third straight Stanley Cup, four games to two.

May 3
Ron Hextall was born in Winnipeg, Manitoba.

November 14
Montreal's Charlie Hodge gave up Gordie Howe's 627th NHL goal (including regular season and playoff games). The goal, scored 20 seconds into a 4-2 Canadiens' win over Detroit at the Forum, moved Howe past Rocket Richard as the league's all-time scoring leader.

December 13
Chicago Blackhawks goalie Denis Dejordy recorded his first NHL shutout, a 5-0 win over the visiting Detroit Red Wings.

1965

January 14
Bob Essensa was born in Toronto, Ontario.

January 30
Jack Norris was scheduled to play for Boston in Toronto but couldn't because his equipment had been stolen from the lobby of the Royal York Hotel. Ed Johnston played despite a fever, then suffered further by breaking a bone in his hand during a 6-1 loss to the Leafs.

February 23
With Terry Sawchuk out with a groin injury and Johnny Bower down with a pulled hamstring, Toronto used a pair of "Smiths" in a game at Chicago. Gary Smith started and when he was injured in the first period, was replaced by Al Smith of the Marlboro Juniors. The Leafs won 3-2.

April 21
Ed Belfour was born in Carman, Manitoba.

March 12
Cesare Maniago was in goal for the Rangers in Chicago when Bobby Hull of the Blackhawks scored at 5:34 of

the first period to become the first player to score 51 goals in a regular season schedule. The Hawks won 4-2.

March 28

Toronto's Johnny Bower shut out the Red Wings 4-0 in Detroit on the final day of the season. That gave the Leaf duo of Bower and Sawchuk the Vezina Trophy by two goals over the Wings' Roger Crozier. But Crozier made the first All-Star team, captured the Calder Trophy as the League's top rookie and was the first winner of the Conn Smythe Trophy as the playoffs' top performer.

March 31

Tom Barrasso was born in Boston, Massachusetts.

1965

May 1

Gump Worsley earned the shutout as Montreal beat Chicago 4-0 in the seventh game of the final to win the Stanley Cup. Worsley had two shutouts in the final series, teammate Charlie Hodge had one.

October 5

Patrick Roy was born in Quebec City, Quebec.

November 3

Bernie Parent played his first NHL game. He helped Boston tie the Blackhawks 2-2 in Chicago. Hall of Famer Parent went on to win a pair of Stanley Cups with Philadelphia.

November 27

Gordie Howe scored his 600th career goal against Gump Worsley at the Montreal Forum. The Red Wings lost 3-2.

1966

April 2

Toronto coach Punch Imlach tried something different: he alternated goalies Terry Sawchuk and Bruce Gamble about every five minutes. The Leafs tied the visiting Rangers 3-3.

April 3

Three goalies played for Toronto in a game at Detroit: Johnny Bower played the first period, Terry Sawchuk the second and Bruce Gamble the third in a 3-3 tie. For the final period, Bower took the place of Leaf coach Punch Imlach behind the bench.

May 5

The Montreal Canadiens beat Detroit 3-2 to capture the Stanley Cup in six games. The Conn Smythe Trophy winner as the most valuable player in the playoffs was Red Wings goaltender Roger Crozier, who posted a 2.17 GAA in 17 games.

June 26

Kirk McLean was born in Willowdale, Ontario.

October 23

Montreal's Gump Worsley had the dubious honour of allowing Bobby Orr's first NHL goal, a 50-foot slapshot. The Habs beat Boston 3-2.

December 7

This was a bad day for the starting goalies at the Montreal Forum. The Canadiens' Gump Worsley had to be replaced by Charlie Hodge after injuring a knee, and Toronto's Terry Sawchuk collapsed with back pain after the match and missed several games. The Habs won 6-3.

December 14

Bill Ranford was born in Brandon, Manitoba.

1967

January 4

During an unhealthy night for goalies at Maple Leaf Gardens, the Rangers' Ed Giacomin was struck in the head by a slapshot, and the Leafs' Bruce Gamble hit his head on a goalpost. Both goalies completed the game after treatment.

January 18

Charlie Hodge and Gary Bauman combined to stop 35 shots in Montreal's 3-0 victory over the NHL All-Stars in the first All-Star game played at mid-season. Henri Richard scored once and was the MVP while John Ferguson scored twice for the defending Stanley Cup champions.

January 29

Sean Burke was born in Windsor, Ontario.

March 4

Terry Sawchuk recorded his 100th career shutout as

Toronto beat Chicago 3-0 at Maple Leaf Gardens.

March 12

Montreal's Gump Worsley suffered a mild concussion when he was struck on the head by an egg thrown by a fan at Madison Square Garden. Worsley was replaced in goal by Rogie Vachon in a game that ended in a 2-2 tie.

May 2

38-year-old Terry Sawchuk was in goal as Toronto beat Montreal 3-1 to win the Stanley Cup finals in six games. Sawchuk and 42-year-old Johnny Bower were brilliant throughout the playoffs.

June 6

At the NHL expansion draft, the six established teams were allowed to protect one goalie. Boston kept Gerry Cheevers; Detroit, Roger Crozier; New York, Ed Giacomin; Chicago, Denis Dejordy; Montreal, Gump Worsley; and Toronto, Johnny Bower. Here are the first goaltending picks of the six expansion clubs: California Seals, Charlie Hodge (from Montreal); the Minnesota North Stars, Cesare Maniago (from New York); Pittsburgh Penguins, Joe Daley (from Detroit); Los Angeles Kings, Terry Sawchuk (from Toronto); Philadelphia Flyers, Bernie Parent (from Boston); and St. Louis Blues, Glenn Hall (from Chicago).

December 9

The St. Louis Blues recorded their first-ever shutout, a 1-0 win by Glenn Hall over the Oakland Seals.

1968

January 16

In the All-Star game, Toronto goalie Bruce Gamble stopped 28 of 30 shots in two periods of the Leafs 4-3 victory over the All-Stars and was named the games's MVP. It was the last All-Star game pitting the defending Stanley Cup champions against a collection of league All-Stars.

February 15

Tim Cheveldae was born in Melville, Saskatchewan.

April 9

Terry Sawchuk was in goal for the Los Angeles Kings when Wayne Connelly of the Minnesota North Stars scored the first-ever playoff goal scored on a penalty shot. Minnesota beat the visiting Kings 7-5 in a quarter-final game.

May 11

Gump Worsley backstopped Montreal to a 3-2 win over St. Louis and a four-game sweep of the Stanley Cup finals. Worsley went undefeated in 11 playoff games. In a rare tribute to a player on the losing team, St. Louis goalie Glenn Hall was awarded the Conn Smythe Trophy as the playoffs' most valuable player.

June 1

Jeff Hackett was born in London, Ontario.

December 4

Pittsburgh goalie Les Binkley had the distinction of giving up Gordie Howes's 700th career goal.

1970

February 1

Goaltender Terry Sawchuk recorded the last of his NHL-record 103 shutouts as the New York Rangers blanked the Pittsburgh Penguins 6-0 at Madison Square Garden.

March 29

The Blackhawks beat Toronto 1-0 in Chicago. It was Tony Esposito's 15th shutout of the season, a record for rookie goaltenders. No goalie had had 15 shutouts in one season since George Hainsworth's league-record 22 in the 1928-29 season.

May 10

Glenn Hall was in goal when Bobby Orr scored his famous goal 40 seconds into overtime giving Boston a 4-3 win over St. Louis and a four-game sweep of the Stanley Cup final. It was the only goal Orr was able to muster against Hall and Jacques Plante during the series. It was a league-record sixth time that Hall was playing goal for the losing team in the final game of a Stanley Cup final. It was also the third consecutive year that Hall found himself in that position, tying a record set by Turk Broda 30 years earlier. Boston goalie Gerry Cheevers got his tenth consecutive win in that game setting a team and goaltending record for one playoff year.

June 17

Stephane Fiset was born in Montreal, Quebec.

December 10

Buffalo goalie Joe Daley faced 72 shots from the Bruins in an 8-2 Boston win at the Boston Garden. The 72 shots were the most taken in a game by one team since the introduction of the red line in 1943.

1971

April 11

Ken Dryden was the goalie for Montreal when Bobby Orr became the first defenceman ever to score three goals in a playoff game—a 5-2 Boston win over the Canadiens. Four others, Denis Potvin, Dick Redmond, Paul Reinhart and Doug Halward, have since tied Orr's mark.

May 18

Chicago goalie Tony Esposito let in an 80-foot shot by Montreal's Jacques Lemaire late in the second period of the seventh game of the Stanley Cup finals in Chicago. It ws the tying goal in a game Montreal went on to win 3-2 on Henri Richard's Cup-winner early in the third period.

June 23

Felix Potvin was born in Anjou, Quebec.

October 23

Los Angeles Kings goalie Gary Edwards was beaten by Montreal's Guy Lafleur, who scored his first NHL goal.

1972

May 11

Gerry Cheevers got the shutout as Boston beat the New York Rangers 3-0 in game six of the final series and took its second Stanley Cup in three years.

September 2

U.S.S.R. goalie Vladislav Tretiak exploded onto the North American hockey scene, stopping 27 shots at the Montreal Forum in a 7-3 win over Team Canada in the first game of the historic eight-game Summit series. It was the first time that the best players from each country went head-to head.

Sepember 4

Chicago goalie Tony Esposito made 20 saves in a 4-1 victory over the U.S.S.R in game two of the eight-game Summit series at Toronto's Maple Leaf Gardens.

September 6

Vladislav Tretiak blocked three shots and Tony Esposito 21 in a 4-4 tie at Winnipeg in game three of the Summit series.

September 22

Tony Esposito was scored upon five times in the third period of the Soviet Union's 5-4 win in Moscow over Team Canada. The decision gave the Soviets three wins and a tie in five games.

September 24

Ken Dryden was in goal when Team Canada beat Vladislav Tretiak and his U.S.S.R teammates 3-2 in game six of the Summit series. For the second game in a row, Paul Henderson scored the winning goal against Tretiak.

September 26

Tony Esposito was in goal for Team Canada's 4-3 win over Tretiak and the Soviet Union in game seven of the Summit series.

September 28

It was Ken Dryden vs. Vladislav Tretiak in the final game of the historic Summit series. Tretiak gave up three third-period goals, including one by Paul Henderson with just 34 seconds remaining, as Canada won the game 6-5 and took the series with four wins, three losses and a tie. Most people remember Ken Dryden as the Canadian goaltender because he played in both the shocking first-game loss at Montreal and the dramatic final game victory. But Tony Esposito played half the games for Canada, had two wins and a tie, and posted the best GAA in the series at 3.25. Dryden, who had two wins and a pair of losses, had a GAA of 4.75, while Tretiak, the Soviet goalie who played all eight games, came in at 3.88.

October 31

Bill Durnan died at the age of 57. Durnan played seven years of goal for the Montreal Canadiens from 1944 to 1950, winning two Stanley Cups, six Vezina Trophies and a half-dozen first team All-Star selections. He is in the Hall of Fame.

1973

May 6

Although both teams boasted future Hall of Fame

goalies, Chicago's Tony Esposito and Ken Dryden of Montreal, the Blackhawks and Canadiens combined for 15 goals in game five of the Stanley Cup final. That was the most goals ever in a final-round game. Chicago won 8-7.

1974

May 19

Philadelphia goalie Bernie Parent got the shutout and was named the Conn Smythe Trophy winner as playoff MVP when the Flyers beat Boston 1-0 in game six of the final at the Spectrum. That made the Flyers the first of the six 1967 expansion teams to win the Stanley Cup.

November 17

Gary Simmons had a bad night in goal for the California Seals when the New York Rangers set a team record for their biggest-ever shutout victory, a 10-0 romp at Madison Square Garden.

1975

January 21

Goalies Rogie Vachon and Ken Dryden stopped 28 shots between them as the Wales Conference beat the Campbell Conference 7-1 in the All-Star game.

March 29

Kansas City goalie Denis Herron was in goal when Montreal's Guy Lafleur reached the 50-goal mark for the first time. Lafleur went on to score 50 or more goals in each of the next five seasons.

April 26

Glen "Chico" Resch got the shutout in the New York Islanders' 1-0 win over Pittsburgh in game seven of the quarter-finals, capping a remarkable Islanders comeback after trailing the series 3-0. The only other team to overcome such a deficit was the 1942 Toronto Maple Leafs, who won the final in seven games after losing the first three.

May 27

Bernie Parent recorded the shutout and won the Conn Smythe Tropy as the playoffs' most valuable player when the Philadelphia Flyers won their second straight Stanley Cup, beating the Buffalo Sabres 2-0 in game six of the finals at the Memorial Auditorium in Buffalo. Parent was the first player to win the Conn Smythe

Trophy in consecutive years.

December 31

In the famous "New Year's Eve game" at the Montreal Forum, Soviet Red Army goaltender Vladislav Tretiak outduelled Canadiens goalie Ken Dryden in a 3-3 tie. The Habs outshot the Red Army 38-13.

1976

February 7

Goaltender Dave Reece played just 14 NHL games, all of them with Boston, but he was part of a big moment for Toronto's Darryl Sittler, who scored six goals and four assists for a league-record ten points in one game. The Leafs won the game 11-4 in Toronto.

April 22

Bernie Parent was the Philadelphia Flyers' goalie when Toronto's Darryl Sittler equalled Rocket Richard's record of five goals in a playoff game. The Leafs beat the Flyers 8-5. Reggie Leach and Mario Lemieux later tied the record.

May 6

Gilles Gilbert was in goal for Boston when Reggie Leach put in a five-goal performance in Philadelphia's 6-3 win over the Bruins in game five of a semi-final series. The five goals tied a record held by Rocket Richard and Darryl Sittler, and later tied by Mario Lemieux.

May 16

Ken Dryden was in goal for Montreal when the Canadiens put an end to Philadelphia's two-year run as Stanley Cup champions. Dryden and the Habs beat the Flyers 5-3 at the Philadelphia Spectrum, completing a four-game sweep. It was the first of four straight Stanley Cups for the Canadiens.

September 7

Team Canada goalie Rogie Vachon got the shutout in a 4-0 win over Sweden in a round-robin game played at Montreal during the first Canada Cup tournament.

September 9

Veteran Czechoslovakian goalie Vladimir Dzurilla shut out Team Canada 1-0 in another round-robin game of the first Canada Cup tournament.

September 13

Canadian goalie Rogie Vachon got the shutout in Canada's 6-0 win over Czechoslovakia in the first game of the best-of-three final in the first Canada Cup tournament.

September 15

The Canada Cup shutout streak of Team Canada goalie Rogie Vachon was broken after 139 minutes and 22 seconds when Milan Novy of Czechoslovakia scored at 9:44 of the second period in the second game of the tournament final. Canada won the game in overtime to take the best-of-three final in two straight games. When the tournament ended, Vachon was named the most valuable player on the Canadian team, although another Canadian, Bobby Orr, skated off with tournament MVP honours.

November 7

Phil Myre was the starting goalie in the only 0-0 tie in the Atlanta Flames' franchise history. Red Wings goalie Ed Giacomin shared shutout honours with Myre at the Detroit Olympia.

1977

February 2

Jim Rutherford was in goal for Detroit when Toronto's Ian Turnbull set an NHL record for goals by a defenceman in one game. Turnbull scored five times in a 9-1 win at Maple Leaf Gardens.

1978

January 24

Billy Smith, who played the first half of the game for the Campbell Conference and didn't allow a goal, was named MVP of the All-Star game. But the Wales Conference won it in the first overtime game in All-Star history when Sabres' star Gilbert Perreault thrilled the hometown fans at Buffalo's War Memorial Auditorium by scoring the game-winner at 3:15 of overtime.

1979

February 8

Ken Dryden was in goal for the winners when Team NHL beat the Soviet National Team 4-2 in the first game of the Challenge Cup series in New York. The series, won by the Soviets 2 games to 1, replaced the usual All-Star game.

February 11

Vladimir Myshkin made 24 stops as the Soviet National Team blanked Team NHL 6-0 to win the third and deciding game of the Challenge Cup series at New York's Madison Square Garden. Gerry Cheevers played goal for Team NHL.

May 21

Ken Dryden was in goal for a 4-1 Canadiens' victory at Montreal in game five of the finals, giving the Habs a Stanley Cup title. The Canadiens won four straight after losing game one at the Forum.

October 14

Glen Hanlon was between the posts when Wayne Gretzky scored his first NHL goal. Gretzky's Edmonton Oilers tied Hanlon's Canucks 4-4.

November 28

Billy Smith of the Islanders became the first NHL goalie credited with a goal. Early in the third period of a game against the Colorado Rockies, with a delayed penalty about to be called on the Islanders, Colorado defenceman Rob Ramage back-passed the puck all the way down the ice and into the empty Rockies' net. Smith, the last Islander to touch the puck, was credited with the goal. The Islanders lost the game 7-4.

1980

January 10

Goalie Jim Stewart played in his first and only game with the Boston Bruins. He gave up three goals in the first four minutes of the game, and a total of five in the first period. He was replaced and never again played in the NHL.

October 12

When Toronto's Wilf Paiement scored the 100,000th goal in NHL history, it wasn't even scored on a goalie. It was an empty-net goal in a 4-2 Leaf victory at Philadelphia.

1981

January 24

Quebec goalie Ron Grahame gave up two third-period

goals to the Islanders' Mike Bossy, who became the second player to score 50 goals in 50 games. Rocket Richard was the first, scoring 50 in a 50-game season in 1944-45.

April 19
Billy Smith gave up three goals to Wayne Gretzky of the Oilers in a 5-2 Edmonton win over the Islanders in game three of the quarter-finals. But Smith and his teammates got revenge, taking the series and going on to capture their second of four straight Stanley Cups.

September 13
Vladislav Tretiak stopped 26 shots in the Canada Cup final game as the Soviet Union beat Team Canada 8-1. Tretiak was named the tournament's MVP.

1982

May 6
Richard Brodeur was in goal for the Canucks when they became the first team to represent Vancouver in the Stanley Cup finals since the Vancouver Maroons of the Western Canada Hockey League lost out to Montreal in 1924. The Canucks lost the game 6-5 in overtime, and the series in four straight games.

1983

January 20
Calgary's Rejean Lemelin gave up the goal which gave Philadelphia's Darryl Sittler his 1,000th career point. It came in Sittler's 927th career game, and made him the 17th NHL player to reach the 1,000 point mark. The Flyers beat the Flames 5-2.

February 3
Boston goalie Pete Peeters extended his unbeaten streak to 28 games, the second-longest in NHL history, when the Bruins beat Quebec 5-3.

February 16
Boston goalie Pete Peeters had his unbeaten streak snapped at 31 games when he lost 3-1 to the Buffalo Sabres. That left him one short of the NHL mark set by his coach, former Boston goaltender Gerry Cheevers, in 1971-72. Peeters went 26-0-5 during his streak, with a 1.94 GAA.

April 6
Billy Smith was the winning goalie as the defending

Stanley Cup champion New York Islanders beat the visiting Washington Capitals 5-2 in the first ever playoff game played by the Caps. Washington entered the League in 1974.

May 10
Billy Smith shut down the Edmonton Oilers in a 2-0 victory in game one of the Stanley Cup finals at Northlands Coliseum.

May 17
Billy Smith was in goal as the New York Islanders won their fourth straight Stanley Cup title, beating Edmonton 4-2 at the Nassau Coliseum in the final game of a four-game sweep.

1984

January 27
Edmonton's Grant Fuhr earned his ninth assist of the season, breaking the record for goalies set by Washington's Mike Palmateer in 1981-82. Fuhr finished the season with 14 assists.

January 28
Markuss Mattson of the Los Angeles Kings put an end to Wayne Gretzky's record 51-game point streak and beat the Edmonton Oilers 4-2. Over the first 51 games of the 1983-84 season, Gretzky scored 153 points.

May 10
Grant Fuhr of Edmonton won a goaltending duel with Billy Smith of the Islanders as the Oilers beat New York 1-0 in the opening game of the Stanley Cup finals. Kevin McClelland scored the only goal midway through the third period at the Nassau Coliseum.

May 12
Edmonton goalie Grant Fuhr gave up three goals to Clark Gillies as the New York Islanders beat the Oilers 6-1 in game two of the Stanley Cup finals. But Fuhr backstopped the Oilers to wins in the next three games as the Oilers ended the Islanders' reign of four straight Stanley Cups and went on to win four Stanley Cups in five seasons.

September 13
Vladimir Myshkin was in goal for the Soviets when they played their first-ever overtime game. Myshkin played well in the Canada Cup semi-final game against Team Canada, facing 40 shots, incuding 17 in the

second period and five more in overtime. But Mike Bossy's goal gave Canada a 3-2 win. Pete Peeters got the win for Canada.

September 16
Goalie Pete Peeters earned two assists in Team Canada's 5-2 win over Sweden in the first game of the best-of-three final in the Canada Cup tournament.

September 18
When Pete Peeters aggravated an ankle injury at 1:40 of the third period, Reggie Lemelin replaced him in game two of the Canada Cup final against Sweden. Lemelin didn't allow a goal as Canada won the game 6-5, and the series in two straight games. The Swedes started backup goalie Goete Walitalo, but he was replaced by Peter Lindmark at 16:44 of the first period after giving up five goals on nine shots.

1985

January 26
Pittsburgh goalie Denis Herron was beaten by Edmonton's Wayne Gretzky, giving Gretzky his 50th goal of the season in his 49th game. It was the third time Gretzky scored 50 goals in 50 or less games to start a season. Edmonton won the game 5-3.

May 21
Philadelphia's Ron Hextall and Edmonton's Grant Fuhr were in the nets for the start of the Stanley Cup final series that began later in the spring than any other, until the strike-delayed playoffs of 1992. The Flyers beat the Oilers 4-1 in that game.

May 23
Ron Hextall was in goal for Philadelphia when Wayne Gretzky of Edmonton scored his 50th playoff goal in the second game of the final series. The Oilers won the game 3-1 and went on to win the series in five games.

May 30
Edmonton's Grant Fuhr stopped a penalty shot by Philadelphia's Dave Poulin and became the first goalie to stop penalty shots in consecutive playoff games. One game earlier, he stopped Ron Sutter.

1986

January 28
Toronto's Tim Bernhardt was in nets when Denis

Potvin of the Islanders scored to eclipse Bobby Orr's career goal-scoring record for defencemen. Potvin scored his 271st career goal at 3:21 of the second period in a 9-2 Islanders rout.

May 18
Calgary goalie Mike Vernon was burned by Montreal's Brian Skrudland, who scored the fastest overtime goal in playoff history. Skrudland scored just nine seconds into the first overtime period as the Canadiens beat the Flames 3-2 in game two of the final. The Habs went on to win the Stanley Cup.

May 22
Montreal rookie goalie Patrick Roy shut out Calgary 1-0 in the fourth game of the Stanley Cup finals at the Montreal Forum. That gave the Canadiens a 3-1 lead in the series which Montreal won in five games.

May 24
Montreal goalie Patrick Roy made a game-saving stop in the final seconds to preserve a 4-3 win over the Flames in Calgary in the fifth and final game of the Stanley Cup finals. Roy was voted the playoffs' MVP.

1987

May 20
Ron Hextall lost to Jari Kurri at 6:50 of overtime as Edmonton beat Philadelphia 3-2 and took a two games to none lead in the Stanley Cup finals.

May 31
Edmonton beat Philadelphia 3-1 to win the Stanley Cup in seven games, but Flyers goalie Ron Hextall set a record for most playoff minutes played by a goaltender in one playoff year. Hextall logged 1,540 minutes over 26 games. Until 1992, it was the latest date on which an NHL game had been played.

December 8
Philadelphia goalie Ron Hextall became the first NHL goalie to score a goal by shooting the puck into the opponent's net. Hextall iced the Flyers' 5-2 win over Boston by shooting the puck into an empty net, joining Billy Smith as the only NHL goalies ever credited with a goal.

1988

November 20
The Chicago Blackhawks honoured two goaltending greats. Glenn Hall (#1) and Tony Esposito (#35) had their numbers retired during pre-game ceremonies. Hall played for Chicago from the 1957-58 season to the 1966-67 campaign. Esposito arrived two years after Hall retired, and played for 15 seasons, setting most of the Hawks' goaltending marks.

November 23
Detroit goalie Greg Stefan was the beaten goalie when Wayne Gretzky scored his 600th career goal in the Los Angeles Kings' 8-3 win over the Red Wings in Detroit. Stefan was a childhood friend and former teammate of Gretzky.

1989

April 1
Goalie Patrick Roy completed an unbeaten regular season schedule at the Montreal Forum when the Canadiens tied Philadelphia 2-2. Roy's record at home was 25 wins, three ties and no losses.

April 25
Ron Hextall helped Pittsburgh's Mario Lemieux tie a couple of NHL playoff records. Hextall was in goal for Philadelphia when Lemieux had five goals and three asssists for eight points in a 10-7 win over the Flyers in game five of the Patrick Division final. The eight points tied the record set by New Jersey's Patrick Sandstrom one year earlier, while the five goals tied a record held by Maurice Richard, Darryl Sittler and Reggie Leach.

May 19
Montreal goalie Patrick Roy raced to the bench in favour of an extra attacker in the final minute of regulation time, and Mats Naslund scored to tie the game 3-3 and send it into overtime. Ryan Walter won it for the Habs with a goal against Mike Vernon at 18:08 of the second overtime. It was the third game of the Stanley Cup finals which Calgary went on to win in six games.

May 25
Mike Vernon was in goal for Calgary when the Flames became the first visiting team to win the Stanley Cup on the Montreal Forum ice. Calgary won the game 4-2 and took the series four games to two.

1990

May 15
Edmonton goalie Bill Ranford made 50 saves in the Oilers' 3-2 victory over Boston in the longest game ever played in the Stanley Cup finals. Petr Klima scored the winner against Andy Moog at 15:13 of the third overtime session at Boston Garden. It was an ironic situation, since Ranford used to play with the Bruins, and Moog formerly played with the Oilers. It was the first game of a series won by the Oilers, four games to one.

May 24
Edmonton goalie Bill Ranford won the Conn Smythe Trophy as the playoffs' MVP after the Oilers beat Boston 4-1 and captured the Stanley Cup final four games to one. Ranford allowed just eight goals in the five games, including a 3-2 triple-overtime win in game one.

1991

May 15
The Stanley Cup finals began and for the first time, two American goaltenders, Pittsburgh's Tom Barrassso and Minnesota's Jon Casey, faced each other in a final series.

September 12
Bill Ranford stopped 30 shots and earned the shutout as Team Canada beat Sweden 4-0 in a Canada Cup semifinal game played at Toronto's Maple Leaf Gardens. Tommy Soderstrom played well for Sweden, stopping all 18 shots he faced in the first period.

September 16
Team Canada's Bill Ranford was named the MVP and All-Star goalie of the Canada Cup tournament following Canada's 4-2 championship victory over Team U.S.A. at Hamilton's Vic Copps Arena. In five round-robin and three playoff games, Ranford allowed just 14 goals, a GAA of 1.75

December 8
New York Rangers' Mike Richter beat the visiting Boston Bruins 4-0. It was the first shutout against

Boston by a Rangers' goaltender since Ed Giacomin did it 22 years earlier.

1992

April 21

The 11-game undefeated streak of Rangers goaltender John Vanbiesbrouck came to an end with a 7-3 loss to New Jersey. He hadn't lost a game since February 20, more than a month earlier. He also hadn't allowed more than one goal in any one game since February 21.

April 27

Buffalo Sabres rookie goalie Tom Draper recorded his first playoff shutout, stopping 28 shots in a 2-0 win over the Bruins in Boston. In the same game, Boston goalie Andy Moog was ejected with 5:06 left in the second period for spearing Wayne Presley.

April 28

Minnesota goalie Jon Casey became the first goalie to have a playoff goal-against count because of a television replay. Detroit's Sergei Fedorov scored 16:13 into the first overtime period, but referee Rob Shick didn't know if the puck entered the net. After the next stoppage in play, Shick checked with supervisor Wally Harris, who ordered the replay that indicated a goal had been scored. Red Wings' goalie Tim Cheveldae got the shutout in the first 1-0 overtime playoff game in 13 years.

April 30

Detroit goalie Tim Cheveldae's playoff scoreless streak was snapped at 188 minutes and 36 seconds when Minnesota's Brian Bellows scored on him during a two-man advantage in the third period of Detroit's 5-2 win over the North Stars.

April 30

In a Smythe Division semi-final, Vancouver goalie Kirk McLean made 33 saves on his way to a 5-0 shutout over the Winnipeg Jets in the first seventh game of a playoff series ever played in Vancouver.

May 6

Chicago's Ed Belfour stopped 29 shots for his first playoff shutout in a 1-0 win over Detroit. That completed the Blackhawks' four-game sweep of Detroit in the Norris Division finals.

May 11

New York Rangers' goalie John Vanbiesbrouck was beaten on a penalty shot by Pittsburgh's Jaromir Jagr in the first period of a 3-2 Penguins win in game five of the Patrick Division final. It was the tenth penalty shot goal in 26 attempts in Stanley Cup history.

May 12

Edmonton goalie Bill Ranford stopped 26 shots as Edmonton beat Vancouver 3-0 to win the Smythe Division final series four games to two. It was Ranford's third career playoff shutout. During the first period of the first five games of the series, Vancouver outshot Edmonton 70-37. But in game six, Canucks' goalie Kirk McLean and his teammates were outshot 18-3 in the opening period.

May 13

Pittsburgh goalie Tom Barrasso stopped 33 of 34 shots as the Penguins beat the New York Rangers 5-1 and advanced to the Wales Conference final. Barrasso stopped 15 shots in the first period and 14 in the third. In the same game, New York goalie John Vanbiesbrouck stopped a penalty shot by Shawn McEachern. It was the Penguins' second penalty shot in as many games, and just the second playoff penalty shot in franchise history.

May 20

Chicago goalie Ed Belfour stopped 21 shots in a 4-3 overtime win over Edmonton at the Northlands Coliseum. That gave Belfour and the Hawks ten straight playoff wins in a single playoff year, tying the record set by Gerry Cheevers and the Boston Bruins 22 years earlier.

May 22

Ed Belfour got the win in Chicago's 5-1 victory over the Oilers in Edmonton to sweep the Campbell Conference finals. It was the 11th straight playoff win for the Blackhawks, setting a record for consecutive wins in a single playoff year. The old record was set in 1970 by Gerry Cheevers and the Boston Bruins. Belfour allowed just 22 goals in the 11 games.

May 30

Tom Barrasso stopped 27 shots to earn the shutout in Pittsburgh's 1-0 win over Chicago in game three of the final series. It was the first final series 1-0 shutout since Montreal's Patrick Roy beat the Calgary Flames in 1986.

June 1

Three goalies from three different countries played in the first NHL game ever played in June. Ed Belfour from Carman, Manitoba started for Chicago but was replaced by Dominik Hasek, a native of Pardubice, Czechoslovakia, at 6:33 of the first period. Tom Barrasso, who was born in Boston, played the whole game for Pittsburgh as the Penguins beat the Blackhawks 6-5 and won the Stanley Cup in four straight games. It was also the 11th straight win for Barrasso and the Penguins, tying the record for consecutive victories in the same playoff year set by Ed Belfour and the Blackhawks just ten days earlier.

July 29

Michel "Bunny" Larocque died of brain cancer at age 40. Larocque played with Montreal, Toronto, Philadelphia and St. Louis over an 11-year career. He won four Stanley Cup rings with Montreal as backup to Ken Dryden, and was a four-time co-winner of the Vezina Trophy.

September 23

Goaltender Manon Rheaume of Quebec City became the first woman to play in an NHL game when she played one period for the expansion Tampa Bay Lightning in a pre-season game against St. Louis. She stopped seven of nine shots in a game Tampa Bay lost 6-4.

1993

February 6

It was a goaltending horror story when the Wales Conference beat the Campbell Conference 16-6 in the NHL All-Star game. The 22 goals were an All-Star record. This and the four previous All-star games produced 87 goals. Ironically, Montreal goalie Patrick Roy did not allow a goal in the first period. The last scoreless periods in an All-Star game had been logged by Wales goalie Mario Gosselin and Campbell goalie Grant Fuhr seven years earlier.

February 10

Calgary goalie Jeff Reese set an NHL record with three assists in one game as the Flames beat San Jose 13-1.

February 11

Montreal's Andre Racicot and Philadelphia's Tommy Soderstrom got the shutouts as the Canadiens and the Flyers skated to the NHL's first scoreless tie in more than three years.

March 17

Edmonton goalie Bill Ranford made a club-record 56 saves to lead the Oilers to a 4-3 overtime victory over the New York Rangers.

April 13

Ed Belfour of Chicago won his 40th game of the season, beating the Minnesota North Stars 3-2. He joined four others, Terry Sawchuk, Bernie Parent, Jacques Plante and Ken Dryden, as the only goalies with back-to-back 40-win seasons.

April 23

St. Louis Blues goalie Curtis Joseph made 34 saves and shut out the Chicago Blackhawks 3-0 for his second playoff shutout in a row. It extended his shutout string to 151 minutes, 9 seconds.

April 25

The playoff shutout streak of St. Louis goalie Curtis Joseph ended when Chicago finally scored against him after 174 minutes, 18 seconds. The Blues swept the Blackhawks in four straight games in the Norris Division semi-final.

May 9

Kirk McLean stopped 29 shots in Vancouver's 7-2 divisional final playoff win over Los Angeles. It was McLean's 15th career playoff victory, the most in Canucks' history.

May 20

Montreal's Patrick Roy stopped 31 shots, including four in overtime, in the Canadiens' 2-1 victory over the Islanders. That gave Roy and the Habs 11 straight playoff wins, tying the record held by Chicago's Ed Belfour and Pittsburgh's Tom Barrasso one year earlier.

June 5

In the first NHL game played on this date, Los Angeles goalie Kelly Hrudey was beaten by Montreal's John Leclair at 34 seconds of overtime in the Canadiens' 4-

3 win at the Great Western Forum. It was the ninth straight victory in overtime games for the Canadiens and their goalie Patrick Roy, a playoff record.

June 7

Patrick Roy stopped 40 shots, including ten in overtime, as the Montreal Canadiens beat the hometown Los Angeles Kings 3-2 and took a three games to one lead in the Stanley Cup finals. It was Montreal's tenth straight overtime victory, a playoff record.

June 9

The first time an NHL game was ever played this late in the spring, Montreal won the Stanley Cup with a 4-1 victory over the Los Angeles Kings. Canadiens goalie Patrick Roy, who had a 16-4 playoff record with a 2.13 GAA won the Conn Smythe Trophy as the MVP.

September 25

Erin Whitten became the second woman to play goal in a professional hockey game. Whitten played the second period for the Adirondack Red Wings in an American Hockey League exhibition game against the Cornwall Aces. She stopped 10 of 12 shots in a 6-4 loss. The game was played in Glens Falls, N.Y., Whitten's hometown. She was a four-time All-Star for the University of New Hampshire women's team.

October 1

Manon Rheaume, the first woman to play goal in a professional game, played in a NHL pre-season game for the second time. She allowed three goals on 11 shots during the first period as her Tampa Bay Lightning lost 4-2 to the Boston Bruins. The game was played before 23,301 fans in the team's debut at the St. Petersburg Thunderdome.

October 5

Andy Moog got the win in the Dallas Stars first-ever NHL game, a 6-4 win over Detroit at Reunion Arena in Dallas. Tim Cheveldae and Vincent Riendeau shared goaltending duties for the Red Wings in front of a sellout crowd of 16,914.

October 8

Guy Hebert was in goal for Anaheim in the Mighty Ducks' first NHL game. Peter Ing and the Detroit Red Wings' spoiled the Ducks' debut, winning 7-2. Aaron Ward scored the first-ever goal against Anaheim, beating Hebert 2:34 into the game. Ing was perfect until Sean Hill scored Anaheim's historic first goal at 4:13 of the second period. 17,174 fans in Anaheim saw Detroit outshoot the Ducks 43-27.

October 9

In a game of firsts, John Vanbiesbrouck recorded the first-ever shutout by a Florida Panthers goalie, beating Tampa Bay Lightning 2-0. It was also the first win by the Panthers, and was witnessed by a NHL single-game record crowd of 27,227 in Tampa Bay's first game at the Thunderdome.

October 23

Toronto's Felix Potvin stopped 24 shots for the shutout in a 2-0 win over Tampa Bay Lightning in front of 22,880 fans at the St. Petersburg Thunderdome. It was the Leafs' 9th consecutive win to start a season, breaking the record of eight straight set by the 1934-35 Leafs and equalled by the 1975-76 Buffalo Sabres.

October 30

Erin Whitten became the first woman goaltender to be credited with a victory in a professional hockey game when the Toledo Storm of the East Coast Hockey League beat the Dayton Bombers 6-5. Whitten replaced the injured Alain Harvey at the start of the second period with the score tied 1-1.

November 5

Erin Whitten became the first female goaltender to both start and win a professional game when her Toledo Storm of the East Coast Hockey League beat the visiting Louisville Ice Hawks 11-10.

November 6

One night after Erin Whitten became the first female goalie to start and win a professional game, Manon Rheaume became the second. Rheaume stopped 32 of 38 shots as the Knoxville Cherokees beat the visiting Johnstown Chiefs 9-6 in East Coast Hockey League Action.

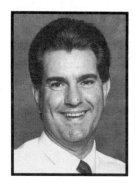

Ian Young (left) is a professional goalie consultant, working with young goalies at the amateur and professional level. He operates a goalie training clinic, has developed goalie training devices, and is the author of two previous books about goaltending.

Terry Walker (right) is a former goalie and a goalie coach, and is the Sports Editor for CBC-TV National News.

Ian Young in 1963 at age 15, minding the nets for the Whitby Dunlops Junior "B" team.

GOALTENDING BOOKS FROM IAN YOUNG

*"I really like what **Behind The Mask** is saying. It stresses the important aspects of goaltending in a progressive and knowledgeable manner, recognizing the goaltender and the coach as equal partners in the successful development of goaltending talent. This book is unique, a must for every goaltender and coach."* —Kirk McLean

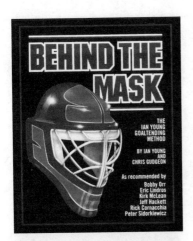

Behind The Mask:
The Ian Young Goaltending Method
Ian Young & Chris Gudgeon
Ilustrations and photos throughout
$18.95 Can/$14.95 US
Drills, practice techniques, equipment considerations and more are part of this unique goaltending guide. Includes advice for coaches and parents about dealing with reactions of a young goalie. Reviews and discusses necessary skills to help young players become the best goalies they can be.

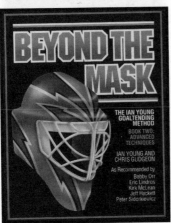

Beyond The Mask:
The Ian Young Goaltending Method, Book Two
Ian Young & Chris Gudgeon
Illustrations and photos throughout
$18.95 Can/$14.95 US
Book Two of this effective goaltending series focuses on intermediate goalies and their coaches, with an emphasis on skill development—specific problem areas are targeted and unique drills are offered to help overcome these problems.

These and other allstar hockey books are available from Polestar Press Ltd.
See reverse page for ordering information.

Polestar publishes best-selling hockey titles. These books are available in your local bookstore or directly from Polestar. Send a cheque for the retail price of the book, plus shipping and handling charges: $4.00 for the first book and $1.00 for each subsequent book. American customers may pay in U.S. funds.

All-New Allstar Hockey Activity Book
Noah Ross & Julian Ross • fully illustrated • $6.95 Can/$5.95 US
A new collection of quizzes, games, radical stats and trivia for young hockey fans.

Allstar Hockey Activity Book
Noah Ross & Julian Ross • fully illustrated • $6.95 Can/$5.95 US
Hockey history, Soviet hockey cards, and hours of hands-on fun for young hockey fans.

The Art of Goaltending
Vladislav Tretiak • fully illustrated • $16.95 Can/$14.95 US
One of the world's greatest goaltenders shares his experience and revolutionary technique.

Basic Hockey And Skating Skills: The Backyard Rink Approach
Jeremy Rose & Murray Smith • fully illustrated • $16.95 Can/$14.95 US
A comprehensive method for learning the fundamentals of ice and in-line skating. Includes plans for building a backyard rink.

Countdown to the Stanley Cup: An Illustrated History of the Calgary Flames
Bob Mummery • photographs throughout • $19.95 Can/$17.95 US
Highlights of nine exciting seasons of this successful hockey club.

Country On Ice
Doug Beardsley • $9.95 Can/$8.95 US
The story of Canada's compelling attraction to the game of hockey.

Elston: Back To The Drawing Board
Dave Elston • $12.95 Can/$11.95 US
Sports-cartoonist Elston's comic view of the world of hockey.

Elston's Hat Trick
Dave Elston • $14.95 Can/$11.95 US
The third in this best-selling cartoonist's collection of irreverent, hilarious hockey cartoons.

Fuhr On Goaltending
Grant Fuhr & Bob Mummery • photographs throughout • $16.95 Can/$14.95 US
The ultimate guide to goaltending from the ultimate goalie.

Hockey's Young Superstars
Eric Dwyer • photographs throughout • $16.95 Can/$13.95 US
Profiles and action photos of Bure, Leech, Lindros, Mogilny, Sakic, Modano and others.

The Rocket, The Flower, The Hammer and Me: An All-Star Collection of Hockey Fiction
Doug Beardsley, editor • $9.95 Can/$8.95 US
Exciting stories from writers like W.P. Kinsella, Hugh MacLennan, Brian Fawcett and others.

Rocking The Pond: The First Season of the Mighty Ducks of Anaheim
Dean Chadwin • 16-page photo section • $18.95 Can/$14.95 US
An insightful look at the eventful season that saw Disney enter the game of hockey.

Taking The Ice: The Mighty Ducks of Anaheim
Dean Chadwin • photographs throughout • $7.95/$5.95
Interviews, exciting photos and informative stats for young fans of the Mighty Ducks.

Order books from:
POLESTAR PRESS LTD.
1011 Commercial Drive — Second Floor, Vancouver, British Columbia, Canada   V5L 3X1